Learning From Failure—
The Systems Approach

About the Authors

Dr Joyce Fortune is a member of the Faculty of Technology in the Systems Discipline at The Open University, UK where her teaching and research interests include systems failures and quality management. She has published widely in both these areas.

Geoff Peters is Pro-Vice Chancellor at The Open University, UK with particular responsibility for strategy and development. He has conducted research and teaching in systems failures since the early 1970s and chaired The Open University's innovative courses on Human Factors and Systems Failures and Complexity, Management and Change.

Learning From Failure—
The Systems Approach

JOYCE FORTUNE
GEOFF PETERS

JOHN WILEY & SONS
Chichester · New York · Brisbane · Toronto · Singapore

Copyright © 1995 by John Wiley & Sons Ltd,
Baffins Lane, Chichester,
West Sussex PO19 1UD, England

National   01243 779777
International (+44) 1243 779777

Other Wiley Editorial Offices

John Wiley & Sons, Inc., 605 Third Avenue,
New York, NY 10158–0012, USA

Jacaranda Wiley Ltd, 33 Park Road, Milton,
Queensland 4064, Australia

John Wiley & Sons (Canada) Ltd, 22 Worcester Road,
Rexdale, Ontario M9W 1L1, Canada

John Wiley & Sons (SEA) Pte Ltd, 37 Jalan Pemimpin #05–04,
Block B, Union Industrial Building, Singapore 2057

British Library Cataloguing in Publication Data

A catalogue record for this book is available from the British Library

ISBN 0–471–94420–3

Phototypeset in 11/13 Palatino by Intype, London
Printed and bound in Great Britain by Biddles Ltd, Guildford

This book is printed on acid-free paper responsibly manufactured from sustainable
forestation, for which at least two trees are planted for each one used for paper
production.

DEDICATION

To Benedict and Lucy
and Gemma, Alexis and Anna

Contents

Preface

Twenty years in the making and a cast of thousands. It sounds like the hyperbole surrounding an epic film, possibly a disaster movie, rather than a serious book by a couple of academics. Nevertheless this book does bring together for the first time the results of a major initiative, stretching back over the past two decades, in which thousands of academics, researchers, teachers and university students have participated. The aim was to discover ways in which failures in organizations can best be understood.

After that mammoth effort we are not the best people to ask if it has all been worth it, but we can at least explain our motivations. We work for a university which like many others is striving to be a learning organization which can develop and change in the light of its own experience in a rapidly moving environment. Perhaps the most valuable way in which people learn is by their mistakes, yet in our experience few organizations seem to bother. There could be a variety of reasons for this absence of learning, but we are convinced that one is a culture of blame and another is the absence of robust methods for discovering anything other than the most superficial lessons.

With this book we want to change both. We want to raise the status of the study of failures to a point where personnel managers, software engineers, teachers, accountants and the like are proud to talk of the lessons they have learnt from the analysis of their own disasters. We hope we will begin to achieve that by providing a highly developed and well-tested method for analysing failures. By bringing complexity and inter-connectivity to the surface we think we can provide a common language in which others can share experiences and benefit from the results of failure.

There is also a social imperative to this work. Many of the most public of failures result in loss of life, injury or income, sometimes for thousands of people. Learning must in the end lead to prevention.

The Open University is of course a learning organization in another sense too. It is the UK's largest single university and has an international reputation as a world leader in the quality of its teaching and learning. It is considered by many to be the most significant and long-lasting achievement of the 1964–1970 Labour Government. When it was established it was specifically aiming to attract students who were post-experience. The study of failure from a systems standpoint matched well with the case-study-based approach which suited their learning needs and varied backgrounds. Subsequently this approach has proved to be popular in many other educational establishments, and so we have chosen here to use that successful formula of case-study-based explanation and exploration to provide what we hope are intrinsically interesting stories and pedagogically sound vehicles with sufficient richness to sustain many opportunities for your own exploration and development of the ideas we present.

We have enjoyed writing this book and hope that it will inspire you to join the growing band who are using these ideas in earnest. We look forward to hearing of your findings and experiences and incorporating them into subsequent editions.

ACKNOWLEDGEMENTS

We have already mentioned the body of people to whom we owe most thanks: Open University academics in the Systems discipline and Tutors on OU Systems courses whom we have worked alongside, and the many hundreds of students we have had the pleasure of teaching, albeit mainly at a distance.

We should also like to thank the many people who have

given us specific help with this book. In particular, thanks are due to:

Alan Bassindale for checking our chemistry;
John Collier and his knowledge of aviation;
Bill Dodd with whom we enjoyed working on the EPR project and the Information Management Group of the National Health Service Executive for permission to publish our study.
Herbert Eisner and Trevor Pearce who shared their expertise on safety in the Channel Tunnel;
Peter Fortune who exercised his keyboard skills to produce the figures;
Tom Horlick-Jones with whom we have done some interesting and enjoyable work, particularly on vulnerability;
Caryl Hunter-Brown and his team at the Open University Library who give us invaluable help year in and year out;
and Roger Stewart who worked with us on the EPR study and who shared some of his other research findings on teams and communications with us.

We should also like to thank our friends and families and Diane Taylor and Claire Plimmer at Wiley for their tolerance and encouragement.

Geoff Peters	Joyce Fortune
Olney	Stamford
	January 1995

1
Failures? Who Needs Them?

INTRODUCTION

It has been forecast that the UK faces at least two, and possibly four, disasters each year in which up to 100 people will be killed each time and that every three or four years there will also probably be a major incident that will kill between 100 and 1000 people (Keller, Wilson and Kara-Zaitri, 1990). 1994, the year this book was written, was unfortunately no exception, though the death toll in the UK was perhaps a little lower than average. Even so:

- 29 died when a Chinook helicopter struck the side of a cliff on the Mull of Kintyre (2 June).
- Six were killed when a passenger walkway collapsed at Ramsgate ferry terminal (14 September).
- Five died and 11 were injured in a head-on rail crash on a single-track line in Kent (15 October).

This grim picture was mirrored elsewhere. For example:

- All 120 on board a Tu154 were killed when it crashed 12 minutes after taking off from Moscow (3 January).
- Over 34 died after Los Angeles was shaken by an earthquake (17 January).
- The concrete roof of a supermarket in Nice, France, collapsed killing three and injuring 94 people (26 January).

- 56 were missing after toxic mud burst through the retaining wall of a dam at a South African gold mine (24 February).
- All 75 aboard a flight between Moscow and Hong Kong were killed in a crash in Siberia (23 March).
- US Air Force jets shot down two US Army helicopters over northern Iraq killing all 26 on board (14 April).
- Tidal waves in Indonesia killed more than 200 people (3 June).
- All 160 on board were killed when a Chinese airline crashed on an internal flight (6 June).
- A DC-9 crashed near Carolina killing 37 (2 July).
- 132 passengers and crew were killed when USAir Flight 427 crashed at Pittsburgh on an internal flight (8 September).
- 912 died when the car ferry Estonia sank on a journey between Tallinn and Stockholm (7 October).

Events such as these where people are killed and maimed attract a lot of media attention, evoking well-placed horror, outrage and sympathy, and are one pinnacle of a mountain of failure. Company collapses, large-scale frauds and massive cost-overruns on big projects form another peak. The vast majority of us will, with luck, avoid direct contact with such disasters but we all rub up against smaller-scale failures. If one reflects back over the failures one has read about and those one has experienced two things become immediately clear. The first is that some failures will always occur and the second is that the vast majority are avoidable. The reasons why they are not avoided are manifold, but a major one is the inability of people to learn from mistakes. This book promotes learning by providing a general understanding of the nature of failure and a systems methodology by which it can be analysed, understood and predicted. The main argument of the book is that through the use of systems thinking it is possible to gain insights into failure that would not otherwise be available. In pursuing this argument it introduces a variety of methods and techniques that have been used and thus allows the reader to see the Systems Failures Method put forward by the authors alongside them.

Throughout, the emphasis will tend to be upon practical application, with the theory underpinning the work being brought in to explain what is being undertaken and why. Case studies are used as the vehicle for introducing the Systems Failures Method and for demonstrating it in action, with further case study material being supplied to enable the reader to try out the ideas, techniques and procedures. A diverse range of case studies has been chosen. This diversity, in addition to demonstrating the range of applicability of the Method, will hopefully ensure that each individual reader finds something that will grab her or his attention and make the journey interesting as well as worthwhile.

WHY STUDY FAILURES?

'There is much to be said for failure. It is more interesting than success.'
(Max Beerbohm, *Mainly on the Air*, Heinemann, London, 2nd edn, 1957)

This 'clever' remark from the man who also gave us: 'I was a modest, good-humoured boy. It is Oxford that has made me insufferable' carries within its glibness a simple statement of a profound truth. Failures are interesting, as the mass media know only too well, but though we hope you will find this book 'interesting' in the entertaining, enjoyable sense of that word, our main aim in writing it is not, of course, to entertain. Nevertheless it is hoped that you will find it interesting and valuable with a part of the value being the role the analysis and understanding of failure can play in learning.

Individual Learning

In many fields practitioners have long recognized learning from failure as a crucial element in their development. Jung (1950) described the process thus:

The psychotherapist learns little or nothing from his successes. They mainly confirm him in his mistakes, while his failures on the other hand, are priceless experiences in that they not only open up the way to a deeper truth, but force him to change his views and methods.

Much more recently, Ackoff (1994) has made a similar point:

> When one does something right, one only confirms what is already known: how to do it. A mistake is an indicator of a gap in one's knowledge. Learning takes place when a mistake is identified, its producers are identified and it is corrected.

More generally, the importance of experiential learning is widely recognized in the literature on adult learning. Simpson (1980), for example, considers it to be one of the two most crucial activities relevant to adult learning (the other is the adult's personal autonomy in learning how to learn) and regards it as 'a unique resource for new learning'. Jones and Hendry (1994, p. 159) describe adult learning as 'characterized by personal autonomy, experiential learning, people seeing connections between different aspect of their work and lives, and by activities that may initially seem irrelevant to the specific job being undertaken.' Systems analysis of failures, by giving people opportunities to analyse and reflect, and thus gain insight, can tap into a number of these characteristics.

Beyond The Individual

The quotations from Jung and Ackoff are both about individuals learning from their own experiences, but learning from failure can be extended, as it will be in this book, beyond direct personal experience so that it encompasses learning from situations in which one played no part, and of which one might have had no direct experience, perhaps by the pooling and sharing of individuals' experiences. It can also take place at the collective level where it might fall within the ambit of the somewhat abstract notion of 'organizational learning'.

The pooling and sharing route is recommended by Parker (1991) in his critique of emergency planning policy. He believes that every policy should include a mechanism for ensuring that the maximum is learned and disseminated from recent accidents, emergencies and disasters, including 'near miss' events. This book aims to support that feedback process. It is clear that there is plenty of scope for improvement. For example, a report by the Marine Directorate of the Department of Transport (1991) noted:

Information about potentially hazardous incidents which do not in fact lead to an accident (near misses) could be a good source of data about the human element, particularly since the chance of prosecution or punishment is rarely an issue. Near miss reports have not been greatly forthcoming from seafarers, however, mainly because they feel that they are given very little feedback on the actions and consequences following the reports that they have made in the past. The view that near miss reporting is largely a one-way communication does not give the mariner much incentive to use it. (Marine Directorate, 1991, p. 8.)

In the air transport industry near miss reporting is well established internationally, with procedures in place to investigate incidents and publicize the findings. For example, British Airways Safety Services produce a quarterly publication, *Flight Deck*, in which they include summaries of accident and air-miss reports and short reports on their own and other operators' incidents which include a statement about any actions taken. However, a paper by MacGregor and Hopfl (1994) on safety management suggests that even British Airways was, at least prior to 1990, a long way from achieving maximum learning and dissemination. They wrote:

The system [for dealing with incident reports] as it operated [prior to 1990] gave emphasis to understanding data that was at best incomplete and at worst totally inadequate. . . . Where human errors were involved, informal communication networks seemed to provide the only means for the dissemination of information. However, the 'grape-vine' operated with inevitable distortions and was at best partial. (MacGregor, C. and Hopfl, H., 1994, p. 3.)

The Learning Organization

The concept of the learning organization has become increasingly widely used in the last few years, particularly in US and UK management circles. It is based on the view that successful organizations respond to differing circumstances in much the same way as that which leads an animal or a human to display adaptability and learning when presented with a challenging environment, and that the absence of such a response is prejudicial to survival. The concept also carries with it the notion that it is probably not practicable, and certainly not desirable, for a modern complex organization to rely on the vision of one grand strategist. Instead the explicit theme is that 'the organizations that will truly excel in the future will be the organizations that discover how to tap people's commitment and capacity to learn at *all* levels in an organization.' (Mintzberg, 1994)

Exactly how a learning organization can be recognized is a matter for some debate; presumably those which do not survive have not learnt. Much of the literature in this area is concerned more with the processes by which organizations increase their ability to learn rather than with the behaviour that would demonstrate that an organization was actually learning and adapting in response to changes in its environment. Attwood and Beer (1990), for example, point to the following as important factors in the learning process:

- Role of management
- Role of organizational development staff
- Shared responsibility for staff learning
- Robustness of learning process
- Continuity of feedback
- Rate of learning.

Senge (1990) has identified five disciplines, or bodies of theory and technique, which when brought together create the capacity to learn.

1 *Systems thinking*—which integrates the other four disciplines. For Senge this is concerned with seeing developing patterns rather than snapshots. 'At the heart of the learning organization is a shift of mind—from seeing ourselves as separate from the world to being connected to the world, from seeing problems caused by someone or something 'out there' to seeing how our own actions create the problems we experience.'
2 *Personal mastery*—a personal commitment to lifelong learning by individuals in the organization. Mastery is seen in the craft sense of constantly striving to improve on the personal skills which the individual has acquired.
3 *Mental models*—Senge argues that there are deeply ingrained assumptions and images which influence the way individuals perceive the world and actions that are taken. These mental

models are different from the 'espoused theories' in that they are based on observed behaviour. In Senge's view these models need to be brought into the open so that they can be subjected to scrutiny.

4 *Building shared vision*—Senge posits that if organizations are to be successful everyone must pull in the same direction towards the same vision of the future, and that they must do so because they want to, not because they are told to. 'You don't get people to buy into a vision, you get them to enrol.' The commitment to learning is a part of that vision.

5 *Team learning*—the team rather than the individual is the key learning unit in most views of a learning organization. Primarily this is because a team is regarded as a microcosm of a whole organization, but it may also be influenced by the knowledge that there was already a body of established management literature on the creation of successful teams.

As can be seen from the above, much of the thrust of Senge's approach is linked to the idea of human centred management; it is about allowing the individuals throughout an organization to contribute fully to its future development, and about making sure that senior management discharge their responsibilities for ensuring that strategy is clearly articulated and that staff are nurtured.

Moving from the theory associated with organizational learning to the actions necessary to facilitate it, the feedback model of learning allied to an awareness of the environmental context in which the organization is operating and the ability to monitor the progress of the organization across a broad range of measures and performance indicators must be fundamental to success. This takes us back to failure analysis with opportunity to learn being in large part dependent on failure being recognized and analysed appropriately. This is not achieved unless individuals are free to share the information they have without fear of recrimination. Again, an example from British Airways can be used to back up this assertion:

> As a decision support system, BASIS [a new British Airways Safety Information System, developed in 1990] has been developed to facilitate and encourage an open reporting-system supported by a company commitment to Penalty Free Reporting. This was deemed necessary because

it was recognised that it was important to encourage crews to report all incidents as fully as possible without fear of recrimination. The success of this has been seen in the improvement (40 per cent) in reports since the beginning of 1991. (MacGregor and Hopfl, 1993, p. 10)

Beyond The Organization

Organizations can also learn one from another. The air transport industry, with its system of near miss reporting as discussed earlier, is one area where this is well established. A failure on an aircraft in one part of the world can result in a carrier on a different continent grounding its aircraft. The capsize of the British ferry Herald of Free Enterprise caused ferry operators, at least throughout Europe, to review their procedures with respect to the closing of bow doors on roll-on-roll-off ferries.

There is also scope for different types of organizations from different sectors of the economy to learn from the failures of one another. To the authors, this type of learning, which we term learning by analogy, offers as many opportunities as benchmarking, the popular quality technique whereby an organization compares its own activities, processes or perform-ance with those of others. Thus instead of Xerox comparing its distribution against 3M in Dusseldorf, Ford in Cologne, Sainsbury's regional depot in Hertfordshire, Volvo's parts distri-bution warehouse in Gothenburg and IBM's international and French warehouse it might look at marketing failures in the soft drinks industry, failed technologies in consumer electronics and the demise of watch manufacturers in Switzerland.

UNCOVERING THE LESSONS

Where people have sought to learn from failures they have tended to draw the lessons either from formal investigations, where the main item on the agenda is often the apportionment of blame, or on partial *ad hoc* recollections of what went wrong. Here we shall look at each of these before putting forward a third way.

The Official Inquiry

In the UK the most rigorous form of formal investigation where failures are concerned is the official inquiry which is automatically triggered by certain types of incidents and which can be called for in others. Taking air transport as an example, under the provisions of The Civil Aviation (Investigation of Air Accidents) Regulations all reportable accidents involving UK registered aircraft and foreign registered aircraft operating in UK airspace have to be investigated. A reportable accident is defined as:

> an occurrence associated with the operation of an aircraft which takes place between the time when any person boards the aircraft with the intention of flight and such times as all persons have disembarked therefrom, in which—
>
> (a) any person suffers death or serious injury while in or upon the aircraft or by direct contact with any part of the aircraft (including any part which has become detached from the aircraft) or by direct exposure to jet blast, except when the death or serious injury is from natural causes, is self-inflicted or is inflicted by other persons or when the death or serious injury is suffered by a stowaway hiding outside the areas normally available in flight to the passengers and members of the crew of the aircraft;
>
> or
>
> (b) the aircraft incurs damage or structural failure, other than:
> (i) engine failure or damage, when the damage is limited to the engine, its cowlings or accessories,
> (ii) damage limited to propellers, wing tips, antennae, tyres, brakes, fairings, small dents or punctured holes in the aircraft skin,
> which adversely affects its structural strength, performance or flight characteristics and which would normally require major repair or replacement of the affected component;
> (c) the aircraft is missing or is completely inaccessible. (Civil Aviation Authority, 1994, p. vii)

The Air Accidents Investigation Branch (AAIB) of the Department of Transport publishes annual summaries of reportable accidents and bulletins on reportable accidents to civil aircraft as well as Aircraft Accident Reports for the more major investigations.

Few would criticize the thoroughness or technical competence with which official inquiries are carried out, but there are three areas where questions about their efficacy have been raised (see, for example, Peters, 1977). The first concerns the amount of time they take.

Chapter 4 of this book uses a report by the Air Accidents Investigation Branch (AAIB) (1989) as its major source. The report, on the aircraft fire at Manchester International Airport in 1985, represented over three years of very careful, painstaking work. During the investigation the AAIB: took evidence from survivors, rescuers, witnesses and others involved; closely examined wreckage, flight recordings, technical logs and other records; sifted through a large amount of research findings on topics such as the emissions from burning aircraft cabin materials and the toxicological effects of combustion gases; and looked at research which was then current.

Just one day after the Manchester fire the United Kingdom Civil Aviation Authority (UK CAA) issued an emergency airworthiness directive requiring checks to be carried out on all aircraft engines of the type involved in the accident, but it was another four years before the AAIB's report was published. It was only after this long wait that the vast majority (26 out of 31) of the inquiry's recommendations became known.

The second reservation about the inquiry is the hiatus that can occur whilst it is in progress, with the inquiry itself sometimes being used as a protective screen. A Minister challenged in the House of Commons may, for example, decline to answer legitimate questions on the grounds that an inquiry is under way.

The third area for concern is that there is no requirement to act on the findings. Two recommendations in particular attracted widespread interest when the Manchester report was published:

1 The Civil Aviation Authority should urgently give consideration to the formulation of a requirement for the provision of smokehoods/ masks to afford passengers an effective level of protection during fires which produce a toxic environment within the aircraft cabin. (Made December 1985) (AAIB, 1989, p. 173)
2 Onboard water spray/mist fire extinguishing systems having the capability of operating both from on-board water and from tender-fed water should be developed as a matter of urgency and introduced at the earliest opportunity on all commercial passenger carrying aircraft. (AAIB, 1989, p. 173)

Writing in 1992 about this second recommendation, Macilwain drew attention, in colourful terms, to the delay between it and a response:

> It is seven years now since 55 people died in a Boeing 737 on the runway at Manchester Airport, engulfed in flames. But time is a great healer—especially where large amounts of money are involved—and the authorities have yet to decide whether sprinkler systems should be installed on planes to prevent a repetition of the accident.... A pronouncement was expected from the CAA almost a year ago, but no decision has been reached. The word is that none is imminent because there is not a snowball's chance in hell of the airlines being able to afford to implement them in the current economic climate. (Macilwain, 1992)

Economic considerations were clearly important, but opponents were also able to bring forward powerful arguments such as the catastrophic effect an inadvertent discharge of the sprinklers might have and the danger of water penetrating electrical systems. However, recommendations from other inquiries which seem far less contentious and much less costly to implement have been ignored too. In 1994 a report was published of an investigation into a very close shave at Gatwick airport (AAIB, 1994). The crew of Boeing 737 operated by Air Malta landed their aircraft on a narrow taxiway instead of on the runway. It was revealed that a very similar incident had happened in 1988 and had led to recommendations that the airport's lighting should be improved. Some changes were made but one key suggestion was not taken up. The CAA 'did not consider that modifications to the green centreline lighting of taxiway 2 and runway 26R ... were necessary.' Six years after one crew had been misled by them, these green lights were to be identified as the major cause of the Air Malta crew's confusion.

Although the public inquiry is a peculiarly British and British Commonwealth device, very large scale-failure investigations are a feature of public life elsewhere. For example, the explosion that killed the seven crew of the US space shuttle Challenger led to a Presidential Commission. This yielded transcripts amounting to 12 000 pages and an official report (Rogers *et al.*, 1986). It also spawned numerous press articles, academic papers and books. The result is that we now have a detailed exposition not just of the causes of the accident, but also of the history of the decision to embark on the project, its evolution, and the state of NASA at the time. So, for example, it can be seen that the late President Nixon's decision to support the project and to opt for the largest design of shuttle was evidently influenced by three factors. It was an election year, so the prospect of 24 000 extra jobs in key states, and support for a prestigious national program, had added significance. Thirdly Nixon was impressed by the support of the Department of Defense. Reportedly this support amounted to little more than a lack of opposition since they had been offered a vehicle for all military missions, whereas they had previously developed their own space launch program. According to John Erlichman (see Logsdon, 1986) the President was also impressed by a list of proposed military missions, such as capturing unfriendly spacecraft, which had been invented by NASA, yet the Department of Defense planned no such missions.

The decision to incorporate military missions changed the specification of the shuttle. The original idea of a reusable space vehicle to support space-station construction had led to a design with a cargo bay 13 m (43 ft) long and a payload of 20 000 kg (20 tons). To cater for all space missions these were changed to 15 m (49 ft) and almost 30 000 kgs (30 tons) respectively, and together with other modifications resulted in the engines being required to produce a thrust equivalent to 109% of their capacity. (Making major changes to specification well after design has begun does tend to be a feature associated with design failures.) The US was also left with no spare capacity in its launch schedule so that when the space shuttle failed to meet its original deadlines commercial users turned elsewhere, to the European space agency, and to the Chinese and Russian space programmes.

Highly Partial Accounts

One of the main blocks to learning from mistakes is post-event rationalization; errors are forgotten, lost opportunities are explained away and poor decisions blamed on the force of circumstances. But even when a genuine attempt is made to reflect on past events it is very difficult to draw out valid lessons without undertaking a proper analysis. First impressions, and the tendency to rush to judgement can be very misleading yet can easily become perceived wisdom as the following two personal accounts by one of the authors show.

Papa India

British European Airways Trident Papa India plummeted into a field near a main road, the Staines by-pass, very shortly after take-off from Heathrow on Sunday 18 June 1972. All of the 118 people on board died. It was a big story; media coverage was extensive.

My own recollection of this accident as reported contained three themes. First, happening as it did on a Sunday and close to London the crash site quickly became a local spectacle. Television and newspaper pictures showed both the aircraft wreckage and the queues of cars blocking the roads and reports were critical of the ways in which these 'ghouls' had impeded the emergency services and rescuers with *The Times* headlining one piece 'Rescue work hampered by gaping crowds' (*The Times*, 1972).

The second theme concerns the part played by poor industrial relations. A dispute was under way between the airline and the trade union which represented the pilots. Graffiti found on a table in the cockpit referred to the aircraft Captain, who was a known opponent of the industrial action being taken, in a critical way, and the conclusion which was widely disseminated was that there had been an argument amongst the crew.

Thirdly it was quickly revealed that the Captain had suffered a heart attack. There was much discussion of the action taken by airlines to check on the health of their staff, and of the possibility that the attack had been precipitated by the aforementioned row.

The impression left on me, and I am sure on many other lay persons, was that the crash was caused by the heart attack suffered by the Captain and that this was probably precipitated by an argument over the industrial dispute. The number of casualties was higher than it need have been because the ambulances and fire engines had been hampered by sightseers.

It might, however, come as no surprise to learn that the official inquiry report showed most of my impressions to be false. The accident investigators' view (summarized in Bignell, Peters and Pym, 1977) was that the aircraft crashed because its droops were retracted too early, causing the aircraft to enter the stall regime, and the crew failed to interpret the stall warnings properly. (Droops, together with flaps, were devices that altered the shape of the Trident's wing so that it would remain aerodynamically stable at low speeds during take-off and landing.) The report identified previous incidents where the same thing had started to happen but had been detected in time to prevent an accident. The graffiti pre-dated that flight; the heart attack probably happened after the accident, though Captain Key's abnormal heart condition may have led to lack of concentration and impaired judgement. Finally, the emergency services had been and gone long before any spectators arrived.

The Design Fire

The second personal account concerns what became known locally as the Great Open University (OU) computer fire of 1987. Once again it was on a Sunday. (An untested hypothesis is that disasters hit the headlines on Mondays more often because of the lower levels of economic and political activity on the preceding day.) A fire broke out and completely destroyed a computer installation. The myths which surrounded this event were not to do with the causes, but with the consequences and remedies. The first reports, that the OU had lost all its student information, were undoubtedly due to poor information links on a Sunday evening and to rapid speculation. This error was quickly corrected. The computer was used entirely for research, but because the whole computer room was destroyed previous versions of programs and data had suffered the same fate. It was therefore concluded that years of research and the life-works of researchers had been lost forever. The human interest was present in the form of stories that the senior researcher responsible for the facility had been taken to hospital in a distraught state. What entered the public domain was what was reported on that day. Newspaper and specialist press articles used this version to support arguments in favour of disaster recovery and contingency plans and other important and worthwhile activities.

However, what happened in reality was somewhat different. The computer which was destroyed was a modest research machine and individual users took responsibility for their own data and programs. They had all acted responsibly and held copies of their material elsewhere, so there were actually no losses at all. Similarly, the 'distraught researcher' who disappeared from the scene of the fire did not need medical attention. He had left to write his incident report and plan the actions that would be necessary over the following days. (A fuller account can be found in Johnson, 1989.)

A Third Way

So far we have argued the case for using failures as learning opportunities and looked at two ways in which the lessons might be drawn out. The first, typified by the official inquiry, is very thorough, but also slow, cumbersome and expensive. As currently practised it also tends to concentrate on individual aspects of a failure rather than considering it as a whole and investigating inter-relationships. The second, relying on impressions and memories, is at best haphazard and at worst totally misleading. This book sets out a third way that in its various stages of development has been applied successfully in an extremely wide variety of situations by many different analysts.

This third way forms the core of this book. It is a systemic method for the analysis of failures called the Systems Failures Method. Because it employs a variety of qualitative modelling techniques it has a major advantage over other methods: in addition to looking back at failures which have already occurred it can be used to look forward to potential failures.

Although emergency planning tends to be the norm in high risk technologies such as nuclear power generation and oil production (though even there it is not always wholly effective as the immediate aftermath of the Piper Alpha oil platform explosion demonstrated), many commercial organizations seem to be remarkably reluctant to anticipate that things might go wrong. One study in the USA (Carreiro, 1991) found that as organizations relied on computer and IT systems more and more, there was a corresponding increase in the frequency of computers causing significant business interruptions. (70% of the incidents in the previous decade had happened in the last three years.) But the study also found that out of 300 000 large and mid-sized computer systems installations less than 3% had disaster recovery plans in place. This must expose them to risk.

The requirement to look forward to failure is essential for good project management, but the high level of failures suggests that attempts to do it are not being undertaken. Morris and Hough (1987), after surveying the literature on project overruns (the literature surveyed in total covered over 3500 projects) concluded:

> Curiously, despite the enormous attention project management and analysis have received over the years, the track record of projects is fundamentally poor, particularly for the larger and more difficult ones. Overruns are common. Many projects appear as failures, particularly in the public view. Projects are often completed late or over budget, do not perform in the way expected, involve severe strain on participating institutions or are cancelled prior to their completion after the expenditure of considerable sums of money. (Morris and Hough, 1987, p. 7.)

The Systems Failures Method

Through the use of case studies this book seeks to explain the third way for uncovering the lessons, the Systems Failures Method, and show how it can be used as a predictive tool. As with other systems methodologies such as Soft Systems Analysis (SSA) and Total Systems Intervention (TSI) the Systems Failures Method takes the analyst from the real world (in this case the situation labelled as a failure or a potential failure) into the conceptual world where systems thinking, qualitative modelling and comparison provide the means by which understanding can be achieved. This understanding is then taken back out to the real world, where it emerges as a set of lessons. This journey is illustrated in Figure 1.1.

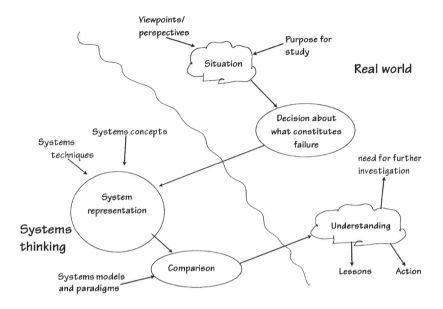

Figure 1.1 *A notional view of the systems failures method*

OVERVIEW OF THE BOOK

Chapter 2 looks at the nature of failure and is followed in Chapter 3 by an examination of various approaches different authors have taken in trying to understand it, explain it, intervene in it and prevent it. It moves from approaches that have tended to concentrate on particular aspects such as reliability, human error, psychological processes and the like to work that considers underlying organizational structure and behaviour. It then introduces systems thinking and describes approaches that draw on this to varying degrees, finishing with a look at the way the method described in this book has developed from earlier work in the systems failures area and from elsewhere.

Chapter 4 is a case study about the aircraft fire at Manchester International Airport on 22 August 1985. The purpose of the chapter is twofold: to provide examples for Chapters 5 and 6 which look at how the Method works; and to provide source material with which others can conduct their own analyses. Thus, the book does not provide a complete analysis of this failure situation which, as mentioned earlier, has already been the subject of an exhaustive study by the AAIB, but instead uses some aspects of it as a vehicle for explaining the Systems Failures Method.

Chapters 7, 8 and 9 are also built around case studies but the slant is different in each. Chapter 7 looks at what is usually described as 'the world's worst industrial disaster', the leak of methyl isocyanate at Union Carbide's plant in Bhopal, from a number of analytical standpoints which to varying degrees are all different from the approach advocated in this book. In Chapters 8 and 9 the direction of the analysis changes from looking backwards to looking forwards. The main purpose of Chapter 8 is to illustrate the process of using the Method. It reports a study that was commissioned by the Department of Health as it embarked upon a large-scale IT project to design, develop and implement an electronic patient record (EPR) system. The study was in two parts. First, the Systems Failures Method was used to analyse published accounts (mainly American and Canadian) of attempts to introduce clinical information systems. Then the findings of the first stage, together with lessons from other large-scale IT projects and information gained from interviews with interested parties, were used to look forward to the development and introduction of the EPR system with a view to predicting the risks associated with it.

For Chapter 9 the topic is again transportation but this time the analysis is left to the reader. Source material is provided in the shape of a case study on the Channel Tunnel. It concentrates particularly on the safety of the Tunnel now that it is in operation.

Chapter 10 looks at the contribution the Systems Failures Method makes within the broad context of quality management, risk analysis, failure and disaster prevention and so on. It picks up many of the themes from Chapters 2 and 3 again and tries to draw the threads together before pointing the way for further exploration.

REFERENCES

Ackoff, R. L. (1994). 'It's a mistake!', *Systems Practice*, **7**, 3–7.
Air Accidents Investigation Branch (1989). *Report on the accident to*

Boeing 737–236 series 1, G-BGJL at Manchester International Airport on 22 August 1985, Department of Transport, HMSO, London.

Air Accidents Investigation Branch (1994). *Report on the incident to Boeing 737–2Y5A, 95–ABA at London Gatwick Airport on 20 October 1993*, Department of Transport, HMSO, London.

Attwood, M. and Beer, N. (1990). 'Towards a working definition of a learning organization', in Pedler, M., Burgoyne, T. and Welshman, G. (eds), *Self Development in Organizations*, McGraw-Hill, London.

Bignell, V., Peters, G. and Pym, C. (1977). *Catastrophic Failures*, Open University Press, Milton Keynes.

Carreiro, E. (1991). 'Disaster recovery—the risks of going naked', *National Underwriter*, **95**(7), 16 and 41.

Civil Aviation Authority (1994). *Reportable Accidents to UK Registered Aircraft, and to Foreign Registered Aircraft in UK Airspace, 1991*, Civil Aviation Authority.

Johnson, J. H. (1989). 'Computer disaster: the experience of having a computer laboratory destroyed by fire', Open University internal report.

Jones, A. M. and Hendry, C. (1994). The learning organization: adult learning and organizational transformation', *British Journal of Management*, **5**, 153–62.

Jung, C. G. (1950). *Modern Man in Search of a Soul*, Harcourt Brace, New York.

Keller, A. Z., Wilson, H. and Kara-Zaitri, C. (1990). 'The Bradford disaster scale', *Disaster Management*, **2**, 207–13.

Logsdon, J. M. (1986) 'The space shuttle program: a policy failure?', *Science*, **232**, 1099–105.

MacGregor, C. and Hopfl, H. (1993). 'A commitment to change: safety management in British Airways', *Disaster Prevention and Management*, **2**(2), 6–13.

MacGregor, C. and Hopfl, H. (1994). 'Beyond the rhetoric of safety management: British Airways', paper presented to Conference on Changing Perceptions of Risk: the Implications for Management, Bolton Business School, 27 February–1 March.

Macilwain, C. (1992). 'Your money or your lives', *The Engineer*, 19 November, 22.

Marine Directorate (1991). *The Human Element in Shipping Casualties*, Department of Transport, HMSO, London.

Mintzberg, H. (1994). *The Rise and Fall of Strategic Planning*, Prentice-Hall, New York.

Morris, P. W. G. and Hough, G. H. (1987). *The Anatomy of Major Projects*, Wiley, Chichester.

Parker, D. J. (1991). 'A critique of UK emergency planning policy', paper presented to The Association of Emergency Planning Officers Annual Study, Gourock, Scotland, 11 April.

Peters, G. (1977) 'Inquiry into failure', *Nautical Review*, **1**(3), 33–4.

Rogers, W. P. (Chair). (1986). *Report of the Presidential Commission on the Space Shuttle Challenger Accident*, US Government Printing Office, Washington DC.

Senge, P. M. (1990). 'The leader's new work: building learning organizations', *Sloan Management Review*, Fall, 7–23.

Simpson E. L. (1980). 'Adult learning theory: a state of the art', in Lasker, H., Moore, J. and Simpson, E. L. (eds), *Adult Development and Approaches to Learning*, National Institute of Education, Washington, DC.

The Times (1972). 'Rescue work hampered by gaping crowds', *The Times*, 19 June.

2
Understanding Failure

As was said in Chapter 1, the main purpose of this book is to give the reader a general understanding of the nature of failure and to provide a systems methodology through which failure can be analysed, understood and predicted. We shall start to fulfil those aims by examining a number of questions. What is a failure? What is an accident? What is a disaster? What is a system and what are systems failures? As we begin to address these questions in this chapter we aim to provide the background and context necessary to enable readers to appreciate the ways in which treatment of these topics has developed over recent years. We shall examine some of the ways in which failures and disasters can be viewed, and in the process develop a working definition of each of the terms used in the questions.

CATEGORIZING FAILURE

A simple definition of failure is something that has gone wrong, or not lived up to expectations. Moving a little way beyond this simple statement, various types or categories of failure can be identified.

In the first, often called type 1 failures, the objectives of the designers, sponsors, or users are not met fully. So, for example, a toll bridge which carried barely any traffic, or an invention which never worked properly, would be type 1 failures. These are the failures which surround us each day. The company which goes into liquidation, the new light bulb which won't shine or the multi-million pound 240–bed hospital near Glasgow, Scotland which was put into receivership less than five months after being opened.

In type 2 failures the original objectives are met but there are also consequences or side effects which are judged to be inappropriate or undesirable. Thus the seemingly beneficial drug thalidomide which was later found to cause birth defects and the mining operation at Aberfan which produced unsafe spoil heaps were both type 2 failures.

These two categories of failure are not mutually exclusive; an object may fail to live up to expectations and have undesirable consequences. For example, the Anglo-French supersonic aircraft Concorde failed to meet cost objectives and turned out to be so noisy that it was banned from some airports.

Even though the term failure may be used to refer to something which no longer functions it is important to note that this meaning is not necessarily synonymous with 'going wrong'. An item may be designed to fail at a particular time or in particular circumstances. Indeed such failure can be an integral part of a safety-based design. A simple example is a fuse in the plug of a kettle which will fail to conduct electricity if the current it is expected to carry rises above a particular limit. The failure of the fuse is a built-in device to protect the rest of the kettle from experiencing that high current and therefore the failure of the fuse is also its successful operation. Something has gone wrong, but the fuse has achieved the design objectives. These could be considered as a third category of failure.

A fourth category of failure can be said to have occurred when the objectives that were set were met without undesirable consequences or side effects but by the time they were achieved there was no longer any merit or satisfaction in achieving them. Examples of these failures are products designed for a market which no longer exists or to meet legal or safety standards which no longer apply. Such failures satisfy their own internal criteria, but those criteria are, at least with the benefit of hindsight, no longer appropriate. For example, in Milton Keynes a well-engineered railway bridge was built to carry the line from Oxford to Cambridge over the London to Manchester line.

Unfortunately by the time it was ready the Oxford to Cambridge line had been closed.

It can be argued that the distinction between type 1 failures and this fourth category hinges on whether the objective setting was carried out correctly in the first place. In defining type 1 failures the objectives are clearly taken as given and a judgement made solely about the extent to which they are met. The definition of the fourth category leaves open the question of whether the original objectives were flawed. What at first appears to be a straightforward categorization rapidly becomes more complicated because it relies very heavily on the view taken of the original objectives which is in turn dependent on the standpoint of the observer.

Table 2.1   *Failure types*

Type 1	Objectives not met
Type 2	Undesirable side effects
Type 3	Designed failures
Type 4	Inappropriate objectives

Almost all judgements about failure are subjective; they are coloured by personal perception, circumstances and expectations. A new play may be a great success for its authors and director and take a lot of money at the box office but fail to meet the expectations of some in the audience who had interpreted the title in a different way. A light bulb may be designed to function for 2000 h but even when it meets this requirement it may still be considered a failure by the householder, left in the dark with no replacement. The manufacturer and the shopkeeper who provide its replacement may, however, take a different view. In engineering, designers talk of mean time between failures (mtbf) as a design attribute. Although what can be thought of as 'designed failures' are not the topic of this book they are an essential feature of design to avoid failure and will therefore be considered later in that context.

So far the examples that have been used have illustrated failures associated with designed objects of some sort, but anything which is perceived to be a failure can be looked at in the same way and regarded as an outcome of a set of activities, just as a designed object is the outcome of a set of design and production activities. For the purpose of the form of analysis recommended in this book these activities are regarded as having taken place within an organized whole which is called a system.

Naughton and Peters (1976) referred to the failures arising from sets of related activities as Systems Failures and characterized them as relying on:

1 human perception and identification as a failure, thereby acknowledging that one person's failure may be another person's success;
   and either:
2 failure to meet system objectives attributed by those involved, such as designers and users;
   or
3 the production of outputs which are considered to be undesirable by those involved.

It is this rather wide definition of systems failures, which only excludes type 3 failures and where significance is entirely in the eye of the beholder, that has been the basis of much of the work referred to in this book.

One term which has been deliberately sidestepped in this discussion of failure is accident. Apart from using it in the everyday sense as a synonym for crash, we avoid it because it can carry with it connotations of unavoidability and unpredictability. In passing, however, it is worth noting that the concept of accident has been developed by some authors to the point where it comes close to the concept of systems failure as used here. One example is Laplat who refers to an accident as 'a consequence of dysfunctioning in the system which does not work as planned'. (Laplat, 1984.)

DISASTERS

There are some failures which have such an immense impact that they inevitably receive widespread public attention and which are almost always the subject of investigation, even if it is only the instant type carried out by the news media. These events, such as oil platforms exploding or collapsing, ferries sinking, and planes crashing, are so momentous that they would create general agreement that something had gone very, very wrong. Much of the research and teaching which the authors have conducted over the past 20 years and which they have used to underpin this book has been concerned with these large-scale catastrophes or disasters. The term catastrophic failures (Bignell, Peters and Pym 1977) has been applied to them (without definition), but the name used more widely for this type of event is disasters.

Throughout the world there are many professionals who work in disaster-related fields. As well as academics, such as those involved in development studies, geography and geophysics, there are practitioners such as aid-workers and emergency planners, and they adopt a variety of definitions of what constitutes a disaster. Amongst the early subjective examples of a definition of a disaster one, due to Cisin and Clark (1962), which is apparently straightforward and relatively all-embracing defines a disaster as: 'an event, or series of events, which seriously disrupts normal activities'. This definition does, of course, imply a personal judgement about that which is serious, and a debate about what activities are normal.

At first glance it might seem that it should be possible to find a quantitative definition such as loss of life or economic damage so that in some sense a disaster is a failure of a particular magnitude. However, in practice, finding such clear and impartial definitions proves to be problematic. Every year thousands of people are killed in Britain as a result of road accidents. The Department of Transport estimate for 1989, for example, was 4907 fatal accidents which cost in the region of £5 million. Yet such accidents are not normally considered to constitute a disaster, except by the people who are personally involved. By contrast, each year some events occur which become universally referred to as disasters even though they involve very little, if any, loss of life.

This difficulty encountered in defining disasters quantitatively is magnified when any attempt is made to measure disasters so as to compare their magnitude. A critique of the failings of such attempts is given in Horlick-Jones and Peters (1991). It concentrates on one example, the Bradford disaster scale (Keller,

Wilson and Kara-Zaitri, 1990). This scale uses the number of fatalities involved in a disaster, with the number of deaths converted to a logarithmic scale (the type of scale used in the geophysical Richter scale which deals with earthquakes), to try to measure its magnitude. Thus a magnitude 1 disaster on the Bradford scale would involve 10 deaths, a magnitude 2 disaster 100 deaths and a magnitude 3 disaster 1000 deaths. Such an approach can be shown to be inadequate in a number of ways. First, the significance of a disastrous event may not lie in the number of fatalities but rather in its economic consequences or the social devastation it causes or its occurrence as part of a series of similar events. The 'disasters' that from time to time have hit the US space programme have resulted in very few deaths, but they have had dramatic impact on the continuation of the programme. Similarly the incident at the Three Mile Island nuclear power plant did not result in any loss of life but had a profound effect on attitudes to nuclear-powered electricity and was largely responsible for the fact that no new nuclear installations were built in California for the next decade.

This particular approach to quantification suffers from other defects too. Because logarithmic scales are unfamiliar to most people a significant public education programme would be required before it became universally recognized that a magnitude 1.3 disaster signified 10 more deaths than a magnitude 1.0 disaster, and that a magnitude 3.1 disaster meant 259 more deaths than a magnitude 3.0 disaster. The public's unfamiliarity with a logarithmic scale might not matter so much were it not that the disasters which result in very high fatalities invariably occur in developing countries, thus giving rise to the impression that the scale places a lower value on life in the Third World.

Even if quantification is difficult it sounds straightforward to at least distinguish disasters according to whether responsibility for their occurrence rests with God or humans. In such a division natural disasters, like earthquakes and hurricanes, which can claim many thousands of lives but which fortunately are relatively infrequent, would be regarded as Acts of God. On the other hand, disasters like rail accidents or chemical plant explosions, though far more common, rarely claim more than a handful of lives, are of human making. However, a simple split into whether the cause of a disaster can be traced back to God or 'Man' soon breaks down. Furthermore, it does not necessarily reflect the way in which people usually think about such things. In Canada, Wapner, Cohen and Kaplan (1976) looked at people's perceptions of hazards. (A hazard is the perceived event which would threaten life or property, whereas a disaster is the realization of that hazard (Whittow, 1980).) Their research indicated that people deploy a more subtle grouping into:

- natural (e.g. snowstorms, tornadoes)
- quasi-natural (e.g. air and water pollution)
- social (e.g. riots and epidemics) and
- man-made (e.g. industrial accidents).

In this book the failures which are considered are those which have been perceived as failures by people. A natural disaster would not therefore qualify if it happened without any significant impact on people. In theory a natural disaster could happen without having any direct influence on people whatsoever, but it is almost a point worthy of philosophical discussion as to whether such disasters can be said to have occurred if they were not perceived by humans and therefore had no impact. In any case, pure natural disasters are rare; and a natural disaster can be regarded as a failure if it could have been predicted and its impact reduced, or if the emergency planning in place to deal with its after-effects proved to be ineffective. So even if a disaster can only be considered as a failure if it is judged to be so by humans, a 'natural' disaster may still qualify because the impact of the natural disaster in terms of loss of life and cost is partially dependent upon factors such as settlement patterns, disaster preparedness and mitigation. Human intervention is at least a partial explanation of why the 6.9 Richter scale earthquake in the San Francisco Bay area in October 1989 resulted in one thousandth of the fatalities experienced as a result of a similar event in December 1988 in Armenia. Figure 2.1 shows the overlapping relationship between failures and disasters. For the purposes of this book disasters, with the exception of natural disasters, will be considered as a sub-set of failures.

The relationship between human perception and natural and quasi-natural hazards can be expressed in a more systemic way.

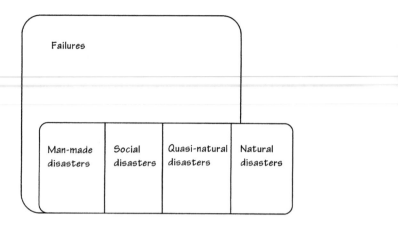

Figure 2.1   *The overlapping relationship between failures and disasters*

Figure 2.2 depicts a systemic model of the interacting features which are at play.

One particularly useful working definition (Susman, O'Keefe and Wisner, 1983) of disaster which keeps the term within the

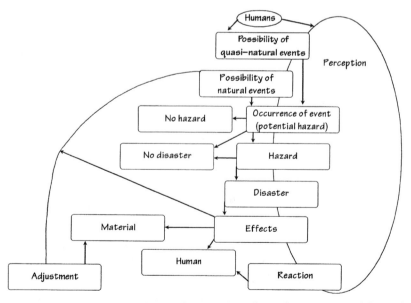

Figure 2.2   *A systems model to illustrate the effect of environmental hazards and the possible adjustments to a disaster (Reproduced by permission of the author from Whittow, 1980)*

scope of this book by acknowledging the human facets states: 'Disasters are the interface between an extreme physical event and a vulnerable human population.' This concept of vulnerability, which will be addressed again in the final chapter, appears to have considerable explanatory power in relation to disasters. When Susman's definition is linked with the idea of systems failures dealt with earlier and a third concept of a human activity system, what emerges is the view that disasters occur when a complex set of internal and external interactions result in a human activity system being (sometimes increasingly) vulnerable, and therefore more susceptible to disturbance by relatively minor events (Horlick-Jones, Fortune and Peters, 1993).

UNDERSTANDING FAILURE

The underlying theme of this book and the work which underpins it is that there are common features which are not specific to the technical or physical aspects of the failure situation. By the end of this chapter the stage will have been set for such an all embracing approach. Armed with working definitions of what is considered a failure and the characteristics of a disaster, the next task is to fill in some of the background and examine some of the different ways in which they have been considered previously and separate ways in which they can be characterized. Much of the work of others has been based upon a narrower focus, either because of the background of the people involved, or the context in which they act. Therefore it is important that the more specific approaches are considered before moving on to the general.

It will be obvious that a failure could be classified according to the type of situation in which it occurs. Thus, a failure in the provision of facilities for the mentally-ill will have certain aspects which are peculiar to the context and different from the failure of a UN peace-keeping mission, which will be different again from a railway accident. It may also be the case that once a preliminary analysis has been undertaken it will be possible to pigeon hole the failure into some classification in terms of the underlying basis of the failure such as whether it has social or technical causes. Neither are the focus of this book, but both may need to be drawn upon in a particular setting. However there are some types of classification which fall midway between the generalized all-embracing approach described later and the topic-specific. The most common is the separation of type 1 failures into those arising during design and development and those which occur during operation.

Design and development failures have received particular attention in the literature and in the public eye because they are usually high-cost and/or high-risk activities in terms of organizational performance. Major projects such as the construction of the Channel Tunnel (the background of which is given later, in Chapter 9) or other civil engineering and transport innovations are conspicuous if they are abandoned or turn out to be late, over budget or fail to live up to expectations when they are completed.

PLANNING FAILURES

One particularly noticeable aspect of design and development failures occurs in the public planning arena. Peter Hall, in his book *Great Planning Disasters* (Hall 1980), sought to analyse planning when it goes wrong. His definition of a disaster was 'any planning process that is perceived by many people to have gone wrong'. These he then splits into two types:

Negative disasters: decisions to take a course of action culminating in a physical result, that was later substantially modified or reversed or abandoned after considerable commitment of effort or resources.

Positive disasters: decisions to take a particular course of action, with physical results that were implemented despite much criticism and even opposition, and which were later felt by *many informed* people to have been a mistake.

One example of a negative disaster quoted by Hall is the abandonment of the third London Airport project. Where the positive disasters are concerned it is interesting to note that Hall's examples at the time of writing were the Anglo-French supersonic aircraft, Concorde, the Sydney Opera house, and the San Francisco Bay area rapid transit system (BART), not all of which would be universally considered disasters today. Indeed, the Sydney Opera House is very highly acclaimed.

Whereas in this book it is argued that failure and disaster are matters of personal perception and judgement, Hall takes a stronger line and considers only cases where at least a significant minority would adopt a similar viewpoint. As he puts it:

> I may think that the Channel Tunnel was thoroughly desirable and its abandonment (in the 1960s) was a disaster; you may think that BART is the finest rapid transit system in the world or the Sydney Opera house is the twentieth Centuries' most distinguished building, but many people criticised these projects and in some case criticism led to abandonment.

Hall analyses these planning failures in terms of a triangle of actors: bureaucrats; politicians; and the public. Put simply he sees decisions arising from the interaction of these three. Bureaucrats who, except when political pressure demands massive expansion, are largely seen as conservative and concerned with the maintenance of existing policies and programmes. The public are regarded as on the fringes and primarily effective in the planning context through pressure groups, and the politicians, in order to maximize votes, are seen as responding to pressure groups in differing ways at different times. Hall considers this arrangement to be unstable because it relies solely on the conservatism of the bureaucracy to provide some counterweight to frequent changes of policy.

Hall considers that this model partially explains cost escalation in public projects, particularly when they benefit a particular group, and it explains how an established bureaucracy can resist pressure for change by letting an issue subside and thereby achieve what is in practice a policy reversal.

A classic case of the way in which a long standing policy eventually prevails was a *cause célèbre* during the second part of the twentieth century. From 1968 until 1971 the Roskill Commission spent millions of pounds considering sites for a third London airport, to complement Heathrow and Gatwick. It recommended Cublington in Buckinghamshire. One member of the commission dissented and supported the choice of Foulness, or Maplin as it became known. The Government, in 1971, eventually supported the Maplin proposal. In 1974 the Government abandoned the Maplin project. In 1975/6 the Government consulted on sites other than Maplin, and in 1978 it reaffirmed Maplin again, only to see a future Government abandon it again.

Meanwhile, amongst the remaining 76 sites that were considered by Roskill was one which had been accepted by an earlier Government Inquiry in 1967 but which had been dropped after public protests. The Roskill Inquiry dismissed it within seven months. That site was Stanstead. Stanstead was already owned by the British Airports Authority, it had been the favoured site of the expert authorities (bureaucrats) and, except when politicians set up the Roskill commission or made political decisions, it was *de facto* the policy from the 1960s.

Hall's case for the persistence of policy is reinforced by subsequent events. In 1991 Stanstead's much heralded new terminal was opened and it is now established in the role of third London airport.

A simplified version of Hall's explanatory model of the actor's role in planning decisions is expressed diagrammatically in Figure 2.3.

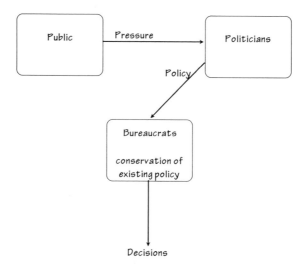

Figure 2.3   *Simple planning decision model*

PROJECT FAILURES

The second major strand to design and development failures consists of information technology projects which, like construction projects, are frequently expensive, and which are increasingly high risk. As organizations rely more heavily on information and computerized transactions in a rapidly changing technological environment, they are faced progressively with new software systems and changes in hardware which, if introduced unsuccessfully, may mean that the organization can no longer transact its business. The computer press is littered with examples of these information technology fiascos or near disasters. An example is the computer aided dispatch system introduced into the London Ambulance Service in 1992. The £1.5 million system was brought into full use at 07:00 hours on 26 October and almost immediately began to 'lose' ambulances. During that and the next day less than 20% of ambulances reached their destinations within 15 minutes of being summoned, a very poor performance when compared with the 65% arriving within 15 minutes the previous May and the target set by the Government of 95%. The service reverted to semi-computerized methods during the afternoon of 27 October and then right back to manual methods on 4 November when the system locked up altogether and could not be re-booted successfully (South West Thames Regional Health Authority, 1993).

More generally Sauer (1988) comments:

> Some systems never work. The full suite of programs and files are never made operational because they will be unacceptable to the user. Some work, but come in either cripplingly over budget, very late, or both. Others are pared down in terms of facilities, while still others are literally forced into place in their host organisation, despite their being either inappropriate or unacceptable. Some perform to specification but turn out to be so inflexible that maintenance and enhancement assume nightmarish proportions. Others are thought to work, but turn out not to. (Sauer, 1988, p. 4.)

Major new developments, products or organizational changes which are crucial to success are frequently treated as 'projects'. Indeed, some organizations such as civil engineering firms live almost entirely by projects, and for them the stakes are particularly high in terms of organizational success. There is a whole literature of sets of techniques and methods for project management and project planning, but projects remain highly vulnerable to failure. (It could be said, though, that treating such activities as projects makes failure more explicit than would be the case if they were a part of normal routine activity.)

Before looking at some particular aspects of project failures, it is worth emphasizing that even labelling a project as a failure can be problematic. It might seem that it is inherent in the nature of a project and its context that agreement about what constitutes failure and success is more easily identified. In theory the project should have had clearly defined objectives and if these were not met fully it can be said to have failed. Fortune (1987) identified the three main threats to project success as cost escalation, delay and client dissatisfaction with the outcome, and a project may not meet expectations on any one or a combination of these three aspects. Because a project may be a success in one arena but not in another, the ambiguity about the extent and nature of failure persists here as elsewhere. Mansell (1993), for example, describes a failures study of an information technology project. The project which 'had become legendary in the company as a failure in the application of information technology' was late and over budget, but on the other hand there was no loss of service to the users. So this project failed on two out of three counts. In this particular context Mansell also reports the existence of type 2 failures, the 'other adverse effects of this project were a loss of staff morale and user confidence'. Though even on this front the messages are mixed since he also reports that 'Staff who left the company had no difficulty in gaining alternative employment.'

With one particular form of information system development that is commonly used the system is completed before it is implemented. This approach is common in other projects too, particularly those where outside 'experts' are called in to devise changes. It would seem that implementation activities are especially susceptible to failure. One of the classic pieces of evidence for this is a survey by West Churchman of the cases reported in the first six years of the *Journal of the Operations Research Society of America*. He did not find a single example where there was sufficient evidence to indicate that the findings had been implemented (Churchman, 1964). Subsequent studies came to more optimistic conclusions, but some showed once again the subjective nature of the judgement about success and failure. An example in Table 2.2 shows the results of a survey conducted by Wedley and Ferrie (1978) of 49 OR/management science projects and how their success was judged by the analysts and the managers responsible for their implementation. Whereas the analysts viewed 63% of the projects as successful and implemented the managers put only 20% into this category.

Table 2.2 *Distribution of projects by implementation status as classified by analysts and managers*

	Analysts' classification		
	Unsuccessful	Successful but unimplemented	Successful and implemented
Managers' classification			
Unsuccessful	6%	6%	10%
Successful but unimplemented	10%	14%	33%
Successful and implemented	0%	0%	20%

There are numerous studies and advice on the causes of project failure, particularly where IT projects are concerned, and frequently 'the best recipe for success' is proffered. A few of these are based upon detailed analysis of a number of failures, whilst others are based more on pragmatic experience. One which is not untypical and which provides a useful framework for the early examination of a failure of this type identifies 12 types of failure in information systems development (Block, 1983). In Table 2.3 these have been grouped under three broad headings which are not those of the original author. The framework is not used explicitly in subsequent chapters, but it is included here so that it can be used as an initial check-list for ensuring that the core features of a failure have been examined.

Both in operational research and information systems projects the avoidance of failure has become an important part of project planning. Ackoff (1960) offered five rules for practitioners:

1 Never sign a contract you cannot break.
2 Never report to anyone lower than the authority capable of controlling all the functions involved in a study.

3 Never report to the responsible authorities through inter-
mediaries.

4 Never fail to complain forcibly to management about undesirable research conditions.

5 Never perform research for anyone at no cost to him or her.

Table 2.3   *Failures in information systems development (after Block, 1983)*

Aims
- Goal failures: inadequate specification of what it is the system has to achieve.
- Requirement failures: deficiency in the more detailed specification of the project.

Organization
- Resources failures: insufficient people time or money to achieve the objectives.
- Size failure: mismatch between the management of the project and the resources available on the one hand and the scope of the activity on the other hand.
- Organizational failures: both internal management of the project team and support from the organization.
- Methodology failures: overall synthesis of software projects involves an explicit method to which the project needs to adhere.
- Planning and control failures: inadequacy in monitoring and control which ideally needs to be coupled to realistic achievable plans.

Methods
- Technique failures: misapplication of particular tools or misjudgment about their appropriateness.
- Technology failures: reliance on technologies such as hardware and software which do not perform as expected.

People
- People management failures: failures in motivation and team building which jeopardize success.
- Personality failures: conflicts between individuals and mismatches between personal attributes and task requirements.
- User contact failures: insufficient checking by designers and builders with those who will use the system.

More recently Pinto and Slevin (1987) asked part-time students
on an MBA programme who were in full-time employment and
who had been members of a project team within the last two
years to consider successful projects (designated as resulting in
organizational change) with which they had been involved and
to identify five actions, in order of priority, a project manager
could take to help substantially the successful implementation
of that project. Their responses were then analysed to give the

Table 2.4 *Critical success factors in projects*
(after Pinto and Slevin, 1987)

Aims
Project goals are clearly defined

Organization
Resources are sufficient
Control mechanisms are in place and used
Project has support of top management
Communication channels are adequate
There is capability for feedback
Contractors are responsive to clients

People
Project manager is competent
Project team is competent

critical success factors shown in Table 2.4. To aid comparison with Block's failure list, the same structure of aims, organization, methods and people has been used, although in this case no success factors relating to methods were identified.

SUMMARY

This chapter has begun the exploration into the nature of failure which is a major feature of this book. Having established some working definitions of failures, a disaster has been specified as a special type of failure that can occur at the interface between an extreme physical event and a vulnerable human population. This chapter has also examined some classifications of disaster and failure and reviewed some relevant work on particular aspects of failure in design and development projects. The next chapter will examine the human and organizational aspects of failure and provide the context for the systemic approach which forms the core of this book.

REFERENCES

Ackoff, R. L. (1960). 'Unsuccessful case studies and why' *Operations Research*, **8**, 259–62.
Bignell, V., Peters, G. and Pym C. (1977). *Catastrophic Failures*, Open University Press, Milton Keynes.

Block, R. (1983). *The Politics of Projects*, Yourdon, New York.

Churchman C. W. (1964). 'Managerial acceptance of scientific recommendations', California Management Review, 31–38 (fall).

Cisin, I. H. and Clark, W. (1962). 'The methodological challenge of disaster research', in Baker G. W. and Chapman, D. W. (Eds), *Man and Society in Disaster*, Basic Books, New York.

Department of Transport (1990). Highways Economics Note No. 1 (November 1990) *Road Accident Costs 1989*, HMSO, London.

Fortune, J. (1987). *Projects and Their Genesis*, Open University Press, Milton Keynes.

Hall, P. (1980). *Great Planning Disasters*, Weidenfeld & Nicolson, London.

Horlick-Jones, T., Fortune, J. and Peters G. (1993). 'Vulnerable systems, failure and disaster', in Stowell, F. A., West, D. and Howell, J. G. (Eds), *Systems Science: Addressing Global Issues*, Plenum Press, New York.

Horlick-Jones, T. and Peters, G. (1991). 'Measuring disaster trends part one', *Disaster Management*, **3**, 144–8.

Keller, A. Z., Wilson, H. and Kara-Zaitri, C. (1990). 'The Bradford disaster scale', *Disaster Management*, **2**, 207–13.

Laplat, J. (1984). 'Occupational accident research and systems approach', *Journal of Occupational Accidents*, **6**, 77–89.

Mansell, G. (1993). 'The failures method and soft systems methodology', *Systemist*, **15**, 190–204.

Naughton, J. and Peters, G. (1976). *Systems and Failures*, Open University Press, Milton Keynes.

Pinto, J. K. and Slevin D. P. (1987). 'Critical success factors in successful project implementation', *IEEE Transactions on Engineering Management*, EM **34**, 22–7.

Sauer, C. (1988). 'The value of case studies in understanding organizational aspects of information systems', internal paper, Department of Computer Science, University of Western Australia.

South West Thames Regional Health Authority (1993). *Report of the Inquiry into the London Ambulance Service*, South West Thames Regional Health Authority, London.

Susman, P., O'Keefe, P. and Wisner, B. (1983). 'Global disaster a radical interpretation', in Hewitt, K. (Ed.) *Interpretation of Calamity*, Allen & Unwin, Winchester, Mass.

Wapner, S., Cohen, S.B. and Kaplan B. (1976). *Experiencing the Environment*, Plenum, New York.

Wedley, W. C. and Ferrie, A. E. J. (1978) 'Perceptual differences and effects of managerial participation on project implementation', *Journal of Operational Research*, **29**, 199–204.

Whittow, J. (1980). *Disasters, the Anatomy of Environmental Hazards,* Allen Lane, London.

3
Approaches to Understanding Failure

This chapter starts by using the simple taxonomy of aims, methods, organization and people, as introduced in the previous chapter in the context of project failures and critical success factors, to examine different ways of looking at failure across a broader spectrum of activities. In this chapter, as in much of this book, the focus is on *post hoc* analysis and understanding linked to some modelling of the context and possible causes of a particular failure. Understanding is a necessary precursor of any action to avoid or alleviate the consequences of future failure.

In the case of methods which are specifically linked to the study of failure the variety is wide, ranging from mathematical treatments of the relationships of abstract systems of failure modes on the one hand, to sociological treatises on the role of the media in disasters on the other. Some approaches are concerned with engineering design and others with the characteristics of stereotypical humans. However, since the failures which are the concern of this book are failures involving human organization and activity, and at this point it is only understanding that is required, this section concentrates on approaches which provide insight into the human aspects of failure and to the related topics of error and disaster. Thus the emphasis is on people and organizations.

The chapter is not designed to provide an exhaustive survey

of all the approaches, methods and techniques for understanding failure which are available. In deciding which material to include an attempt has been made to illustrate the range of what is available but inevitably the chapter concentrates upon the work which the authors have found to be particularly useful and informative and is thus biased towards material which draws on systems thinking.

The structure of the following sections of this chapter derives from a simple model of human involvement in failure. The starting point is individual humans and the characteristics which they can display in failure situations. The remainder of the sections are concerned primarily with people collectively, whether in groups, organizations or whole societies. Inevitably such a simple hierarchy does some injustice to the original authors whose work has been used, and so to minimize this some overlap has been allowed between the levels.

INDIVIDUAL FACTORS AND HUMAN ERROR

For the past 50 years as technology has become more sophisticated and widespread in its use there has been a matching development of a body of knowledge about how people behave when working and interacting with it. Much of the emphasis has been on determining how machines or environments or work layouts can best be organized to enable humans to perform more effectively and to make their lives more comfortable. The driving force behind the research, much of which has been carried out in the industrial or military context, has usually been greater efficiency and productivity.

In the United Kingdom the term ergonomics was originally coined to mean the study of man and machines in the working environment. It brought together physiologists and psychologists in a problem-solving framework. In the United States the more familiar term for this area of study is human factors, although it places greater emphasis on the psychological aspects of human-machine interactions. There are other similar approaches—for example human-computer interaction (HCI)—which can cover much of today's technology, and de Greene

(1970) coined the term *systems psychology* to capture the whole area of the human as the crucial element within a system.

Probably the aspect of human factors which is most central to the understanding of failure is the concept of human error. In its everyday context the term 'error' covers the widest variety of mistakes or misjudgements on the part of operators, designers or maintainers of systems and equipment. In the more specialist human factors disciplines the term is usually applied to circumstances where a human being acts in a manner inappropriate to a particular situation, perhaps by deviating from the prescribed practice by omitting or adding some action, or failing to respond to a change in the setting in which the task is being undertaken. There is a considerable body of research on the topic of error, much of it concerned with the human operator in complex technological environments (often military) such as aircraft cockpits and power station control rooms. Excellent and thorough treatments of the current state of knowledge in this area are available, and the authors would particularly recommend interested readers to refer to Reason (1990) for a systematic synthesis. Reason uses a framework, originated by Rasmussen and Jensen (1974), which distinguishes between three levels of performance, each of which is liable to different types of error: skill-based performance, rule-based performance and knowledge-based performance. Skill-based performance is concerned with what are, in effect, stored patterns of behaviour which can be likened to the simplest straightforward computer programs. Rule-based performance is concerned with the situation where there is a set of patterns for dealing with familiar scenarios or problems. It encompasses the routine application of well-rehearsed procedures, but also incorporates elements where alternative courses of action are required, the appropriateness of each depending on the particular circumstances. To continue the computer-programming analogy, rule-based performance is the equivalent of a program with branches which say 'If . . . then . . .'

Knowledge-based performance is necessary where no set pattern of behaviour exists, and where the situation, because it is novel, requires recourse to more basic principles. Over a period of time, knowledge-based performance may migrate to rule-based performance as patterns recur and become familiar. The way in which the situation is dealt with may then evolve to a stereotype and, in time, even become so automatic as to qualify for the description skill-based.

Errors in skill-based performance are essentially simple: either something can be missed inadvertently or something can be added to the normal routine accidentally. Reason calls these 'inattention' and 'overattention' respectively, and goes on to classify different aspects of each, giving examples based upon actual cases reported to him (Table 3.1).

Table 3.1 *Skill-based errors (Reproduced by permission of the author from Reason, 1990)*

Inattention
Omissions following interruptions—phone rings part way through an action
Reduced intentionality—opening the refrigerator and failing to remember why
Perceptual confusions—pouring tea into the sugar bowl
Interference errors—trying to do two things and partially doing each, like making
    tea and feeding the cat and ending up putting cat food in the tea pot
Double-capture slips—writing one's old address on a letter

Overattention
Omissions—failing to boil the water when making tea
Repetitions—pouring water into an already full teapot
Reversals—taking off shoes intending to put on slippers only to put shoes back on

Rule-based errors and knowledge-based errors are also different from skill-based errors in that the first two are associated with dealing with problems while the third is concerned only with monitoring progress. Reason divides up rule-based errors into the misapplication of 'good rules' and the application of 'bad rules'.

However, it is the knowledge-based errors which are the most relevant to the failures being considered in this book. These are also the most difficult to classify. Reason proposes the ten types given in Table 3.2.

Reason has come to this classification of the types of errors which can occur from the study of individuals operating in a variety of conditions. However, as will be seen later, there is considerable similarity between the types of human error he identifies and the failure types identified by others who have taken a very different initial perspective. Indeed, Reason's subclass of knowledge-based error, which is concerned with com-

Table 3.2 *Knowledge-based errors (Reproduced by permission of the author from Reason, 1990)*

1 Selectivity—attending to the 'wrong information'
2 Workspace limitations—selecting an inappropriate framework or model for understanding the situation at hand
3 Out of sight out of mind—ignoring data which is not readily available and giving undue weight to that which is readily discernible
4 Confirmation bias—having made a preliminary judgement on a small amount of information, being unwilling to move from it as more information comes to light
5 Over-confidence—particularly in one's own knowledge
6 Biased reviewing—less than thorough checking back over the process of problem solving
7 Illusory correlation—misjudging a cause and effect relationship
8 Halo effects—faced with different orderings individuals will be inclined to reduce these to a single order
9 Problems with causality—general oversimplification of relationships
10 Problems with complexity—a major grouping which includes difficulties associated with handling multi-causality and lags in feedback
11 Problems of diagnosis in everyday situations—difficulties arising from trying to assess symptoms and simultaneously develop an hypothesis.

plexity and diagnosis, will be addressed repeatedly throughout this book.

PEOPLE IN GROUPS

The disasters and failures under consideration here are inextricably linked with people. According to the definition being used as set out in the previous chapter, they do, for a start, require humans to perceive them. People also play significant parts in failure situations. Their roles can range from being the victims and rescuers to being the original designers or decision-makers. They may be the current operators and maintainers or face the task of emergency planning and disaster response. As well as looking at the role played by people as individuals, it is also necessary to look at the way they act as part of wider groups. A wider group could be a small *ad hoc* rescue team, a project team or the maintenance crew in a company which owns a plant which explodes.

Models, such as transactional analysis for example, have been developed for explaining the nature of one-to-one interaction

between people, but they have limited relevance to the understanding of failures. The next level of human interaction, which
has come to be known as the 'small-group' interaction, can,
however, yield considerable insights.

A small group can be defined as a dynamic system of interaction between at least two people. Group life involves a continuous process of adaptation by individuals to one another
and to their mutual needs and problems (Lewin, 1948). Social
psychology has been much concerned with this level of human
activity in a variety of contexts stretching from therapy groups
to factory production teams. One important aspect of this work
has been the development of models of successful groups. If a
successful group is defined as one which succeeds at its tasks
then it is not surprising that a group which is deemed to be
successful has members who place a high value on their membership of the team. A successful group can, therefore, be judged
at least to a partial extent according to the level of allegiance
that individuals within it feel to one another. In many aspects
of human existence being a part of a successful group can be
regarded as crucial. Drug takers or alcoholics, for example, may
be helped to modify their behaviour by becoming members of
a group which they value highly and which frowns upon the
behaviour they have previously exhibited. Similarly a small
company may be more successful in business terms if everyone
within it feels part of a team and works closely with other
members to achieve the best for each other and the group.

In general, groups which are found to be most successful
display certain characteristics. For example, a successful group
is likely to feel autonomous from its surroundings, with an
obvious boundary surrounding the group which makes clear
who is inside the group and who is outside. It is also found
that the more difficult it is to obtain entry to a group, the more
membership of it is valued.

Strong groups also display behaviour which encourages
members of the group to conform to the group's own view
of the world. Members develop a view of outsiders which is
stereotypical, and put internal pressure on members who do
not share the group view of a situation. Although the origin of
this and similar findings is work with successful groups, an
important downside of their success that has been observed is

that strong group coherence, and other attributes associated with it, can result in the group becoming less successful at dealing with environmental changes and the task in hand. Janis (1972, 1982) has, in the context of work on public policy making, given the name 'groupthink' to this phenomenon. He uses it to refer to 'a mode of thinking that people engage in when they are deeply involved in a cohesive in-group, when members' strivings for unanimity override their motivation to realistically appraise alternative courses of action'. He goes on to say that groupthink 'refers to a deterioration of mental efficiency, reality testing, and moral judgement that results from in-group pressures.' (Janis, 1972, p. 9)

Janis has examined a series of American policy 'fiascos', and discovered strong evidence for groupthink with defective decisions being seen to arise from very cohesive groups. The examples he cites include the Kennedy administration's unsuccessful orchestration of the Bay of Pigs invasion of Cuba and the attack on the US Navy at Pearl Harbor by the Japanese. Unfortunately, even if groupthink provided a perfect explanation of poor decision making it would be difficult to establish it was occurring because, as Janis acknowledges, the link between decision making and outcomes is itself not perfect. A sound decision may still result in a debacle if poorly implemented, and a flawed decision may still be followed by a successful outcome if luck or the behaviour of others has a major, beneficial impact. However, by looking both at fiascos and policy successes Janis has been able to arrive at eight symptoms of groupthink which he has combined to form three main types. These symptoms help define the groupthink syndrome by observation. They are summarised in Table 3.3.

Although Janis developed this framework in the context of US policy making, it has not proved at all difficult for him to extend the model to the UK. He considered the members of the Chamberlain Government's inner circle who supported the policy of appeasement and concluded that they were probably dominated by groupthink. A more recent example in which it may well provide a description and at least a partial explanation of a group's problems concerns the Poll Tax (Community Charge) and its hasty withdrawal soon after its introduction

Table 3.3 *Symptoms of groupthink (after Janis, 1982)*

Type I Overestimates of the group: its power and morality
1 An illusion of invulnerability, which creates excessive optimism and encourages taking extreme risks.
2 An unquestioned belief in the group's inherent morality, inclining the members to ignore the ethical or moral consequences of their decisions.

Type II Closed-mindedness
3 Collective efforts to rationalize an order to discount warnings or other information that might lead the members to reconsider their assumptions before they recommit themselves to their past policy decisions.
4 Stereotyped views of enemy leaders as too evil, weak or stupid to counter the risky attempts to defeat their purposes.

Type III Pressures toward uniformity
5 Self-censorship of deviation from apparent group consensus, thereby minimizing the importance of any self doubt.
6 Shared illusion of unanimity partially resulting from self-censorship and partially from the false assumption that silence means consent.
7 Direct pressure for loyalty on members expressing arguments counter to the prevailing view.
8 The emergence of 'mindguards' who protect the group from adverse information.

and, indeed, the subsequent downfall of the then Prime Minister, Margaret Thatcher.

> 'Is he one of us?' was asked by Mrs Thatcher of colleagues about other colleagues . . . The criteria were political or economic rather than social. 'Wet' was used by her to rebuke colleagues who lacked her singleness of purpose or disagreed with her economic or social policy. (Watkins, 1991)

Those who have studied the pattern of many large scale accidents will recognize that the significance of groupthink in the context of systems failures is that it is a phenomenon which can potentially be associated with the behaviour of any groups. If coal-mine managers, safety engineers, or systems analysts isolate themselves from aspects of their environment then they become highly vulnerable. Groupthink may not be the underlying cause of major failures, but later in this chapter you will see examples of disasters where if groupthink was not occurring then behaviour that was remarkably similar was apparent.

ORGANIZATIONAL PHENOMENA

Having looked at individuals and groups, the next level of granularity is the organization. A particularly significant contribution to the literature which looks at disasters as organizational phenomena can be found in the work of the late Barry Turner (Peters and Turner, 1976; Turner, 1979). Using the official enquiry reports of three contemporary accidents he undertook a comparative study of disasters in order to try to find underlying thematic similarities. The three cases used were:

1 The 1966 Aberfan tip disaster in which a portion of the waste tip of the local colliery slid down into the village of Aberfan and in so doing killed 144 people, 114 of whom were children in the village school.
2 The Hixon level crossing accident in which a train hit a large road transporter in 1968. The incident occurred at a new type of automatic level crossing where the times allowed for the warning period were insufficient for such a slow-moving transporter.
3 The Summerland fire at a newly built holiday leisure complex on the Isle of Man. The complex was of a novel acrylic-covered steel-frame design. 3000 people were inside the building at the time and 50 of them died in the rapidly spreading fire.

Turner concluded that although the detail of the three failures were very different there were eight classes of similarity amongst them.

1 Rigidities in perception and beliefs in organizational settings. Within an organization there will, to some extent, be a similarity of approach and a distinctive culture which distinguishes it from others, and which may contribute to its success. Turner argues that this commonality may also lead to narrowed perceptions and may restrict the decision making of the organization. One example he quotes from the Aberfan Tribunal report illustrates how the colliery workers were concerned with coal production and not the dangers associated with the disposal of the waste products. This common perception seemed to make them oblivious to the dangers associated with the tip.

We found that many witnesses, not excluding those who were intelligent and anxious to assist us, had been oblivious of what lay before their eyes. It did not enter their consciousness. They were like moles being asked about the habits of birds.

2 Decoy problems. Difficulties and potential problems may be identified and dealt with, but these often turn out not to be the ones which lead to the accident. For example, there was concern about tipping at Aberfan, but when the tipping was stopped the danger was assumed to have passed even though the tip itself was still present.

3 Organizational exclusivity. The employees of an organization will be expert in its activities, therefore they may devalue the concerns expressed by outsiders.

4 Information difficulties. There is a tendency for any accident report to identify poor information and communications as contributory factors and to recommend better communications. Turner went beyond this to analyse the necessary features of secure communication and the potential for failure at various points. (Communications is dealt with in Chapter 6 of this book.)

5 The involvement of 'strangers', especially on complex 'sites'. The concept of a site arises from a physical situation which, as well as being designed for one purpose, has features and characteristics which make it apparently suitable for other purposes. Turner identifies strangers as another common feature. These are groups who are outside the immediate control and influence of an organization. They may be the general public or employees of other organizations, but briefing them and being certain of their levels of knowledge is problematic. As a simple example, a tractor may be designed for farm work, but to a young child it may look like an attractive piece of play equipment. The child then is a stranger on this site.

Strangers have been defined as people who have access to a part of a system, not necessarily legally, and who cannot be adequately briefed about the situation because they are not sufficiently clearly identified to enable training to take place, or because the 'keepers of the system' do not have sufficient influence over them to be informed. A site is a concrete subsystem the components of which have additional properties to those required by the system (Peters and Turner 1976).

6 Failure to comply with regulation. Turner identifies the inadequacy of existing regulations and the failure to revise and control the implementation of regulations.

7 Minimizing emergent dangers. Turner demonstrates a consistent pattern of underestimating the dangers as they become apparent. This pattern stretches from the initial recognition of the possibility of a hazard through to the first signs of the accident itself and a reluctance to call immediately for help. Even when the full potential of the danger is recognized the action taken may be inadequate and defensive. Turner quotes the British Railways fiat 'vehicles must not become immobilised on these crossings' as an example of the latter.

8 Nature of the recommendations: well-structured problems. A final aspect of Turner's findings was that the recommendations of the Inquiry were concerned with the avoidance of similar incidents. However, in the main the recommendations assumed that the problem had been identified and, as he puts it, 'structured', whereas the situation faced by the participants in the disaster had been ill-structured. This eighth point is included for completeness, although it is really a commentary on the learning process associated with failures rather than on the failures themselves.

PEOPLE, GROUPS AND ORGANIZATIONS

Although the approaches which have been outlined so far stem from a variety of disciplines and contexts and operate at different levels there are a number of similarities between them which are worth summarizing.

1 There is a strong similarity between Turner's rigidities in perception and beliefs in organizational settings, those aspects of Janis' conception of groupthink which are associated with closed mindedness, and some of Reason's knowledge-based errors (notably, selectivity, out of sight out of mind, and confirmation bias).
2 There are similarities between Turner's decoy problems and Reason's selectivity.
3 Turner's organizational exclusivity is linked both to type I

overestimates of the group, its power and morality, and type II closed mindedness in groupthink.

4 Minimizing emergent dangers ties in with Reason's knowledge-based error, biased reviewing.

In Chapter 5 considerable space will be devoted to the conceptualization of contexts in ways which have regard to the wider environment and influences. Although the ideas will be being applied to the *post hoc* analysis of failure the approach is relevant to points 1, 2 and 4 above.

SOCIETAL ASPECTS

The approach used by Turner (and, indeed, others) to the study of accidents, failures or disasters at the level of the organization was to try to identify underlying or common themes which can be found again and again in different situations. The method he used to try to identify these themes took the form of a systematic and scholarly enquiry into a small but carefully selected sample of disasters.

Cook (1989) has conducted a similar search for underlying or common themes but she has looked beyond organizational boundaries to study societal aspects and she has used an alternative method for conducting the search. Her investigative methods were essentially journalistic, relying on personal judgement rather than on the rigorous application of a particular social science method. She examined a series of case studies of accidents in the UK and drew conclusions that were primarily about the then state of the country and its administration:

> ... I do not believe that it is fortuitous that we have had three major disasters ... in as short a period under the Thatcher administration. This government has made an idol of profit. What is not profitable is worthless in every sense of the word. Alongside this belief goes another—all state or nationalised industries and services are bad, all privatised industries and utilities are good—gas electricity oil, all forms of transport, even water, have been or are to be sold off for quick cash returns.
>
> There is a direct link between profitability and Zeebrugge, King's cross and Piper Alpha. Those industries originally in private hands or already privatised must put their profit to shareholders first. Those

industries waiting to be privatised, like London Transport, must be made economic and fattened up ready for sale so that sufficient funds can be attracted when sale day comes.

The wreck of the Herald of Free Enterprise was, in part, brought about by three individuals, but overwhelmingly it was the result of 'sloppy management' described at the Inquiry, and the cost cutting that had put profit first. The continual overloading of the ferries against every rule of the sea was overlooked because it meant more money taken from fares. It became the norm, not the exception, to clip over a quarter of an hour off the turn-round time to keep profits up. Who knows, had the ship been turned around in the time properly allowed for the job then it might well be that there would have been ample time to check the bow doors. (Cook, 1989, p. 147)

The views which Cook voiced about the relationship of the prevailing ethos of the UK in the 1980s and the potential for accidents were not confined to her. A more detailed treatment was provided by Horlick-Jones (1990) who mounted a comprehensive account of UK disasters during the period. In an attempt to capture these apparent social changes in the UK in the 1980s, Hood and Jackson (1991) used the concept of the 'new public management' which they summarize as an administrative doctrine whereby a disaggregated approach to public sector management involving arms length and user-pays relationships between corporatized and privatized entities coupled with a strong emphasis on cost-cutting and cheap administration is preferred to investment in administrative systems. These factors, coupled with a penchant for deregulation, are seen as hallmarks of the 1980s which may have contributed to what some (for example Parker, 1991) saw as an unprecedented spate of major incidents.

By way of a specific illustration, Parker reports that during the lead up to the privatization of the water industry in England and Wales he and other researchers and engineers were actively discouraged by the Department of the Environment from discussing dam safety and the risks and possible consequences of a dam-break. Furthermore, he says that the Financial Services Act 1985 effectively precluded Government officials from commenting upon dam safety on the grounds that such comments might adversely affect share prices. In his view 'the judgment of government was that share prices were more important than sharing information about the risks to the public.' It is not the intention in this book to dwell on the distinctive circumstances of recent UK history and its impact on failures and disasters, but the work outlined here does illustrate how comparative studies can yield a thematic view of a set of occurrences in a specific country at a particular time.

SYSTEMS AND FAILURE

In general it should by now be apparent that commentators have found that disasters are complex in origin. The degree of simplicity or sophistication of the approaches already outlined in this chapter varies considerably, but so far none of them are systemic, nor do they claim to address issues of complexity specifically. But though certain approaches may make it possible to identify common themes, those themes alone are not sufficient in themselves to explain all disasters. Further analytical tools are needed and this book seeks to provide them.

Most of the remaining material in this book is concerned with analysing the complexity of individual situations which result in disasters and failures. One example is Bhopal in India where, in the early hours of 3 December 1984, a gas leak occurred at the Union Carbide of India Ltd pesticide production plant in India. In terms of the number of fatalities this was still at the time of writing this book the worst industrial accident in history.

It is possible to analyse this disaster in scientific and engineering terms which attempt to demonstrate how the gas came to be generated in the plant and how it escaped. The management can be examined to see whether the relationship between the Union Carbide Corporation in the USA and UCIL worked effectively and whether local arrangements to handle maintenance were at fault. Explanations can be sought in the nature of Indian politics, looking at aspects such as planning, industrial and even military policies. On a global scale there are those who see what was happening at Bhopal as a part of a trend whereby the West exports hazardous technologies to the developing world with inevitably disastrous outcomes.

One analysis of the Bhopal tragedy (Bogard, 1989) acknowledges the complex and different perceptions of the situation and the variety of standpoints and disciplines that can be employed. Bogard takes the view that there is no single explanation of an incident such as the Bhopal gas leak, but that on one hand there are systems of interacting social, technological and ecological hazards and on the other there is a similarly complex discursive network of conflicting and contradictory interpretations of these systems. The rest of this chapter will pick up Bogard's use of the word system as a trigger to start building upon ideas from the systems world which have been found to be valuable in the failure context. Chapter 7 describes the Bhopal tragedy in detail and presents some of the analytical treatments to which it has been subjected.

BASIC SYSTEMS CONCEPTS

Perception and Appreciation

The complex nature of failures and disasters has been a recurring theme so far and at this point it is appropriate to develop the beginnings of a tool chest of concepts and methods for dealing with this complexity. Before examining the applicability of these systems tools we shall be using it is necessary to gain some familiarity with them and to develop an appreciation of their accompanying health warnings. In the previous section attention was drawn to Bogard's framework which refers to systems of interacting social, technological and ecological hazards and to the complex discursive network of conflicting and contradictory interpretations of these systems. The implication of these words and similar utterances by many other writers is that whatever systems are, they exist in some objective sense. An alternative view, which is held by the authors, is that 'system' is a notion which is applied to a situation, often with the aim of understanding it or explaining it more easily. The difference in these two views—whether systems exist or not —is far more than a philosophical argument of the type which would have occupied the Nominalists and the Realists in the Middle Ages. It has practical implications for the way in which systems ideas are handled and influences the extent to which their use in a particular application can be regarded as valid.

To take the view that a particular system exists implies that, once the definition of a system has been agreed and the information about a candidate for the descriptor 'system' is known, there will be agreement about whether or not it is a system. Inherent in this approach is not just the assumption that a concept such as system has a public currency but also the view that individuals share a single unambiguous perception about the features of a specific situation. As illustrations, the term system is widely used in everyday speech in relation to transport or education, but while two people may both complain about the poor state of the education system it is unlikely that they would both include the same features in their descriptions of this system. They may both recognize teachers and school premises as parts of the system but may disagree over the inclusion of parents, pupils, politicians, publicly funded and privately-funded schools, and the broadcasters. Even when there is agreement over what constitutes the system there is seldom a single view as to the nature of the relationships between its components. It is far safer, therefore, to take the view that though systems concepts such as component, sub-system and system itself may be defined, they will be applied by individuals to different features of a specific context. Thus whatever one's views on the philosophical argument about whether systems are or are not constructs it is, as a matter of practical expediency, better to subscribe to the view that the systems identified for the purpose of analysis do not actually exist as systems. Certain individuals are deciding to treat particular features of a situation as if they conform to a (sometimes personal) set of rules and definitions for the concept 'system' so as to be able to further their understanding.

Now for a health warning. When these ideas are applied they are often found to be particularly rewarding and capable of providing powerful insights. In such circumstances it is remarkably tempting for the practitioner to slide into a way of working which comes close to assuming that the systems do actually have some objective reality. The authors of this book are firmly of the opinion that systems are only constructs—indeed, one of the strengths of the idea is that what is taken to constitute the system can be experimented with and changed—but of course there will sometimes be a close and deceptive correspondence between the elements that the practitioner would together choose to consider as a system and what might commonly be called a system. Experience suggests that it is all too easy to describe and write about systems as though they exist, and what is more, the linguistic manoeuvres required to avoid this misrepresentation become very tedious. Therefore the words used to identify, describe or investigate systems in this book may not always remind the reader of the authors' standpoint despite their best intentions. Furthermore when other authors are quoted it will not always be known or made explicit how they are using such terms, so particular caution will sometimes be needed.

The term 'system' refers to an 'organized whole' or a set of components that are interconnected. The decision as to which, if any, aspects of a scenario can be regarded as constituting a system will depend upon the interest and background of the viewer as well as the purpose of the study. Vickers (1963) uses the term 'appreciative system' to describe a state of readiness to distinguish some aspects of a situation rather than others and to classify and value these in this way rather than that. In applying systems ideas it is important that analysts are both aware of their own appreciative systems which give rise to the values and norms which they apply, and are also aware of the appreciative systems of other participants in the situation.

A related concept is *Weltanschauung*, the German word for world view, which in general usage refers to a personal philosophy of life and the universe. It is used in much the same way by systems practitioners to make explicit their view that different individuals have a distinct set of values, different perceptions and distinct expectations. Appreciative system and *Weltanschauung* thus both attempt to provide mechanisms which explain why perceptions and interpretations differ from individual to individual.

Holism

A further application of the above concept is found in the work of Churchman (1971) and others who use contrasting *Weltanschauungen* to widen the conception of a situation or problem in order to provide a broad understanding. The two fundamental aspects of the systems approach are organization and wholeness and it is this wholeness to which Churchman strives with multiple *Weltanschauungen*; consideration of the whole is an essential precursor to considering individual parts. A systems perspective thus has to start from trying to ensure that all the likely angles have been covered, all the potentially fruitful ways of looking at a situation have been explored and all the features which may be relevant have been examined. Note that in this last sentence every 'all' has been deliberately qualified by 'likely', 'potentially fruitful' or 'may be relevant'. It is neither feasible nor desirable to examine every feature of a situation whatever its relevance. It is always necessary to employ judgement, but one important aspect of a systems approach is this striving for a comprehensive overview of relevant aspects before any detailed investigation is undertaken. This deliberate taking of an overview is commonly called holism.

Readers should note that there is also a more specialized use of the term holism. Checkland (1981) would wish to reserve use of the term 'holism' for the far more precise scientific sense of being concerned with wholes as opposed to a reductionist approach which builds up understanding and models from the individual parts. This is not the usage adopted here where the term system is used to mean discrete but interconnected entities.

Environment and Boundary

If a system is to be identified and considered as a clearly defined entity within some context, then it needs to be distinguished from its surroundings. This requires two further concepts: environment and boundary. The boundary is the imaginary line which delineates what is considered to be the system from that which is outside. However, the environment is not the rest of the world which lies outside the system; whether something is judged to be part of the environment is determined by whether or not it influences or is influenced by the system which has been perceived. The environment can also exert a degree of control over the system but the environment cannot be controlled by the system.

These three basic concepts of system, boundary and environment are remarkably powerful tools for reaching an understanding of or explaining failures. If for example a factory manager does not fully consider all the external factors which may influence her department, she may find that a failure occurs because she has not allowed for the disruptive impact of a strike at a key supplier. Similarly a company which does not consider Parliament or the changing legislative framework when it decides to embark on a new product may find that its market no longer exists, in the same way that in the 1970s and 1980s some UK car manufacturers were unable to respond to the rapidly changing environmental standards in California.

A simple example of the strength of the concepts can found by looking at the requirements for emergency planning. Emergencies very seldom come to the emergency services. Fire fighters and ambulances need to get to the scene of a disaster. Therefore they need fuel and roads which are passable. Many people trying to look at this as a system might locate the road network and the petrol supply in the environment, but it is less apparent that the electricity supply must also be in the environment. Electricity is needed for a variety of reasons; providing the energy for petrol pumps is one example. It might seem that such considerations are unimportant, but now imagine an earthquake where roads are destroyed or blocked and electricity supplies are cut. Unless the planning had included these two aspects of the situation the effectiveness of the plans would be somewhat diminished to say the least.

Closed and Open Systems

There are of course many other systems concepts, some of which will be introduced as this book progresses. The concept of environment brings with it the theoretical possibility that a system might not have an environment. Such theoretical abstractions are useful in physics and thermodynamics. A system which does not interact with anything else, and which thus does not have an environment, is termed a closed system. It is hard to imagine a scenario where whilst trying to be holistic it proved to be insightful to consider a system as closed. If, however, a closed system was perceived it would have very different properties from the more normal open system. Because a theoretically closed system imports or exports nothing, not even energy, materials or ideas from its surroundings, the second law of thermodynamics says that it can only deteriorate. This disorder is called entropy, and in a closed system it can only increase.

Although it is not helpful to consider a system as closed when trying to capture all the relevant features for a full understanding, the concept can prove penetrating as an explanation of the behaviour of people in a situation. One example is the work of Kirschman-Anderson (1980) who used a few basic systems concepts to try to explain the Jonestown massacre in which 913 followers of the Reverend Jim Jones' religious cult the 'People's Temple' died, apparently after drinking a mixture of cyanide and soft drink. She found that systems concepts like open and closed systems, entropy and feedback provided an adequate framework for analysis and explanation. Her use of closed system mirrors the groupthink symptom of closed mindedness whereby the group overestimates its power and morality and then becomes inclined to ignore the ethical or moral consequences of its decisions.

Systemic and Systematic

There are two more systems ideas which it is necessary to explain before introducing the background to the systems method which is the core of this book. Like many other systems methods the Systems Failures Method is both systemic and systematic. Both these features have system at their core, but there the similarity ends. Systemic means pertaining to system. In this case it means a method which applies the concept system, and related systems ideas such as those mentioned already to an actual or potential failure situation. Systematic means organized and following a pattern. All but the most chaotic or creative of methods would be systematic, incorporating procedures which are to be adhered to, even if they also allow multiple branching and a variety of paths through them. One of the advantages of a systematic method is that it causes users to follow a path which may force them to confront difficult but important issues. A further advantage is that it allows someone else to examine the way in which the method has been applied and by examining the process arrive at some view of the likelihood that the application was sufficiently comprehensive to warrant confidence. These features would be true of most methods; it is the systemic aspects of a systems approach which makes it distinctive. The method described in Chapters 5 and 6 is systemic in the classic sense. Put simply it involves expressing a situation in systems language and then, once a system has been identified, scrutinizing it, first to see if it holds up as a system, and secondly to see how it compares with an idealized model of a system.

The systemic method for failure analysis described in Chapters 5 and 6 also provides a framework within which other ideas can be applied. As with many other systems approaches, one of its major strengths is that it is both eclectic and multidisciplinary. In both its development and its subsequent use it borrows freely from and builds on the work of other disciplines.

SYSTEMS MODELS AND FAILURE

As well as concepts such as complexity and environment and an overarching commitment to holism, the systems movement brings to the study of failures a set of models and techniques and the framework of a method for their incorporation. These are discussed fully in Chapters 5 and 6. For now, the final section of this chapter gives a brief overview of the method and outlines its history.

The relevant linkages between the study of failures and disasters and systems concepts, techniques and methods have been forged over a quarter of a century. Jenkins (1969), the founding Professor of Systems at Lancaster University, quoted four examples of the dire consequences that can follow from the absence of a systems approach to engineering. The examples, which were mainly drawn from his long experience in the chemical engineering industry, were presented under the heading of 'Disasters that could have been avoided with Systems Engineering'. They were as follows:

1 A plant translated too quickly from laboratory stage to full-scale plant, without a proper systems study, failed to operate at all on a large scale and had to be redesigned at considerable expense.
2 A plant, which had been engineered excellently, was built but was written off immediately and did not manufacture a single ton of product. This was because the firm's assessment of the market had been at fault and was outstripped by the assessment of a rival company.
3 A large integrated plant complex lost a great deal of money during the first two years of its life because plant reliability and raw material availability had not been assessed properly.
4 A fibre manufacturer responded quickly to an increase in demand by installing additional spinning capacity without ensuring that its raw material supply was adequate and so lost money by tying up valuable capital resources.

He went on to suggest:

> Mistakes of this kind, which are so obvious with hindsight, are caused by the piecemeal approach to problems. It is such disasters that the disciplined approach of Systems Engineering is designed to prevent and can prevent.

In a similar vein de Greene (1970) pointed to a catalogue of disasters, primarily in the US military and aerospace industries, which resulted in loss of life or dollars, decreased operational efficiency and, in one case, led to near national chaos. de Greene's intention was to demonstrate the need for the inclusion of human factors in the design and operation of systems, an activity which he termed 'systems psychology'. To this end he cited some straightforward and relatively simple mistakes such as:

- A transcription error in the coding of a computer program for the guidance system of the Atlas rocket which was to launch a Mariner probe to Venus. The error was the omission of a single hyphen, but the cost was in excess of $35m because the rocket went off course and had to be destroyed.
- The installation upside down of a yaw rate gyro in the rocket which launched what was then NASA's most heavily instrumented meteorological satellite. Again it had to be destroyed shortly after take-off. This time the cost was said to be $62m.

de Greene also detailed other disasters which were of greater systemic interest. The first, the 1965 Northeast power failure, was the largest of its type in American history. It was triggered by an unexpected flow of power which caused a circuit breaker to trip in a hydroelectric power plant in Ontario. But the integration of many individually designed and managed electricity supply systems in Canada and the United States resulted in the occurrence of what is now known as a cascade failure. The circuit break in Ontario caused other circuits to became overloaded, and they subsequently tripped, thus causing further overloading. A string of similar incidents followed in quick succession; within 12 minutes of the initial event, 30 million people were without electricity.

The second, the 1967 Apollo command module fire which resulted in the death of three astronauts, also involved an electrical fault. This fault, together with other contributing factors such as the use of a pure-oxygen atmosphere, non-fireproof space suits and an escape hatch which took some time to open, caused a disaster which had dramatic after-effects. The space programme was delayed by about a year, there was widespread managerial reorganization in NASA and the contracting companies, and there was a loss of public confidence in the programme.

Amongst many observations about the nature of failure and disaster, de Greene also referred to 'the unequivocal pedagogical value' of the cases he cited. It was this interest in pedagogy which led the founders of the Open University Systems group to select the study of failures as a teaching vehicle for systems concepts and techniques. Over and above their intrinsic academic interest, the use of case studies based upon disasters had the dual advantages of being well researched and documented mappings of the internal and external workings of socio-technical systems, and being potentially more motivating and apparently applicable to a mature audience than stark theoretical discourse (Beishon, 1972; Peters, 1973). Early experience in the Open University had already shown that with a student body drawn from a wide variety of backgrounds, case studies were a valuable device for providing a common experience (Peters and Blackburn, 1978). The use of disasters and catastrophes as case studies generated an even stronger general motivation.

Although the first intentions were primarily pedagogical, and involved using disaster cases to develop skills in the students which would enable them to more fully understand systems terminology and to describe real world situations using those systems terms, it was soon realized that the work had potential value in its own right. This lay in the benefits to be derived from studying failures as set out in Chapter 1. In order to start to realize this potential the application of concepts was structured into a systematic framework (Naughton and Peters, 1976) and subsequently a simple method for student analysis of case studies was devised (Spear, 1976). In the main it served well its dual purpose of providing a vehicle for the introduction and assimilation of systems concepts and techniques and showing that it should be possible with further development to devise a systems method for the analysis of failure which would be capable of full-scale application.

Over a period of about six years, during which it was used by over 1500 students in their undergraduate project work, the strengths and weaknesses of the simple method were examined, and refinements introduced. Finally, in 1984, a revised method was published (Bignell and Fortune, 1984). Since then a number of published studies, the experiences of the authors and of 2000 students and further research have resulted in the method which is the basis of this book. A fuller history, including descriptions of earlier methods, can be found in Peters and Fortune (1992).

THE SYSTEMS FAILURES METHOD

Any method for examining the real world with a view to intervening in it can be considered to have the stages of abstraction, modelling, manipulation and evaluation. In simple terms the analysts decide which parts of the real world they are going to consider, they model them in some way, perhaps mathematically or verbally, then they manipulate that model in order to obtain greater understanding, and, in some situations, designs for different formulations. Then having undertaken the modelling they return to 'reality' to compare the results of the previous stages and, if appropriate, decide upon or recommend or facili-

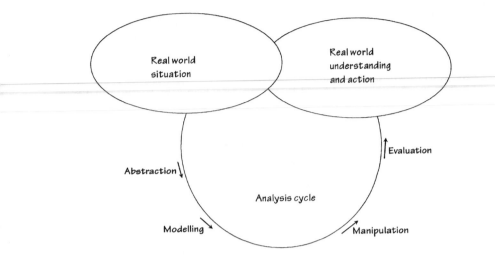

Figure 3.1   *The analysis cycle*

tate action. Figure 3.1 shows this classic cycle in diagrammatical form.

In the case of the Systems Failures Method the goal is a systemic interpretation of a failure and its context which could in turn lead to some action. The abstraction is achieved by considering a situation and using a variety of diagrammatic techniques to depict it in a way which improves the initial understanding and enables conceptualization of the system or systems that can be said to lie at the core of the failure. This system is then modelled, in this case being described in the format of a stereotypical system. This formulation of the real world as a system is then manipulated by comparing it with an idealized model of a system and the results of this comparison used to identify further comparisons with other system-related models concerned with control and communications. This evaluation can then lead back to further investigation of the scene or to an explanation which is satisfactory for the purposes of the analysis.

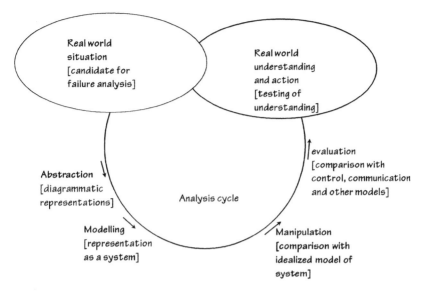

Figure 3.2   *The failures analysis cycle*

Figure 3.2 maps the method on to the analytical cycle in Figure 3.1.

So at its heart the Systems Failures Method has two key features: conceptualization and modelling of the failure situation as a system(s); and comparison of that system(s), first with a model of a robust system that is capable of purposeful activity without failure, and subsequently with other models based on typical failures. Its full diagrammatic representation is shown in Figure 3.3.

Before any full description of the Failures Method can be attempted it is first necessary to describe a situation to which the method can be applied. The first case study in this book, which concerns an aircraft fire at Manchester Airport, will be set out in the next chapter. Although only parts of it are drawn on to provide examples for Chapters 6 and 7, a lot of detail has been included so as to allow the partial analysis conducted by the authors in those chapters to be used as a basis for the reader's first attempt at a full application.

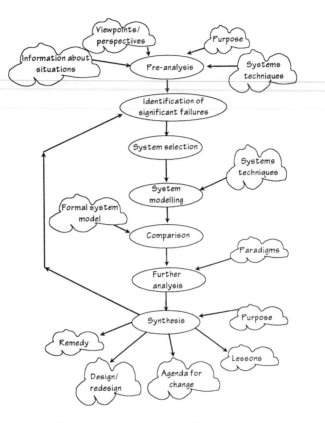

Figure 3.3   *The Systems Failures Method*

REFERENCES

Beishon, J. (1972). Systems File, *Open University Press*, Milton Keynes.

Bignell, V. and Fortune, J. (1984). *Understanding Systems Failures*, Manchester University Press, Manchester.

Bogard, W. (1989). *The Bhopal Tragedy*, Westview Press, Boulder.

Checkland P. B. (1981). *Systems Thinking, Systems Practice*, Wiley, Chichester.

Churchman C. W. (1971). *The Design of Inquiring Systems*, Basic Books, New York.

Cook, J. (1989). *An Accident Waiting To Happen*, Unwin, London.

de Greene, K. B. (1970). (Ed.) *Systems Psychology*, McGraw Hill, New York.

Hood, C. and Jackson, M. (1991). 'The new public management', in

Parker, D. J. and Handmer, J. (Eds) *Hazard Management and Emergency Planning Perspectives on Britain*, James and James, London.

Horlick-Jones, T. (1990). *Acts of God? An Investigation into Disasters*, EPI Centre, London.

Janis, I. (1972). *Victims of Groupthink*, Houghton Mifflin, Boston.

Janis, I. (1982). *Groupthink: Psychological Studies of Policy Decisions and Fiascos*, Houghton Mifflin, Boston.

Jenkins, G. M. (1969) 'The systems approach', *Journal of Systems Engineering*, **1**, 3–49.

Kirschman-Anderson, E. (1980). 'Jamestown, Guyana—a systems autopsy', *Proceedings of the 24th Annual meeting of the Society for General Systems Research*, SGSR Louisville, USA.

Lewin, K. (1948). *Resolving Social Conflict*, Harper, New York.

Naughton, J. and Peters, G. (1976). *Systems and Failures*, Open University Press, Milton Keynes.

Parker, D. J. (1991), 'A critique of UK emergency planning policy', paper presented to The Association of Emergency Planning Officers Annual Study, Gourock, Scotland, 11 April.

Peters, G. (1973). *Air Traffic Control*, Open University Press, Milton Keynes.

Peters, G. and Blackburn, D. (1978). 'The teaching of technology in the Open University (UK)', *Proceedings of American Society of Engineering Education*.

Peters, G. and Fortune J. (1992). 'Systemic methods for the analysis of failure', *Systems Practice*, **5**, 529–42.

Peters, G. and Turner, B. A. (1976). *Catastrophe and its Preconditions*, Open University Press, Milton Keynes.

Rasmussen, J. and Jensen A. (1974). 'Mental procedures in real-life tasks', *Ergonomics*, **17**, 293–307.

Reason, J. T. (1990). *Human Error*, Cambridge University Press, Cambridge. •

Spear, R. (1976). *The Hixon Analysis*, Open University Press, Milton Keynes.

Turner, B. (1979). *Man-made Disasters*, Taylor and Francis, London.

Vickers, G. (1963). Ecology, planning, and the American dream, in The Open Systems Group (Eds), (1984) *The Vickers Papers*, Harper and Row, London.

Watkins, A. (1991). *A Conservative Coup, the Fall of Margaret Thatcher*, Duckworth, London.

4
Fire at Manchester International Airport

With the First Officer at the controls, flight KT28M to Corfu began its take-off from runway 24 of Manchester International Airport at 0612 hours on Thursday 22 August 1985. The aircraft, registration G-BGJL, was a Boeing 737–236 series 1, operated by British Airtours, and it was carrying 131 holiday-makers, 6 crew and over 12 000 kg of fuel. Before it had even left the ground it was in flames. What happened?

The two flight crew and the purser had carried out their usual pre-flight checks before the passengers had boarded. Nothing unusual had occurred, although one of the plane's two engines, the No. 1 (left) engine, had been giving problems the day before during a flight from Barcelona to Manchester. According to the technical log, remedial action had been necessary because of slow acceleration but this action had apparently been successful and no further problems had been reported during a subsequent flight to Athens and back.

When all the passengers and crew were fastened in their seats, the Captain lined the aircraft up on the runway prior to the First Officer assuming control. As soon as clearance for take-off was given the First Officer requested take-off power, the Captain advanced the throttles and then selected the auto throttle, and the engines began to increase their speeds towards the required take-off power. The Captain remarked that the No. 1 engine acceleration was acceptable and the First Officer agreed, saying it was better than the previous day when he had been flying the same aircraft.

As the plane continued its take-off run, all seemed well and the Captain's routine call of 'eighty knots' signifying that the aircraft's acceleration was up to standard was confirmed by the First Officer. But 12 seconds later (that is 36 seconds after the start of the take-off) the flight crew heard a 'thump' or 'thud' which they though was a tyre bursting or a bird-strike. This caused the Captain to signal abandonment of the take-off immediately by ordering 'stop'. He closed the throttles, selected reverse thrust on both engines and checked that the speed brakes (spoilers) were extended. Meanwhile the First Officer applied maximum wheel braking until the Captain, fearing the possibility of tyre failure and noting that there was plenty of runway left, said, 'Don't hammer the brakes, don't hammer the brakes', at which point he eased off.

The sequence of events shown in Table 4.1 then occurred in quick succession.

Straight after the Captain ordered the passenger evacuation

Table 4.1 *Sequence of events in the Manchester airport incident*

Number of seconds after thud heard that event started	Event
9	Captain informed Air Traffic Control (ATC) by a Radio Telephone (RTF) that the take-off was being abandoned. The fire bell on the flight deck started to ring, so he added 'it looks as though we've got a fire on number 1' to the end of his message and cancelled reverse thrust.
19	ATC transmitted, 'right there's a lot of fire, they're on their way now.' The crew silenced the fire bell.
25	In response to the query from the Captain as to whether the passengers should be evacuated ATC replied 'I would do via the starboard side [i.e. right-hand side]'.
31	The Captain initiated the turn into link Delta (see Figure 4.1) and broadcast the following message to crew over the cabin address system: 'Evacuate on the starboard side please.'
35	The purser opened the flight deck door and asked for confirmation of the evacuation order.
37	The Captain repeated 'Evacuate on the starboard side'.
45	The aircraft stopped. The Captain shut down the right engine and ordered the First Officer to carry out the engine fire drill on the left engine.

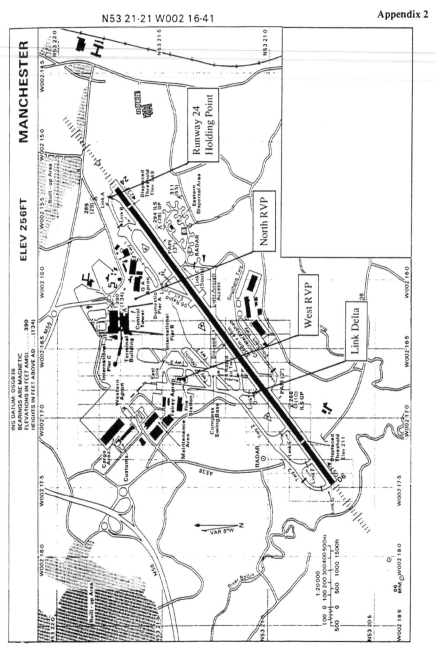

Figure 4.1   *Runway 24 and its surrounding area. Crown copyright is reproduced with the permission of the Controller of HMSO*

the First Officer began to read out the non-memory 'Passenger Evacuation (Land) Drill' from the *Quick Reference Handbook*. However, before this somewhat lengthy drill, which called for 'passenger' evacuation as item fourteen, could be completed, the Captain, seeing fuel and fire spreading forward on the left side of the plane, decided he and his First Officer should get out. They slid down an emergency strap from a cockpit window.

Interestingly, the Captain's decision to leave the aircraft and supervise the evacuation from outside was in accordance with the operator's (British Airtours) procedure but at variance with the aircraft manufacturer's recommendation which was that flight deck crew should complete the cockpit drills and then move to the passenger cabin to assist in the evacuation.

Of the passengers, the first to be aware of the fire were those sitting in the back eight rows on the left-hand side. Very soon after the thud they began to feel the heat of the flames and to see the window transparency panels start to crack and melt. Some passengers had stood up and began to move into the aisle before others even realized that a fire had started.

As more people became alarmed, a male passenger shouted 'sit down, stay calm', but although his call, which was taken up by others, did cause some passengers to sit down, others ignored it and continued to move forward.

The purser and a stewardess who were sat on the left-hand side of the galley at the front of the plane also thought that a tyre had burst. They, of course, realized that the take-off would have to be abandoned and recognized the sound of the engines being put into reverse thrust as soon as they heard it. They did not, however, know about the fire until the sounds of distress from the passengers alerted them to it. On hearing the cries the purser moved forward in his seat until he could see into the main passenger cabin. When he saw that some of the passengers were standing up he made a call over the Public Address (PA) system for them 'to sit down and remain strapped in'. Some did not hear the call. When the purser left his seat to investigate further he soon saw the fire which by then was coming up over the leading edge of the wing and flowing back over its top surface.

As shown in Figure 4.2, the passenger cabin had four main doors and two overwing emergency exits. The latter were each

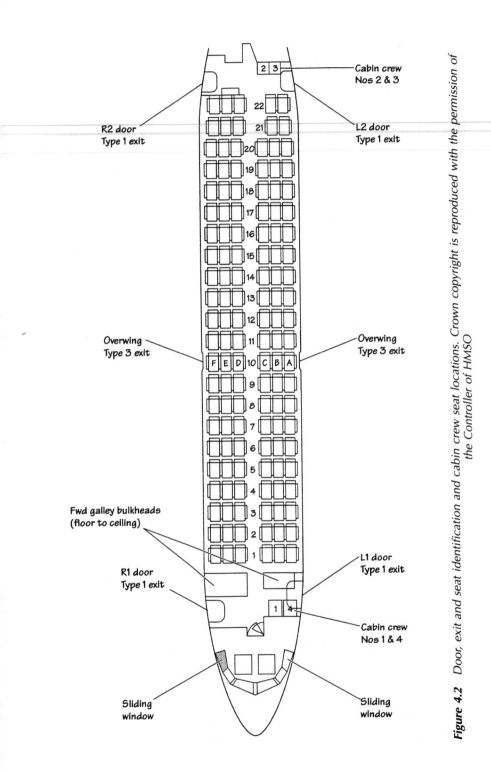

Figure 4.2 Door, exit and seat identification and cabin crew seat locations. Crown copyright is reproduced with the permission of the Controller of HMSO

fitted with a webbing-type escape rope for use after a sea-ditching.

The purser quickly confirmed the evacuation order with the Captain and then repeated it over the PA system a number of times. Again, though, not everyone could hear what was being said. As the aircraft was coming to a halt the purser moved towards the right front door (R1 in Figure 4.2) ready to open it. He unlocked the door, but as it began to open inwards the hinged lid of the container in which the escape chute was held jammed on the door-frame preventing the door from opening further. He tried to free it, but after a short while decided to leave it until he had got the left front door open (L1 in Figure 4.2). He opened the left door, just a little at first to make sure that the forward spread of the fire was slow enough to allow people to get out, and then fully. At the same time as the purser was checking that the escape chute was inflating the first fire vehicle to arrive on the scene was just starting to discharge its foam onto the fire. Approximately 25 seconds had elapsed since the aircraft had come to a halt.

Many of the passengers from the rear of the aircraft tried to move up the aisle towards the centre cabin area but the smoke filling the cabin caused them to stumble and collapse. Others attempted to clamber over the backs of seats as a way of moving forward.

Something that was moving forward without difficulty was a roll of thick black smoke. It clung to the ceiling until it reached the forward bulkheads, then it curled downwards and started to fill the whole of the cabin. As it did so it generated an immediate sense of panic. Passengers from the front section tried to move forward, some of them clambering over the seats to avoid the crush in the aisle—the aisle width, measured at arm rest level, was between 39.4 and 44.4 cm (15.5 and 17.5 in) wide. They saw the front left-hand door as their way out. But before the first ones could get out the No. 4 stewardess who was supervising that exit had to do something to get them moving. A crush had developed between the forward galley bulkheads where the aisle was only 57.2 cm (22.5 in) wide. Fortunately, she was able to clear the jam by pulling one young passenger forwards and people were then able to start leaving.

A total of 17 survivors left the aircraft by the front left-hand

door. Some of them would not have got out without considerable help from the stewardess. One young girl, for example,
had collapsed on the cabin floor. The stewardess pushed a youth
back so that she could grab the girl's collar, heave her forward,
and push her down the slide. The stewardess herself was the
last of the seventeen to leave. Unable to locate any further
passengers she went down the slide, urged on by a fireman
who was very concerned that she would not survive if she
stayed any longer.

Meanwhile the purser returned to the right hand door. He
managed to clear the obstruction 'with difficulty' and get it
open. By the time he had done this about 70 seconds had elapsed since the plane had stopped. He confirmed the inflation of
the slide and then stood, his back to the galley bulkhead and the
door to his right, and pushed passengers past him towards
the chute. The smoke quickly became so dense and acrid that it
prevented him from even seeing the chute and so he too had to
leave the aircraft. Altogether 34 survivors left by this exit.

Some passengers used the right overwing exit in the middle
of the aircraft to escape. This had been opened about 45 seconds
after the plane came to a halt at the instigation of some of
the passengers who could see that the aisle was already too
overcrowded for them to get to the front of the plane. They told
a young woman sitting in row 10, seat F (see Figure 4.2) to open
the exit hatch. She pulled on her right hand arm-rest, which
was mounted on the lower part of the hatch, and at the same
time her friend from seat 10E stood up and reached across to
pull the handle marked 'Emergency Pull' at the top of the
hatch. Immediately the hatch, which weighed 22 kg (48 lb), fell
inwards on top of the young woman from seat 10F, trapping
her in her seat. A man from row 11 helped to move the hatch
which he then lifted over the back of row 10 and placed on a
vacant seat in row 11.

The two young women from seats 10E and 10F and 24 other
people, including two young children, were able to escape via
this overwing exit despite the fact that it became shrouded in
dense black smoke soon after it was opened and the gap
between the two rows of seats which allowed access to it was
only 26.7 cm (10.5 in) wide. The atmosphere in the cabin was so
poor that even many of those who did finally reach safety

collapsed temporarily from the effects of smoke inhalation on their way out. Indeed, some of those who managed to move forwards from the worst area of the rear cabin did so only to die in the central area.

A white canvas strap or piece of webbing (probably a ditching-strap) had fallen across the overwing exit. For some of the survivors this was a final obstacle to overcome as they became entangled in it as they left. For one passenger, though, it proved to be her salvation; as she collapsed near the exit she was able to grab it and hang on until she came to with her head outside the exit. Others failed to make it. When the aircraft was examined later a male passenger was found to have died wedged in the same exit.

Before the aircraft had come to a halt the right rear door (R2 in Figure 4.2) had been opened and its slide inflated by one of the rear cabin crew. People on the ground had seen a stewardess in the doorway, but by the time the aircraft stopped the exit was so engulfed in the thick black smoke which suddenly filled the aft cabin that no-one was able to use it.

Meanwhile, the fire and smoke trailing behind the plane as it sped along the runway had been clearly visible to the air and ground movement controllers in their control tower. They initiated 'full emergency' action. The air controller summoned the Manchester International Airport Fire Service (MIAFS), whose fire station was only 825 m (902 yd) from where the aircraft had stopped, by activating the alarm siren which was connected directly to the station. He also rang MIAFS' watchroom over the direct telephone link to give brief details of the emergency whilst the ground movements controller rang the emergency telephone operator at the Manchester International Airport Exchange.

Even before the siren sounded, however, some of the firemen had started to respond; they too had heard the bang and seen the smoke and flames as the aircraft decelerated along runway 24.

The fire station ambulance and an Airport Police escort vehicle left immediately. According to the emergency orders that were current at the time, the ambulance should have gone straight to the incident, but instead it accompanied the police vehicle to the West Rendezvous Point (RVP) where they waited for appliances from the Cheshire Fire Service and Greater Manchester Council (GMC). Neither vehicle's crew knew that the escort arrangements had been changed. At a meeting on 25 July attended by the Head of Airport Services, the Airport Fire Service and a Senior Fire Officer from the GMC it had been agreed that from then on the external emergency services would be met by a police escort at the North RVP instead of the West. (The RVPs are shown on Figure 4.1.) The GMC appliances were contacted by land line and reminded to go to the North RVP, but no-one told the police, who had not been represented at the meeting on 25 July, of the change.

Two Rapid Intervention Vehicles (RIV1 and RIV2) reached the stationary aircraft first, arriving only 25 seconds after the aircraft had stopped and just after the L1 door had been opened. The purpose of an RIV is to reach an incident quickly so as to give 'first aid' fire protection until major foam tenders arrive. RIV2, which arrived ahead of RIV1, discharged its foam onto the left side of the fuselage at first, then onto the left engine, and finally into the rear fuselage which by then had collapsed onto the tarmac. RIV1 positioned itself just to the left of the aircraft's nose and discharged all its foam along the left side of the fuselage in an attempt to protect the passengers who were leaving by the L1 chute.

About 30–40 seconds later, just as door R1 was opening, the RIVs were joined by two major foam tenders named The Protector and Jumbo 1. Each of these carried sufficient foam concentrate for two full water tank loads and 9080 and 13 620 litres (2000 and 3000 gal) of water respectively. When it arrived The Protector first took up position well to the right of the nose and began spraying foam on the right overwing exit and the right rear fuselage. These appeared to be well alight. It changed its position twice, each time moving nearer to the apparent seat of the fire on the right rear fuselage and continuing to discharge its foam until its water ran out.

Jumbo 1 was unable to take up the position on the nose that was normally reserved for a major tender because RIV1 had already positioned itself there, so it had to stop further off the nose. It delivered its foam down the length of the right hand side of the fuselage, driving the flames back and keeping them clear of the forward and overwing exits. After about a minute of this Jumbo 1 was re-positioned onto the left side to attack the fire in the left engine and fuselage.

A third major foam tender, Jumbo 2, arrived 3 or 4 minutes later (i.e. about 5 minutes after the aircraft had stopped). It had to be retrieved from the paint shop before it could hurry to the scene. As it drove up, its driver saw a hand move in the right overwing exit. He leapt from his cab and clambered onto the wing to free the hand's owner, a 14 year old boy, whom he was able rescue after pulling him clear of the body of a man trapped in the exit.

Jumbo 2's driver was then forced off the wing by smoke so he returned to his tender and applied foam to the top of the fuselage. Side-lines were also used from Jumbo 2 to cool a running fuel fire which was burning near the left engine.

As soon as it became apparent that no-one else was likely to emerge from the aircraft without assistance (some seven minutes into the fire), firemen, wearing breathing apparatus, went on board via the R1 entrance. The cabin was thick with smoke and a fire was still burning strongly at the rear. Almost immediately one of the fire-fighters was injured; an explosion (possibly caused by the rupture of an aerosol can or a thera-peutic oxygen cylinder) blew him back out of the door and onto the tarmac. The officer in charge, increasingly worried because there was very little water left on the fire fighting vehicles, ordered that no-one should try to enter the cabin again until a reliable water supply had been secured. Soon after they got down a fire was seen to flash briefly along the cabin.

Because of the water shortage Jumbo 1 was sent to the nearest fire hydrant on the airfield to refill. But when it got there its crew found that hydrant, and the two others they tried, empty. After spending ten minutes looking for water Jumbo 1 returned empty and was then sent to the hydrant behind the fire station. If the hydrants had been operating normally it would have taken between 15 and 18 minutes to refill Jumbo 1 completely.

It later emerged that the lack of water in the hydrants was the result of some engineering work that was taking place at the airport. Contractors were in the process of connecting the existing water main south of the runway to an additional main which had been laid alongside it to increase flow rates. In carrying out their work they had ignored the proper procedures and isolated parts of the water hydrant system themselves. A system of work permits, which were issued solely on the authority of the Head of Engineering Services, should have been used to exercise control over the work, but no permit relating to activities involving the serviceability of the hydrant system had been issued. If permission to isolate parts of the system had been granted, such permission would have only been given on condition that the isolation was not carried out by the contractor's personnel. Furthermore, the established practice of notifying the Senior Fire Officer before any isolation had not been followed either.

The GMC appliances arrived at the airfield's North RVP at 0621 hours but, as explained earlier, they had to wait there until their escort, redirected from the West RVP, arrived. After a delay of about 3 minutes, during which time the effectiveness of the airport fire service was suffering as a result of the shortage of water, they set off, reaching the plane at 0626 hours (i.e. 13 minutes after the aircraft stopped). At first the Station Officer (SO) in charge found it difficult to identify the officer commanding the airport fire service. This led to a delay in the identification of the water requirements and in the subsequent transfer of 7300 litres (600 gallons) of water from the GMC appliances to Jumbo 2.

Once Jumbo 2 had been replenished, side-lines from it allowed two firemen equipped with breathing apparatus to board the aircraft through the R1 door and begin to tackle the internal fire.

The next person to arrive on the scene was a GMC Divisional Officer (DO). He then took command of the emergency services and, unaware of the earlier hydrant problems, ordered that a hose relay be set up. One of the RIVs was used to carry hose across to hydrant 130. Unlike earlier, the hydrant was now working; contractors arriving for work had seen the earlier attempts to obtain water from the hydrants and had reconnected them to the system.

Shortly afterwards the GMC DO and SO put on their breathing apparatuses and entered the cabin through the R1 door. Despite the very limited visibility they saw two bodies, so the DO left the cabin to transmit the message that there were fatalities. A couple of minutes later when he re-entered the smoke had cleared somewhat. With the improved visibility the officers were able to discover one person (from seat 8B) still alive, but unconscious and badly burned. He was to be the last passenger to leave the plane alive, but he died in hospital 6 days later as a result of severe lung damage and associated pneumonia.

About 4 minutes after the aircraft stopped a British Airways crew coach carrying a Tristar cabin crew arrived on the scene. They had been on the way to their flight office until their driver, seeing the aircraft on fire, had set off to try to help the survivors. After the Tristar team had helped a number of people on the ground they assisted some 40 survivors onto their coach. They took them first to a departure lounge where British Airways cabin crew staff were waiting to help them, and then on to Wythenshawe hospital. Three Manchester Airport Authority coaches also ferried survivors, taking them to the fire station crew room before going on to Wythenshawe Hospital.

The 14 year old boy whom the Jumbo 2 driver had pulled from the overwing exit was one of those taken on board the Tristar crew's coach. He was given some treatment for burns to his hands in the departure lounge and then, as his condition deteriorated, driven in a catering van by a British Airways stewardess to the fire station where he was reunited with his father before being taken to the hospital.

Of the 54 people who died on board only 6 were actually burnt to death. The remaining 48 died as a result of smoke/toxic gas inhalation.

> The seats do not appear to have played a significant part in the production of the heavy smoke which suddenly engulfed the aft cabin immediately after the aircraft stopped, and yet this smoke was very potent in its debilitating effects. It is thus probable that the smoke was largely from the external fuel fire, with significant amounts entering through the open R2 door, and the air conditioning grills located at floor level from the fire which had penetrated the outer skin adjacent to the aft cargo compartment. (Air Accident Investigation Branch, 1989, p. 144)

Of the 51 passengers and crew who escaped by the two front exits, 25 (18 of whom were sat in the front three rows of seats) were unaffected by smoke, having left the aircraft before it reached them.

A scale of rescue and fire fighting (RFF) is used to specify the protection required for different types of operation. Whilst the protection required for operation of a Boeing 737 was set at the category 6 level, the overall requirements for Manchester International Airport were higher. It was a category 8 airport and was thus, under clause 2 of the aerodrome licence, required to provide the following minimum amounts of fire fighting media:

- 18 200 litres (4000 gal) of water for production of fluorochemical foam;
- 1080 litres (238 gal) of fluorochemical foam concentrate;
- a discharge rate of water/foam of 7200 litres/min (1600 gal/min);
- 450 kg (1000 lb) of Dry Powder or 450 kg (1000 lb) Halon (BCF) or 900 kg (2000 lb) carbon dioxide or a combination equivalent thereof.
  (50% of the final requirement on this list could be substituted by water for the production of fluorochemical foam at a substitution rate of 1 kg per 1 litre (10 lb/gal) of water.)

At the time of the accident all of these requirements were exceeded comfortably at Manchester even without the involvement of Jumbo 2 (the tender which had to be retrieved from the paint shop) and without a Land Rover fire vehicle that attended but was not used. It had moved to the scene from the apron area where it had been providing fire cover and although it had no foam capability it was carrying Monnex powder which is designed to tackle running fuel fires. The official report into the accident noted that 'There had been no recent training in the use of Monnex powder . . .' and implied that this may have been the reason why it was not used.

After the fire was extinguished the extent of the damage to the aircraft became clear. As Figure 4.3 shows, it was extensive. The right engine and wing were intact, but those on the left were severely damaged with parts of them melted or burnt away. Inside, the most badly affected area was the rear of the passenger cabin, though there were other isolated pockets of severe damage such as seats 8C and 9C which were completely burnt. Most of the cabin roof and the left sidewall of the rear fuselage between seat rows 17 and 21 were destroyed and the

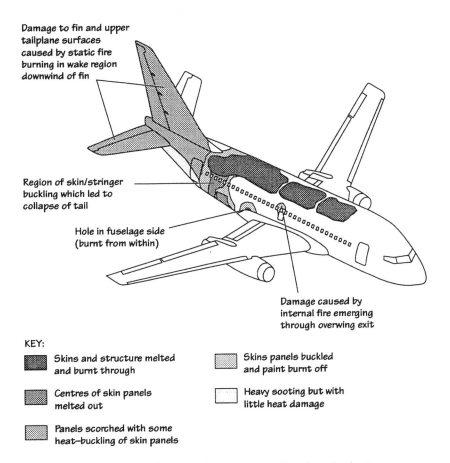

Damage to fin and upper tailplane surfaces caused by static fire burning in wake region downwind of fin

Region of skin/stringer buckling which led to collapse of tail

Hole in fuselage side (burnt from within)

Damage caused by internal fire emerging through overwing exit

KEY:

Skins and structure melted and burnt through

Centres of skin panels melted out

Panels scorched with some heat–buckling of skin panels

Skins panels buckled and paint burnt off

Heavy sooting but with little heat damage

Figure 4.3 *Principal fire damage—fuselage and tail starboard side. Crown copyright is reproduced with the permission of the Controller of HMSO*

rear fuselage aft of row 19 and the tail section had collapsed. The floor in the rear had also collapsed, landing in the rear cargo hold.

Parts from the left wing and engine were found scattered on the runway between link 'C' and runway 06 rapid exit (see Figure 4.1). The runway and taxiway link Delta were also damaged by the fire and by the solvent action of the spilled fuel; a trail of damage could be followed from the area where the first engine debris landed to the aircraft's final resting place.

That was a broad description of the sequence of activities.

Now let us look at some aspects of the situation in greater detail.

The aircraft was four years old and had flown for a total of 12 977 hours, completing 5907 cycles. (One cycle is a take-off and a landing.) As permitted under the regulations, it was fitted with 130 passenger seats and five cabin crew seats and was powered by two Pratt & Whitney JT8D-15 engines complete with thrust reverser systems. Each engine had been fitted to one of a pair of similar aircraft (G-BGJG or G-BGDE) when it was delivered new to British Airtours in 1980. There is no evidence that the aircraft's right engine played any significant part in the sequence of events which led to the accident so this account will concentrate on the left engine (serial number P702868).

The Pratt and Whitney JT8D-15 is a two-shaft turbofan engine. Its combustion system is illustrated in Figure 4.4. The combustion process takes place in the nine combustor cans which are contained within the combustion chamber outer case (CCOC). Compressor delivery air, which is at a pressure of roughly 1650 kpa (240 psi) at take-off, enters the CCOC and is used in both the combustion of the fuel in the combustor cans and in the cooling of the cans—by flowing around the inner and outer walls of the cans it prevents them from melting. The cans themselves are complex constructions whose design has been modified since their first introduction so as to improve durability.

In September 1983 engine P702946 was removed from its aircraft as a result of a pilot's report of high exhaust gas temperatures and visible compressor damage. The engine was stripped down and given the light maintenance inspection which would normally have been carried out after between 10 000 and 12 000 running hours. The problem reported by the pilot was found to be due to failure of the thirteenth stage compressor outer shroud which had damaged the thirteenth stage compressor blades. However, the LMI revealed a further problem: considerable burning and cracking around one particular area could be seen to differing degrees on five of the nine combustor cans. Can No. 9, which will become important later in this account, showed most cracking in the 3/4 liner joint. It contained one circumferential crack that was 160 mm (6.3 in) long and another of 25 mm

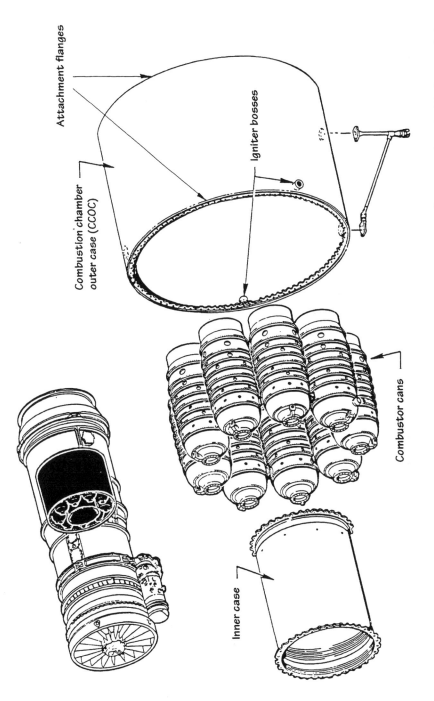

Attachment flanges

Combustion chamber outer case (CCOC)

Igniter bosses

Combustor cans

Inner case

Figure 4.4 The combustion system of the Pratt and Whitney JT8D-15 engine. Crown copyright is reproduced with the permission of the Controller of HMSO

(1 in). Direct fusion weld repairs were used to address the cracks in all five cans but neither pre-weld solution heat treatment nor post-weld stress relief were carried out.

After running 9892 hours, engine P702868 was removed from aircraft G-BGJG for its first scheduled check in the winter of 1983/1984. After a light maintenance inspection had been carried out it was re-assembled using the repaired cans from engine P702946 and fitted to aircraft G-BGJL on 2 February 1984. Between that date and 22 August 1985 when it caught fire the engine ran for a further 4611 hours/2036 cycles, giving a total of 14 503 hours/6552 cycles. The total hours/cycles run on the combustor cans were 12 093/5397.

Between February 1984 and the beginning of August 1985 flying crews reported a number of defects on the left engine. In his Report on the accident, an Inspector of Accidents of the Air Accidents Investigation Branch of the Department of Transport picked out a number of defect reports that he felt were of particular interest. These related to:

- throttle stagger—2 incidents;
- slow acceleration—10 incidents, one of which was accompanied by a report of low ground idle;
- slow acceleration and throttle stagger—2 incidents;
- slow start—2 incidents.
  (Throttle stagger is a mismatch in the position of the throttle levers when the engine pressure ratio (EPR) for both engines are matched. EPR is the ratio of the compressor delivery pressure to the air intake pressure and is an important engine parameter.)

In all the reported cases of throttle stagger the left engine lever was forward of the right to achieve the same engine pressure ratio.

These 16 reports were dealt with in a variety of ways. In some cases no positive action was taken, the crew being asked to accept the aircraft and report further. On other occasions, minor actions were taken that appeared to cure the symptoms so no major steps such as checking the engine combustion section for a disrupted gas path were undertaken. No references were made in any Pratt and Whitney communications to low idle speeds or throttle stagger as symptoms of a disrupted can; although British Airways, who controlled British Airtours engine maintenance and repair, made sure that trouble-shooting guidance was available in respect of slow acceleration nothing was provided on what to do about low ground idle defects; and the Boeing maintenance manual did not mention combustor can defects in its section dealing with throttle stagger nor give any indication that the various symptoms might be inter-related.

Although British Airways/Airtours had a repetitive defect alerting procedure in place, this was not triggered by the persistent problems with the engine because they were spread out over an eighteen-month period and did not appear to cause a lot of disruption.

Trim runs, in which the aircraft's engines were run on the ground with a test-set of reference instruments connected so that various engine parameters could be recorded and checked against data tables in the maintenance manual, were carried out on 16 February 1984 and 18 June 1985 but no record was made of any fuel control unit adjustments having been made.

During August the three engine-related reports shown below were recorded in the aircraft's technical log. The third of these was the final flight crew report in the log concerning the condition of the engine; the aircraft only flew for a further 2 hours and 14 minutes after it was made.

Date	Defect	Action
5.8.85	No. 1. (left) engine very slow to accelerate both forward and reverse	No. 1 FCU damper versilubed (lubricated) PS4 line blown through
20.8.85	No. 1 engine slow to spool up on take-off and about 1½–2 inches throttle stagger at 1.4 EPR	PS4 pipes checked for leaks. Fuel system bled. Please give further report
21.8.85	No. 1 engine does not accelerate for 5 or 6 secs with thrust lever half-way up quadrant. Ground idle is very low: 28% N1 and 50% N2. Autothrottle drops out due to amount of stagger at first. In the air, No. 1 engine slower than No. 2 as well.	ADD raised for full trim run with test set to be carried out on No. 1 engine. PS4 filter water drain trap removed – some water found. Ground idle adjusted 1 turn increase. Now matches No. 2 engine but still seems slow to No. 2 engine. Would crews please report further. (ADD – Acceptable Deferred Defect)

Contrary to the Pratt and Whitney and Boeing maintenance manuals, adjustment of the engine idle trim was not followed by a part-power trim run, but the Air Accidents Investigation Branch report does conclude that 'it is difficult to state that implicit following of the existing Maintenance Manual guidelines, and in particular performance of a part-power trim run, would have revealed the defect in can No 9.'

Failure of the left engine started with a 360° crack around the circumference of the No. 9 combustor can. (Can No. 9, you may remember, was the can which had been most cracked prior to the repair in November 1983.) This crack was the result of thermal fatigue, though there was also evidence of mechanical fatigue which had probably occurred as the can lost structural strength due to the thermal fatigue cracks. After the crack had run the full 360°, or perhaps even as it did so, the dome fractured its locating pin as it started to tilt outboard. When it became canted by about 11° from its normal axis it allowed hot combustion gases to heat the inner surface of the CCOC. The CCOC bulged, and then split open explosively along an axial line next to the No. 9 combustor can. As it did so it struck the inner surface of the aluminium alloy fan case, shattering it. The upper section of the CCOC blew upwards onto the underside of the engine pylon, striking the fire/overheat detection system electrical loom, whilst the lower section blew downwards and outwards.

The engine cowlings were damaged in a number of ways: parts were shattered; overpressure caused a large single piece to be blown off; and the rest suffered severe fire damage, as did the remainder of the engine. The thrust reverser, which was later found to be still deployed, was also badly burned and the in-fill panels on the engine pylon were damaged by overpressure.

As a result of the extremely rapid escape of high pressure combustion air through the ruptured CCOC, the dome was ejected through the disrupted engine casing. It was found on the runway afterwards, comparatively undamaged. When the aircraft was inspected after the event, other parts of the No. 9 combustor could be seen, crushed and burnt, through the CCOC rupture and the No. 1 and No. 8 cans were found to have pieces missing having suffered from being adjacent to No. 9, but the remaining six cans were intact though they showed varied amounts of cracking.

Not surprisingly, the aircraft was extensively damaged by fire. The mechanical damage to the airframe, however, was confined to the left wing which had contained one of the main fuel tanks (capacity 4950 kg) (10 900 lb). None of the three fuel tanks had been damaged by fire, but an access panel belonging to the left one had been hit by the No. 9 combustor can dome and a fan case fragment. The resulting hole which led directly into the tank interior was approximately 270 cm^2 (42 in^2) in area. (No impact criteria had been laid down for the design of the wing skin or the access panel.) Fuel escaped from the tank directly into the path of combustion flames from the damaged engine and ignited.

Whilst the aircraft continued to speed down the runway its turbulent wake entrained much of the fuel and the fire took the form of a 'dynamic plume', but as its speed reduced the turbulent wake declined too and the fire became a 'quasi-static fire burning above the increasingly large pool of fuel trailing behind the aircraft'. As the aircraft turned right into link Delta its position relative to the light wind that was blowing (260°/6 kt) changed too; what was a slight crosswind component from the right became a larger, though still slight, crosswind component from the left. Thus as the aircraft moved towards its final resting place it did so with the cabin downwind of the fire. Whilst the aircraft had continued to move forward it had generated sufficient forces to keep the fire plume trailing behind the wing, but as it came to a halt the force of the wind took over and the fire was driven against, under and over the fuselage. Witnesses on the ground saw the rear fuselage become completely enveloped in smoke. The path the fire took is shown in Figure 4.5.

Once the fire started to attack the fuselage its destruction proceeded as follows:

- 20 seconds after aircraft stopped—initial penetration—fire burnt through to cavity surrounding the cargo hold and then entered aft cabin via floor-level air-conditioning grills.
- Within an estimated 1 minute of aircraft stopping—fire penetrated passenger cabin sidewalls at just above floor level next to seats 17A, 18A and 19A and windows.

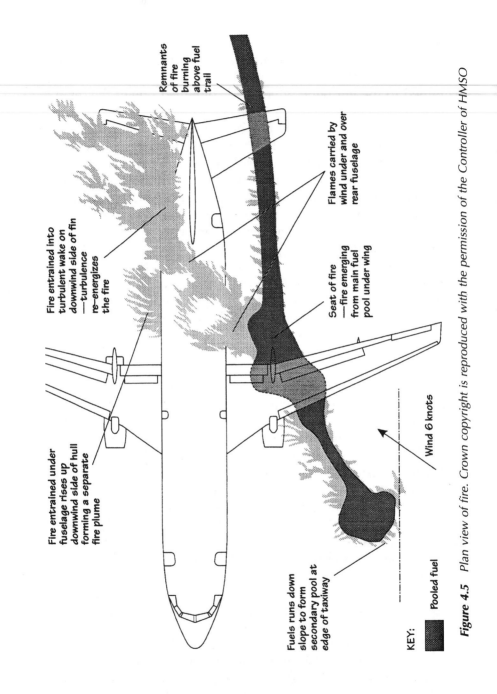

Remnants of fire burning above fuel trail

Fire entrained into turbulent wake on downwind side of fin —turbulence re-energizes the fire

Flames carried by wind under and over rear fuselage

Fire entrained under fuselage rises up downwind side of hull forming a separate fire plume

Seat of fire —fire emerging from main fuel pool under wing

Fuels runs down slope to form secondary pool at edge of taxiway

Wind 6 knots

KEY:

Pooled fuel

Figure 4.5   Plan view of fire. Crown copyright is reproduced with the permission of the Controller of HMSO

- Fire under fuselage caused rear fuselage and tail to collapse.
- Internal fire in aft section of cabin spread forwards as roof panels and overhead lockers fell onto seats after being set alight.
- Further localized damage caused as a result of aerosol sprays and therapeutic oxygen cylinders rupturing.

Contrary to the predictions of experts in the air safety field a fully developed flashover did not take place, though a number of brief flash fires did occur.

In total, it was estimated that 2109 kg (4640 lb) of fuel were lost from the left wing tank.

After the fire had been burning for some time the left fuel tank suffered from a rapid overpressure of the tank cavity caused by the ignition of fuel vapour in its outer section.

The aircraft was fitted with separate fire and overheat detection systems to trigger visual warning messages, plus auditory messages in the case of the former, to the flight deck in the event of excessive temperatures being generated in the engines. It was also fitted with a conventional 'two shot' main engine fire suppression system. The flight data recorder revealed that the left engine fire detector had triggered 9 seconds after the combustion case had ruptured but the overheat detector had not triggered at all. Subsequent examination showed that the power supply cable feeding the left engine overheat detector elements had been severed and the upper detector module overheat element had been damaged. Both main engine fire extinguisher bottles had been discharged fully into the left engine, but the extinguishing agent had not been contained by the enclosure formed by the left engine cowls, as it should have been, because they had been badly damaged when the combustion case burst. The auxiliary power unit fire extinguisher bottle had also been discharged completely, but none of the extinguishers within the passenger cabin had been used.

The next two chapters will use this description of what happened at Manchester to illustrate the stages of the Systems Failures Method. Although this first pass through the Method is not intended as a thorough systems study of the failure it is hoped that some light will be shed on the reasons why the outcome of the events was so unexpectedly tragic.

REFERENCE

Air Accidents Investigation Branch (1989). *Report on the accident to Boeing 737–236 series 1, G-BGJL at Manchester International Airport on 22 August 1985*, Department of Transport, HMSO, London.

5
The Systems Failures Method
Part 1: From Situation To System

The Systems Failures Method as a whole was introduced in outline at the end of Chapter 3. Drawing on the fire at Manchester airport case study in the previous chapter as a source of examples, this chapter and the next will look at it in much greater detail. The purpose of these two chapters is to explain the Method rather than to provide a full analysis of the fire at Manchester Airport, but readers may wish to practise the Method by extending the examples given. To facilitate this a single theme of analysis has, where possible, been followed through the two chapters.

The stages of the Method covered in this chapter are highlighted in Figure 5.1.

PRE-ANALYSIS

As was seen in Chapter 3, the concept of 'system' is central to the approach that forms the core of this book; abstract notions of wholes are used as devices through which understanding of the real world is achieved. Application of the Method relies on being able to conceptualize systems in the situation being studied. The systems themselves are personal intellectual constructs, conceived by individual observers in order to assist in the study. There may sometimes be a measure of agreement, even total

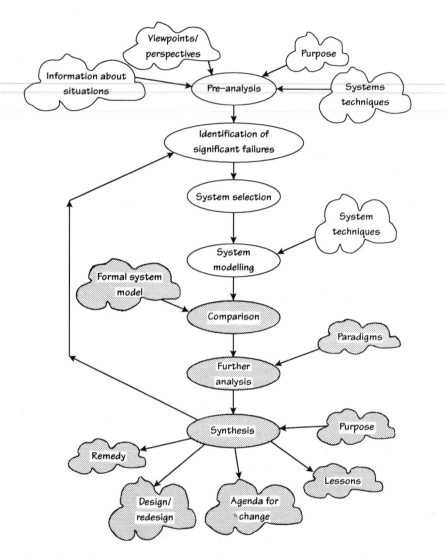

Figure 5.1   *The stages of the Systems Failures Method covered in Chapter 5*

agreement, amongst observers about what a 'system' contains, but there could well be none. Similarly, there may be many different aspects which could be labelled as failures, or disagreement as to whether particular aspects deserve that label or not. The first task is to decide which aspects of a situation are being regarded as the failure(s), and hence the focus of the application, and which of the many systems which could be conceptualized are likely to advance understanding. This task requires the purpose of the study and the different viewpoints and perspectives that must be taken into account to be specified and information about the situation and its history to be gathered and brought together. This early work is called the pre-analysis.

In the Manchester case, for example, a firm that manufactures smokehoods might have commissioned a study so that it could use the findings to support the case that the Civil Aviation Authority should require carriers to provide all passengers with smokehoods. For such a study the perspectives and viewpoints of the client, passengers and carriers would be of primary importance. However, if the Civil Aviation Authority itself commissioned a systems failures study of the accident with a view to examining the adequacy of existing British Civil Airworthiness Requirements, then many more viewpoints and perspectives would have to be taken into account. The fewer the viewpoints and perspectives, the more partial the picture, so a four-way balancing act is always necessary between the requirement to be holistic which underpins systems work, the purpose of the study, the time and cost constraints imposed by the client and the need for the investigation to be manageable. Level of analysis also becomes important here and forms a bridge between purpose and the many different ways of structuring the situation into systems and, by implication, wider systems, sub-systems, sub-subsystems and so on. Thus the smokehood study might operate at the escape system or evacuation and rescue system level and disregard engine maintenance entirely, but an investigation into the adequacy of airworthiness requirements would need to incorporate all of these aspects as subsystems within a much bigger system or as a series of nested systems.

For that strand of pre-analysis which is concerned with the gathering and organization of information about the failure situation, a wide variety of techniques are available. These include: spray diagrams; relationship diagrams; multiple-cause diagrams; rich pictures; and non-diagrammatic methods such as lists, data-bases, charts and the like. The decision about which techniques to use in the pre-analysis of any particular failure rests with the people carrying out the study but there is one important rule: *the situation must not yet be represented in terms of systems.*

Diagrams of various sorts play a big part in the Method. During the pre-analysis stage they allow information to be organized and stored and provide working tools for checking that all aspects of the situation are considered and for generating options. They allow experimentation with different boundaries and configurations when systems are being conceptualized and, later in the analysis when systems are being represented and modelled, they provide a means of showing not only structure and process but also interconnectedness. In trying to learn about failures the interactions between the system and the environment, between subsystems and between components within subsystems are at least as important as the components and subsystems themselves. Because diagrams are so useful they will be considered at some length in this chapter, starting with those which can be used during the pre-analysis stage.

The descriptions of diagram types given here are based on a series of rules and guide-lines originally developed within the Systems Discipline of The Open University. They stem from considerable experience of using systems diagrams and of trying to pass on to students the necessary skills to draw them and to interpret them. The development of a common approach to diagramming is regarded by some as overly prescriptive, but having clearly defined conventions does make it easier for groups of people to work together on diagrams and for them to be more easily understood by others with whom one might wish to share ideas.

Spray Diagrams

A spray diagram is used to record ideas about relationships in the very early stages of analysis, often as a preliminary to drawing a relationship diagram or a multiple-cause diagram. Figure 5.2 shows an aircraft-centred spray diagram of the Manchester incident, including the evacuation of the aircraft. It shows one reading of the various factors which came together, such as the engine problem and the difficulties faced in trying to evacuate the plane, and either looks at them in greater detail or traces

them back through chains of events or to the different organizations or people involved. The amount of detail included in
Figure 5.2 has been limited deliberately in order to make its
structure clearer, but as a working tool it would be added to
and revised as the information gathering proceeded until it
contained all the key pieces of information. For example 'emergency services' would be further subdivided.

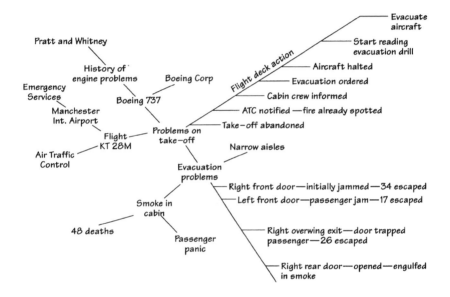

Figure 5.2 *Spray diagram—the Manchester incident, including evacuation*

Rich Pictures

'Rich picture' is a term normally associated with Checkland's
soft systems methodology (SSM) where it refers to a representation of a problem situation which aims to answer the following questions:

1 What resources are deployed in what operational processes under
   what planning procedures within what structure, in what environments and wider systems, by whom?
2 How is the resource deployment monitored and controlled?
   (Checkland, 1972, p. 100)

There is now some controversy over the precise meaning of the term rich picture in SSM with some interpreting it literally as a physical picture and others considering it to be an abstract understanding of a problem situation. (Lewis, 1992). Taking the abstract meaning of the term in the context of the Systems Failures Method, the whole of the output of the pre-analysis could be said to be a rich picture. Interpreted as a picture or diagram it becomes one of the tools that can be used during pre-analysis. A diagrammatic rich picture seeks to get onto one sheet of paper all the salient features of a situation in a way which is insightful and can be easily assimilated. It is common to use cartoon-like encapsulations of key ideas or pieces of information, as in the example in Figure 5.3.

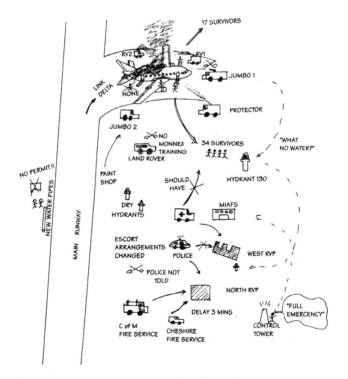

Figure 5.3   *Rich picture—the Manchester Airport situation*

Relationship Diagrams

Relationship diagrams provide snapshots of situations. Lines are drawn to connect components which are significantly related in some way. Although the nature of the relationships are not specified, different lengths of line can be used to imply different degrees of closeness. An example is shown in Figure 5.4. When trying to structure a situation as a prelude to conceptualizing systems within it, clusters of components on relationship diagrams may suggest where system or subsystem boundaries could usefully be drawn. For example, Figure 5.4 could give rise to the two possible groupings denoted by dotted lines in Figure 5.5.

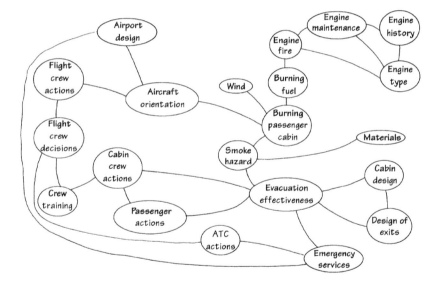

Figure 5.4 *Relationship diagram—the fire at Manchester Airport*

Multiple-cause Diagrams

Multiple-cause diagrams explore why a given event happened or why a certain class of events tends to occur. They are not intended to predict behaviour, but may be used to develop a

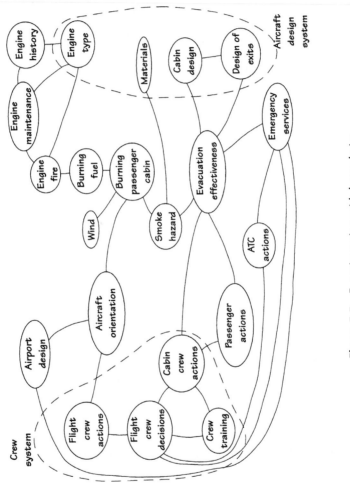

Figure 5.5 *Experimenting with boundaries*

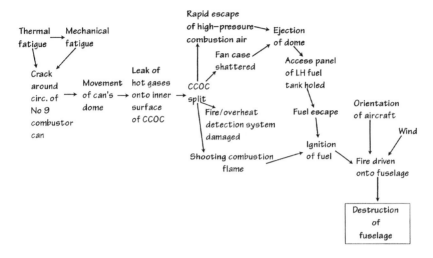

Figure 5.6 *Multiple-cause diagram—the destruction of G-BGJL's fuselage*

list of factors to bear in mind when considering comparable circumstances in the future. Construction normally begins at a single factor/event, such as the destruction of the fuselage of G-BGJL as shown in Figure 5.6, and this is then traced backwards. The elements of the diagram are phrases and arrows. The phrases may be names of 'things', with or without their relevant associated variables, or events. The arrows may represent causes or may mean 'contributes to', 'is followed by', 'enables', or something similar. Unless annotation indicates otherwise, no distinction is drawn between necessary and/or sufficient causes.

IDENTIFYING SIGNIFICANT FAILURES AND SELECTING A SYSTEM

Chapter 2 discussed the notion of failure and argued that the extent to which something can be judged a failure must depend upon the standpoint from which it is viewed. Chapter 3 presented the idea of failures being regarded as the outputs, or lack of outputs, of the transformation processes being carried out within systems. These ideas are combined in the next stage of the Systems Failures Method where all aspects of the pre-analysis are brought together to identify the focus for the analysis and to allow the systems from which the failure(s) can be said to have emerged to be specified.

The situation will have already been labelled a failure or a potential failure in general terms, otherwise the Method would not be being used, but now it is necessary to move towards a more specific statement of the focus of the analysis. (The words 'move towards' have been chosen carefully to try to reflect the uncertainties of definition (uncertainties which are inevitable given the nature of the concept of failure) and the need for iteration which this method shares with most other systems approaches.)

Following the fire at Manchester airport, 55 people lost their lives and the aircraft was destroyed. The uncontained rupture of the left engine could be identified as the significant failure upon which the analysis is to be focused, with the loss of life being regarded as a result of that failure. Another view may be that the inability of passengers to escape from the aircraft constituted the significant failure, and that the shattering of the engine, whilst important as the cause of the accident, should have been survivable; though it was the trigger for the failure it was not part of the failure. This apparent contradiction between the nature of the incident and its outcome was one of the issues that was raised in the official report on the accident. It said:

> Many of the factors which affected this accident should have biased events towards a favourable outcome. The cabin was initially intact, the aircraft remained mobile and controllable and no one had been injured during the abandoned take-off. The volume of fuel involved, although capable of producing an extremely serious fire, was relatively small compared with the volume typically carried at take-off, the accident occurred on a well equipped major airport with fire cover considerably in excess of that required for the size of aircraft and the fire service was in attendance within 30 seconds of the aircraft stopping. However, 55 lives were lost. (Air Accidents Investigations Branch, 1989, p. 97)

One way of looking at the Manchester situation would be to separate it into three distinct phases, each containing an apparently significant failure:

1 the engine failure
2 the handling of the aircraft after the engine failure
3 the fire-fighting and rescue.

Within the first, for example, the uncontained failure of the left engine, and within that again the failure to diagnose the symptoms of the disrupted can earlier, the lack of effectiveness of the repair to the No. 9 combustor can and the lack of impact resistance which led to the fracture of the underwing fuel tank access panel, could each, or all, be regarded as the subject for analysis. Faced with ranges of options such as this, people using the Method have no hard and fast rules to tell them where to begin; a judgement has to be made. This judgement has to be based on purpose, viewpoint and perspective, but there are no objective criteria for it. The concept of 'top event' which dictates the starting point for a fault tree analysis has no equivalent in this approach. Even after embarking upon an analysis it may become necessary to widen the scope or narrow it down or to switch between levels, but again this will be based on subjective judgement.

A whole range of systems relevant to the failures could be conceptualized from within the Manchester situation. These include:

- a passenger transport system
- an aircraft propulsion system
- an aircraft maintenance and repair system
- an aircraft design system
- an emergency rescue system
- an airport system
- a survival system
- a firefighting system
- a crisis management system.

Within the Method failure is regarded as an output, or lack of outputs, of transformation processes carried out by a system. By putting trial systems boundaries around aspects of the situation, experimenting with various configurations, permutations and combinations, it should be possible to delineate a notional system which carried out, or was supposed to carry out, those transformations. Most importantly, the system which is conceptualized must also look a likely candidate to take the analysis forward. It is probable that because of the complexity of the situation the analysis will have to be conducted at a number of levels within any system. It may also be necessary to select a number of interacting systems and carry them all forward through the subsequent comparison process, looking at them individually and as a whole. Considerable care is needed at this stage since splitting a failure up into different phases or different aspects could inhibit a full investigation without this notion of interacting systems. Important inter-relationships might be lost and the analysis cease to be holistic.

The system(s) which have been selected need to be modelled in some detail. This process is described in the next section which uses the authors' conceptualization of the emergency rescue system at Manchester as an example.

MODELLING SYSTEMS

Models of any systems used in the analysis have to be sufficiently detailed to enable switching between levels to be carried out and to allow structure and process to be represented in the formats necessary for later comparisons. (These comparisons are dealt with in the next chapter.) As a minimum, this requires:

1 naming and defining of the system(s)
2 description of the components of the system(s)
3 description of the components and relationships in the environment of each system
4 identification of the wider system
5 description of the inputs and outputs
6 identification of the system(s) variables
7 the structural relationships between components to be established
8 some indication to be given of the relationships between the variables which describe the behaviour of the system(s).

For example, the components of the emergency rescue system might be said to include:

- the Fire Services of Manchester International Airport, Greater Manchester Council and Cheshire, each with its own personnel, management, vehicles, other equipment, and so on;
- Air Traffic Control
- the Airport Police
- the Ambulance Service
- the infrastructure of the airport, including the water supply subsystem
- the Head of Airport Services and his team
- the communication subsystem.

Within the environment the following might be identified:

- the aircraft involved in the incident
- the people at risk or already dead or injured
- aircraft operators and manufacturers
- engineering services
- contractors such as those working on the water supply subsystem.

Important variables might be: the number of fire-fighting and rescue vehicles available; the fire-fighting capacity of those vehicles; their response times; and so on.

Systems diagrams, particularly input-output diagrams, systems maps and influence diagrams are the main modelling tools at this point in the Method.

Input-Output Diagrams

An input-output diagram is a simple form of flow block diagram with the system represented by a single box, and inputs and outputs shown as labelled arrows. For an example, see Figure 5.7. Although this diagrammatic form is very simple it is a very effective way of showing what the system would or should do, that is take inputs and transform them into outputs.

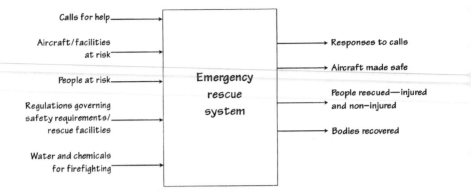

Figure 5.7   *Input–output diagram—emergency rescue system*

Systems Maps

A systems map is essentially a snapshot showing the components of a system and its environment at a point in time. Primarily it shows structure, but the positioning of components provides some information about the relative strengths of relationships. The only elements allowed are named components; linking lines, arrows, etc., are not permitted.

Within the Systems Failures Method, systems maps are very useful when experimenting with trial boundaries, for communicating the structure of the system which is being used to others, and for deciding at which levels the analysis should be conducted. Figure 5.8 shows a map of the emergency rescue system outlined earlier. The boundary of the system encloses the subsystems and elements which are its components and separates it from the components that make up its environment.

Influence Diagrams

An influence diagram is also a snapshot based on structure, but its prime purpose is to explore relationships. It is often the case that closer examination of interactions, perhaps also using a matrix of interactions, leads to redefinition of the system or regrouping of its components.

The elements of an influence diagram are named compo-

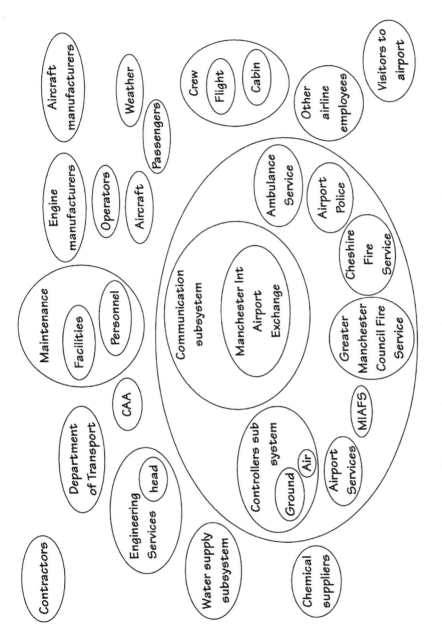

Figure 5.8 Systems map—the emergency rescue system

nents and arrows. The arrows may be labelled to distinguish between different types of influence such as influence via finance, information, statutory regulation or so on and variation in thickness of line used to indicate different strengths of influence. As in systems maps, space and relative distance reveal information about the nature of the relationships shown, so, for example, a component that is shown as important in terms of the amount of influence it has could from its position also be seen to be isolated and remote.

An influence diagram of the emergency rescue system is shown in Figure 5.9. A one-way arrow such as that joining the contractors to the water supply subsystem shows that the former can or does influence the latter, but the latter has no significant influence over the former. Double-headed arrows denote two-way influences.

SUMMARY

The activity of conceptualizing and modelling systems as a prelude to studying a failure situation can itself be likened to a transformation process. It begins with users of the Method being confronted with a situation that someone has identified as a failure or potential failure and ends with sufficient knowledge of the situation in systems terms to be able to represent it, or aspects of it, in the appropriate format to allow the comparison stage of the Systems Failures Method to begin. It is achieved using the following process:

Stage 1 Pre-analysis. Define the purpose of the analysis and the viewpoints and perspectives from which it is being carried out. Gather together source material and investigate the situation, examining it from the various viewpoints that have been identified as important. Organize the information into forms that will render it usable. This may involve the use of rich pictures, spray diagrams, multiple-cause diagrams, databases and so on. Exact methods for pre-analysis are not prescribed, but systems analyses are proscribed.

Stage 2 Identify significant failure(s) and select system(s). The situation itself will have already been labelled a failure or potential failure in general terms, but now the failure(s) must be

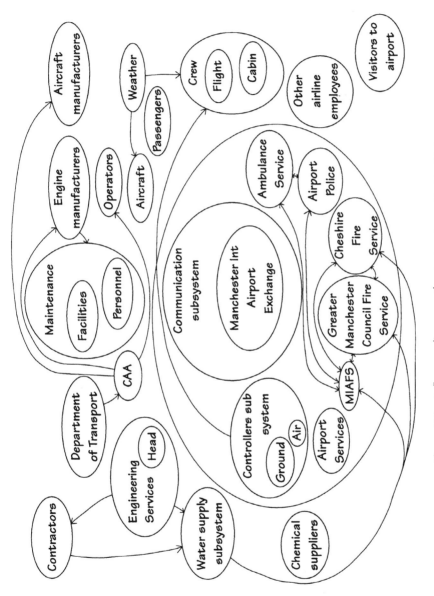

Figure 5.9 Influence diagram—the emergency rescue system

specified more precisely in accordance with the outcomes of the pre-analysis.

Use trial boundaries to structure relevant aspects of the situation into a range of systems and select the system(s) to be carried forward to the next stage. For the purposes of analysis, the significant failure(s) will be regarded as the outputs of the system(s).

Stage 3 Model the system(s). Clarify the nature of the system(s) using a set of systems questions and build diagrammatic models of structure and process as a precursor to representing various aspects of the system(s) and its behaviour, possibly at different levels, in the formats required for comparison.

REFERENCES

Air Accidents Investigation Branch (1989). *Report on the accident to Boeing 737–236 series 1, G-BGJL at Manchester International Airport on 22 August 1985*, Department of Transport, HMSO, London.

Checkland P. B. (1972) 'Towards a systems-based methodology for real-world problem solving', *Journal of Systems Engineering*, 3, 87–116.

Lewis P. J. (1992). 'Rich picture building in the soft systems methodology', *European Journal of Information Systems*, 1, 351–60.

6
The Systems Failures Method
Part 2: Comparison and
Synthesis

The process that lies at the heart of the Systems Failures Method is comparison. Understanding is achieved by comparing systemic representations of the failure situation with models of how a situation should be structured and managed if it is to be capable of operating without failure. The previous chapter looked at how the systems representations are set out. This chapter describes some of the models which can be used and explains the process of comparison. It then examines the final stage of the Systems Failures Method, synthesis. Thus the stages of the Method which are covered in this chapter are those highlighted in Figure 6.1. And once again, the case study described in Chapter 4, the Manchester fire, is used to provide examples where appropriate.

THE FORMAL SYSTEM MODEL

The first comparison which must be carried out is made at the level of the system. The system as a whole (or each system if there was more than one) which was conceptualized following the pre-analysis and which was then modelled is tested against a model of a robust system that is capable of purposeful activity

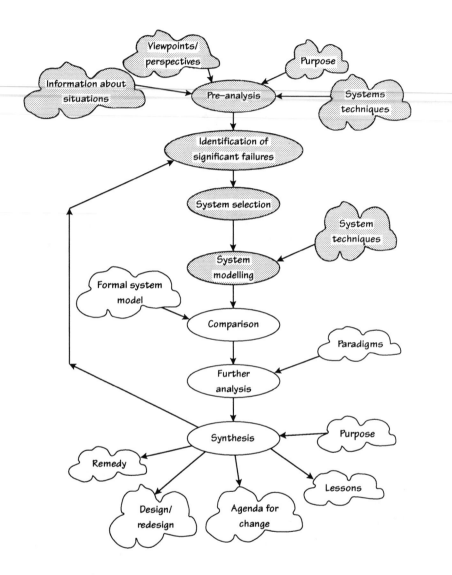

Figure 6.1   *The stages of the Systems Failures Method covered in Chapter 6*

without failure. This model is called the Formal System Model (FSM) and is shown in Figure 6.2. It is adapted from Checkland (1981), who in turn drew on the ideas of Churchman, particularly his concept of a teleological system (Churchman, 1971, pp. 42–78), and Jenkins (1969).

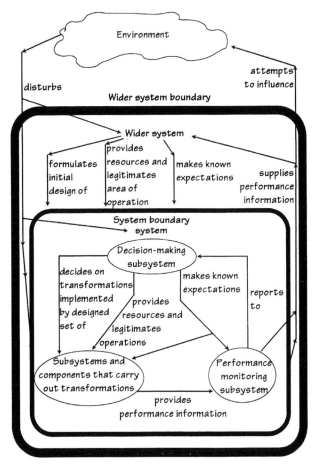

Figure 6.2 *The Formal System Model (from Fortune 1993)*

In the model as used within the Systems Failures Method the Formal System itself comprises a decision-making subsystem, a performance-monitoring subsystem and a set of subsystems and elements which carry out the tasks of the system and thus effect its transformations by converting inputs into outputs. Other features it incorporates include: a continuous purpose or mission; a degree of connectivity between the components; an environment with which the system interacts; boundaries separating the system from its wider system and the wider system from the environment; resources; and some guarantee of continuity.

A comparison of the features of the Formal System Model with the mapping shown in Figure 6.3 reveals that the FSM does in fact unite most of the concepts which are widely accepted as being central to systems thinking.

Although a Formal System would, by definition, have requirements of its subsystems, such relationships would not preclude each subsystem having a certain amount of autonomy in deciding how those expectations were met. An equivalent relationship could be said to exist between the Formal System and its wider system; a powerful wider system might constrain the activities of a system by defining goals and exercising control and only providing those resources necessary to the achieve-

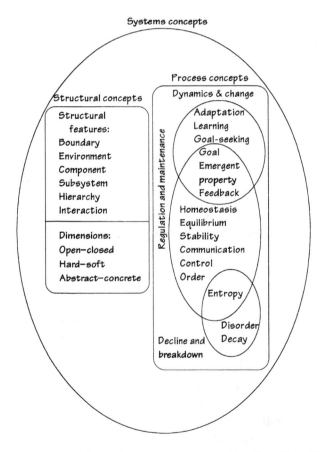

Figure 6.3   A map of the main systems concepts using the categories of Young (1964) (Cameron, 1983)

ment of those goals, but it could also enhance the authority of the system. If the legitimacy of the objectives and activities of the wider system had been established this legitimacy could be extended to justify the activities of the system and its subsystems.

Because of the hierarchical nature of the FSM each of its subsystems could also be perceived as a Formal System with its own decision-making, performance-monitoring and transformation-effecting components, and each one of those could then, in turn, also be regarded as a Formal System, and so on, until the level was reached where the components must or need only be regarded as elements. This notion of hierarchy is an important aspect of the Method. Unless it is taken on board and applied it is difficult to avoid the charge that the model is a unitarist one which ignores concepts such as conflict and power. The decision-making subsystem is itself just that—a subsystem. It may, at one extreme, be made up of people who share a single world view and are united in some common purpose, or it could be a changing balance of forces such as that suggested by Hall (see Chapter 2) in his references to a triangle of actors: bureaucrats; politicians; and the public. It could comprise disparate groups who are constantly forming and reforming and making temporary alliances as they jockey for position.

Wide experience (see Peters and Fortune, 1992) of comparing systems representations of failure situations with the Formal System Model has shown there to be recurring themes which emerge from comparisons with the FSM. The following are typical points of difference:

1 Deficiencies in the apparent organizational structure of the system, such as a lack of a performance-measuring subsystem or a control/decision-making subsystem.
2 No clear statements of purpose supplied in a comprehensible form to the system from the wider system.
3 Deficiencies in the performance of one or more subsystems— for example the performance-measuring subsystem may not have performed its task adequately.
4 Lack of an effective means of communication between the various subsystems.
5 Inadequate design of one or more subsystems.

6 Not enough consideration given to the influence of the environment, and insufficient resources to cope with those environmental disturbances that were foreseen.

7 An imbalance between the resources applied to the basic transformation processes and those allocated to the related monitoring and control processes, perhaps leading at one extreme to quality problems and at the other to cost or output quantity problems.

In order to undertake the process of comparison it is first necessary to represent the system which has been conceptualized in the same format as the FSM. Figure 6.4 shows the emergency rescue system, still as conceptualized in Chapter 5, but now reordered into the format of the FSM.

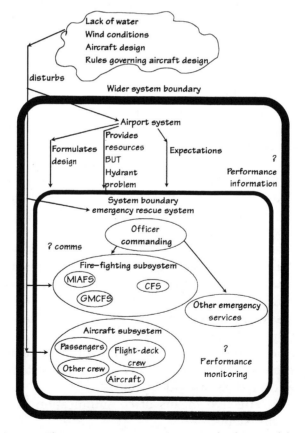

Figure 6.4   *The emergency rescue system in the format of the FSM*

The next stage is to compare the FSM with the system which has been conceptualized. This process identifies discrepancies and reveals gaps in one's understanding of the situation. In the case of the emergency rescue system comparison with the FSM shows three main areas where there appear to be discrepancies. The first concerns aspects which are shared between the decision-making and the control functions. In considering these in more detail it is necessary to make distinctions between the functions and the individuals performing them. For about the first 20 minutes of the incident the officer commanding the airport fire service appears to have been in charge, and thus responsible for decision-making. When the Greater Manchester Council (GMC) fire officers and appliances arrived about 13 minutes into the incident their Station Officer had difficulty in identifying the officer commanding the airport fire service. Thus there was a communication breakdown. Control and decision-making switched again later, passing to the GMC Divisional Officer when he arrived. This whole area of decision-making and control appears to merit further investigation and analysis.

The second area of interest to emerge from the comparison involves the relationships between the system and the wider system. The discrepancies, all of which merit further investigation, are shown in Table 6.1.

Table 6.1 *Discrepancies revealed by comparison with the FSM*

Aspect of the FSM	Discrepancy
'Formulates initial design of'	Certain aspects of the design of the emergency rescue system, namely the escort arrangements
'Provides resources'	Water was not available from the hydrants
'Supplies performance information'	The extent to which there was a link between the performance monitoring subsystem and the wider system is not known

The third area for further consideration which emerges from the comparison concerns the effects of the environment on the system. Two particular disturbances from the environment should be investigated further. The first is the weather; although the slight crosswind was perhaps not perceived as being strong enough to be of consequence, its impact was significant. The second is the bodies who set the rules governing aircraft design and the aircraft's manufacturer, the Boeing Commercial Airplane Company; cabin design and construction and the choice of materials used within it made a major contribution. Design decisions were remote from the situation with respect to time and place, but that does not limit their importance. Could their consequences have been predicted, mitigated, or prevented?

As in the above, insights gained from comparison between the FSM and the system conceptualized from a failure situation will either be found within subsystems or be associated with one or more of the many interfaces:

- environment—wider system
- environment—system
- wider system—system
- interfaces between subsystems.

To investigate further it is usually appropriate to stay with the FSM as a basis for comparison and move up and/or down a level. When moving up, the system which has just been considered will next be viewed as a subsystem of a higher-level system. Moving down a level, what was regarded as a subsystem will be perceived as the system. Judgement about whether a change in level is appropriate, and if so whether it should be up to a wider system or down to what was a subsystem will need to take account of the nature of the system(s) as conceptualized earlier in the Method and the results of the first comparison.

OTHER BASES FOR COMPARISON

When the usefulness of the FSM appears to be exhausted it is appropriate to move to an alternative basis for comparison. In the terminology of the Method the other bases which are used are called 'paradigms'. The word paradigm is used to denote a pattern or example of good practice; use of the word 'models' as the collective noun for the bases for comparison would not be legitimate because they are not necessarily all 'models'. (Readers who are familiar with Kuhn's use of the word 'paradigm' in relation to the methods of science (Kuhn, 1970) should be aware of the different usage here.)

CONTROL

In systems terms control is an action that a system or subsystem applies to its own activities in order to reach or maintain a desired state. For the purposes considered here, the need for control is brought about either by the influence of the environment on the activities that are being undertaken or by variations within a subsystem which are due to its complexity or to its stochastic nature. Control is achieved by either modifying activities or by changing inputs.

The Formal System Model specifies one particular control mechanism—the performance monitoring subsystem—but many others can be inferred. For example, control loops are almost certain to be necessary within the subsystems that carry out transformations. Lack of control can be both a symptom and a cause of failure, but through use of the various aspects of the control paradigm, which are set out below, it should be possible to distinguish between the two. By comparing those aspects of the situation where control was being exercised or where a need for it was indicated with various aspects of the control paradigms it becomes possible to identify those areas where control was lacking, incomplete or inappropriately applied.

The paradigm incorporates three types of control model:

- classical feedback control
- modern feedback control
- feedforward control.

Classical feedback control, also often known as the engineering control model, is depicted in Figure 6.5. Measured values of the outputs of activities are compared with desired values, or reference levels, either continuously or at intervals, and the activities or the inputs to them are modified (increased, reduced, or their nature changed) as necessary in order to bring the outputs to their desired levels. The aim is thus to remove dis-

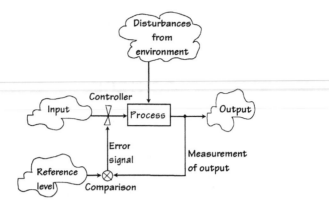

Figure 6.5   *Classical feedback control*

crepancies between actual and target outputs. (This is some-times referred to as error-nulling.)

In so-called modern feedback control (see Figure 6.6), action is based not on simple error-nulling but on the best estimate of the true current state and the likely effects of any changes. The best estimate is generated within the control system itself, using a model of the system. This internal model, which is continually updated so as to reflect the changes that are taking place, evaluates the various control actions which could be taken in order to examine the trade-off between each action's effectiveness and the costs associated with it.

In feedback control the emphasis is on reacting to events after they have happened. In certain situations, however, where disturbances can be anticipated and steps taken to counter them

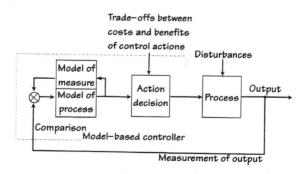

Figure 6.6   *Modern feedback control*

before they affect output, feedforward control, as shown in Figure 6.7, can be more effective. For example, one may anticipate a mismatch between income and expenditure after retirement and begin to save now so as to be able to supplement income to match expenditure later. Feedforward control is sometimes used in combination with feedback.

For very complex systems, Volta (1988) has proposed an extension of these cybernetic-based models of control. He suggests that control be regarded as 'triggering actions that modify behaviour' and that 'control is activation, by internal factors, of the evolution of a system in a given direction' with communication being 'one of the basic mechanisms of activation'. He links this with the concept of controllability and states that 'a system is controllable not only when it allows recovery, after an error, but when it is capable of being improved through errors'. Thus, in Volta's terms, a complex system that lacks controllability is not learning and is susceptible to failure.

For control to be successfully established and maintained a number of preconditions must be satisfied:

1 The processes being controlled must be understood, at least to some degree. The inputs which affect the outputs and the directions in which they cause variation must be known.
2 An appropriate form of control must have been selected.
3 It must be possible to sample the inputs and outputs repeatedly and at suitable intervals.
4 There must be adequate communication between the measuring devices and the decision-taker.
5 The reference levels must be achievable and must be specified

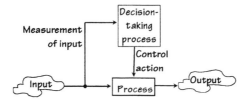

Figure 6.7 *Feedforward control*

in forms compatible with those in which the outputs are to be measured.

6 The changes in the level of inputs must not be greater than the range of variation for which control actions are capable of counteracting disturbances.

7 The time interval between a measurement being taken and control action being initiated must be appropriate.

8 The decision-taker must be of an appropriate level of sophistication for the activities and/or processes being controlled.

9 Agreement must be reached over what constitutes an acceptable trade-off between error, resources required and time-pattern factors.

In passing it is worth noting that this notion of controllability and the preconditions of successful control could be applied to the process through which an organization or society learns from its mistakes and failures. Items 3, 4 and 7, taken together, for example, imply that analysis of failures, and hence knowledge about them, must be timely and open and available to those responsible for decision making.

A major cause of failure to control is instability due to positive feedback, whereby the signal that is fed back leads to actions that increase the deviation from the desired level. Depending upon the circumstances, the output may move quickly to one extreme position or begin to fluctuate violently. For example, a petrol retailing system would normally operate with a large number of individual decision-takers acting independently. However, if rumours of a shortage occurred, motorists who normally drove with petrol tanks less than half-full would flock in great numbers to fill up, thus guaranteeing that the rumoured shortage would occur. This example is illustrated in Figure 6.8.

For large and complex transformation processes there is often delay before control actions take effect. Therefore it is necessary to take account of the dynamics of the activities being controlled in order to prevent too-frequent control actions and the 'hunting' (illustrated in Figure 6.9) to which they lead.

Problems can also occur when control is based on an inadequate model of the situation. Even where the level of understanding is very good over the typical range of inputs and

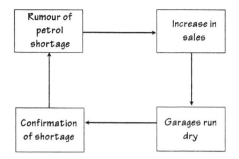

Figure 6.8 *Positive feedback loop for petrol shortage*

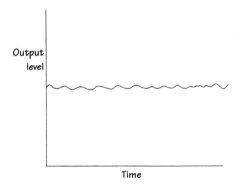

Figure 6.9 *Hunting*

outputs it may be less good over the full range of options and thus unable to cope sufficiently well with rare events.

Poor communication within a feedback loop can lead to a variety of problems. 'Open loop' or 'broken loop' control results when no information about the current state of the output is received by the decision-taker and thus when no informed control actions are possible. If information collected about the current state becomes distorted 'control' actions may be taken that cause the outputs to deviate even further from the desired state. If information relayed about the outputs of a process is accompanied by amplified 'noise', inappropriate control actions may be triggered which may in turn cause severe random variations in the output. Such variations may be greater than those caused by the influence of disturbances from the environment.

These difficulties can also manifest themselves in physical

installations. For example, measuring devices can be prone to decay as a result of ageing, corrosion and so on, especially in hostile environments. As the deterioration proceeds, instruments may deviate more and more from their correct readings but the discrepancies not be detected until serious faults occur which make it all too clear that the instruments are no longer working. If instrumentation problems occur frequently, operators may begin to assume that all unexpected readings are due to instrument failure rather than investigating the causes. This can lead to unwarranted and unacceptable delays before appropriate actions are taken. The equivalent problem can be seen in computerized commercial information systems where data that is inputted or processed incorrectly give rise to misleading answers when databases are interrogated. As research has shown (see, for example, Koester and Luthans, 1979), the authority carried by computer-generated information just because it is computer-generated renders it less liable to challenge.

A common source of error is misreading of the output. Where physical measurements are concerned this may arise in some cases because instruments are badly designed and difficult to read, but in others it may caused by operator error, perhaps resulting from stress, distraction or boredom. It can also apply to people who are 'reading' situations and trying to judge the reactions of others. Human factors relating to the control paradigm will be considered later in this chapter.

Communication failures within control can relate to the physical hardware involved and/or to the people receiving and acting upon the information. Both can be investigated further using the communication paradigm which will be dealt with in the next section.

Good examples of the interweaving of control and communication can be found in the Manchester air crash case study. For example, picking up the resource provision problem identified earlier, the control paradigm can be used to explore further the lack of water in some of the hydrants. The contractors should have obtained a work permit, issued solely on the authority of the Head of Engineering Services, before starting work on the hydrant system, and should not have carried out the isolation themselves. Clearly, there was no effective control over this aspect of the contractor's work; they apparently did isolate parts of the water hydrant system themselves without securing the necessary permission and without any notification of the proposed work being given.

In thinking about why there was no control it might be useful to pursue the communication aspects of the problem further. The Engineering Services Department was unaware that the hydrants were out of service at the time of the fire, but did they know in general terms that work involving the water main, and hence the hydrant system, was in train? Who did know? If permission had been sought was the communication network in place that would have enabled notification to be received by all those with a need to know? The accident report notes: 'in the case of any work affecting the serviceability of hydrants, it was established practice for the Senior Fire Officer to be informed in advance and the information promulgated on the fire station notice board.' Was there any evidence that this 'established practice' had broken down in the past? Was the procedure itself subject to any form of control? Why did it break down on this occasion? In looking at these questions, control and communication are linked inextricably.

Control models are, of course, derived from engineering perspectives in which the purpose of a control device is to ensure that the system or subsystem moves towards the goals that have been set for it. In an organizational context, however, there can be a more sophisticated form of control in which the system selects different goals in the light of knowledge about environmental conditions and the way they are changing. In applying control models as discussed in this chapter it is assumed that at a particular point in time the system is striving for some known, i.e. fixed, goals.

COMMUNICATION

Communication occupies a central role in the Formal System Model. In addition to the communication aspects of control just discussed, the following are highlighted:

1 communication between the system and its environment;

2 the flow of information from the wider system, via the system, to the subsystems, and vice versa;
3 numerous communication links within the system and the subsystems.

If comparison with the FSM reveals that any of these links were missing, or inadequate, or simply not used, then further analysis using a more specialized communication paradigm is indicated.

Guetzkow (1965, p. 534) has said that 'the communication system serves as the vehicle by which organizations are embedded in their environments.' If he is correct, the high frequency with which failures can be traced back to inability to monitor what was happening in the environment or to lack of influence over it must be evidence of widespread communication problems. And unfortunately, communication problems within what can be perceived as 'the system' are no less rare. As in the Manchester disaster, examples of lack of communication are all too easy to find, whilst the opposite problem, information overload, though perhaps less immediately apparent, is also common.

It can be very difficult to achieve a balance between too much information and too little. As Rogers and Agarwala-Rogers (1976, p. 93) point out, on the one hand 'the solutions to problems of information overload in an organization which restrict communication flows, such as gatekeeping, filtering and queuing, tend to cause problems of distortion and omission', but on the other, 'methods of coping with distortion and omission depend upon creating a larger volume of messages and thus a greater potential for overload.' (Incidentally, this dilemma does provide an excellent example of a positive feedback loop as a 'vicious circle'—see Figure 6.10.)

A simple communication model is shown in Figure 6.11. A variant of this was used by Shannon in the work he did to establish a mathematical theory of communication (see Shannon and Weaver, 1949). His interest was to determine, in a purely technical sense, the maximum capacity of a channel for transmitting messages. He was thus concerned with the process of 'reproducing at one point either exactly or approximately a message selected at another point' and not with the meaning of

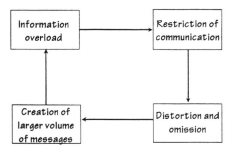

Figure 6.10 *Restricted communication versus information overload*

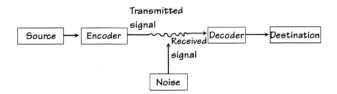

Figure 6.11 *Simple communication model*

the signal nor the capacity of a human to process the information being transmitted.

According to this simple model, successful communication between people requires that:

1 The sender makes an appropriate selection from the agreed 'alphabet'. (The 'alphabet' is the set of signs from which the message may be constructed.)
2 The message can be transformed into a form of physical energy for transmission. With speech the message is first encoded into nerve impulses that activate the mechanisms involved in voice production, and then transformed into vibrations of the atmosphere.
3 The channel is capable of transmitting the signal. This will depend upon the channel capacity (which may vary according to the information code used), the level of noise, and the amount of distortion. In fixing channel capacity at design, exceptional circumstances, such as those pertaining at the time of an emergency, must be taken into account. For example, a telephone system which may appear perfectly

adequate in normal situations may be unable to cope with a sudden upsurge in calls when a serious operating problem occurs.

4 The received signal can be transformed back into a message using the same code. For speech the message produces vibrations in the eardrum of the recipient and is transmitted up the auditory nerve before being decoded at some high level in the nervous system.

5 The receiver has the same 'alphabet' as the sender and can therefore reconstruct and interpret the original message.

There are plenty of examples in the Manchester air disaster where this model could be applied and the communication seen to have worked successfully. Indeed, much air traffic communication works on this basis. A common and limited alphabet/language is used across the world for air navigation. It is transmitted by radio and decoded by the recipient.

Although the simple communication model is a useful starting point for thinking about communications failures it does have severe limitations. One of these is its linearity. Addition of a feedback loop, as shown in Figure 6.12, converts the model into a dynamic two-way process in which the sender and the receiver can adapt to changes in context such as those brought about by alterations in the level of noise. Also, the receiver's response to the sender's message can be used to modify subsequent messages.

A drawback which also applies to the modified model is that it is only concerned with the transmission and receipt of a

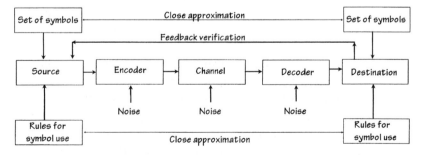

Figure 6.12　*Modified communication model*

message and thus ignores a number of factors which may be of great importance in the study of failures. For example, it does not take account of the context in which the communication is taking place apart from those aspects which increase the level of noise. Nor is it concerned with the values, beliefs and circumstances of the people who are communicating, which, as Rogers and Agarwala-Rogers (1976, p. 14) point out, can have important implications:

> communication within a heterophilous source-receiver pair [a pair which are different in certain attributes such as values, beliefs, education or social status] is generally less effective than that within a homophilous pair [a pair which are similar in those attributes]; when source and receiver share meanings, communication is more facile. Heterophilous communication . . . often leads to message distortion, delayed transmission (because of longer reaction time), restricted channels, and cognitive dissonance.

Human attributes such as beliefs and values may perhaps shed light on why, in a particular situation, communication that crosses the boundary from system to environment or vice versa is more problematic than communication within the system itself.

As a starting point for building a more useful model, Lucas (1986) draws on the work of Mason and Mitroff (1973) to identify a list of factors that influence the interpretation and use of information:

1 The nature of the decision problem. How serious is the decision? What are the consequences of an incorrect decision? What benefits will derive from a correct decision? And so on.
2 The organizational setting. This becomes particularly important as individuals become socialized by the organization.
3 Personal and situational factors which lead, for example, to financial executives seeing finance problems and sales executives seeing sales problems even when both groups are given the same information.
4 The cognitive style of the decision maker. The easiest to recognize distinction appears to lie between the analytic decision maker who looks at quantitative information and the heuristic decision maker who is more intuitive and more interested in general concepts.

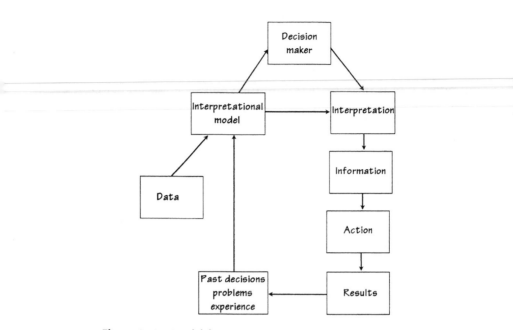

Figure 6.13   *Model for interpreting information (Lucas, 1986, p. 26)*

Lucas suggests that a decision-maker draws on personal beliefs and analyses of historical data and observations to develop an internal model of the type shown in Figure 6.13 and then uses the model to interpret information. Citing the example of a decision-maker who observes data on sales and production over time and finds that the data appears to predict customer reaction to a product, he suggests that such a view, once formed, is used to build the model which is then tested. After the initial design has been finalized, the model is then continually updated in the light of experience. Thus if sales increase after a product has been modified in line with sales and production data the model is reinforced, but if sales decrease the model may be called into question. In the Manchester example the model could have been about the site of the fire.

In spelling out the implications of such a model, Lucas makes two important points:

> The presence of different interpretational models creates many serious problems for the designer and user of information systems. First, the meaning of information is clearly in the mind of the recipient. What

one party perceives as useful and relevant information may be meaning-less to another person. Even more serious is a situation where two individuals agree on the importance of information but develop com-pletely opposite interpretations of what the information means. (Lucas, 1986, p. 27)

He also points out that the effect of the model might be to restrict the amount of information derived from data. For example, the decision maker who perceives that sales and pro-duction data is collected to provide information on product acceptance may ignore other information that can be derived from the data.

In making these points Lucas does appear to assume that people are trying to be rational, informed decision-makers. Although this view may be applicable to much behaviour it does not encompass it all. Deliberate or unintentional filtering may occur for a whole host of reasons. (Further discussion of the biases that may be associated with judgement and choice can be found in Sage, 1981.) Nevertheless, Lucas's work can provide insight into failures involving communication. Further-more, his notion of a decision-maker drawing on personal beliefs and analyses of historical data and observations may be particularly helpful when looking at behaviour during a catastrophic failure. It has been argued elsewhere that people interpret observations in the light of what they expect to happen so when an unexpected, rare event such as a disaster occurs they are not predisposed to believe it (Auf der Heide, 1989) and that if there is doubt as to whether the danger is real, people will tend to assume it is not and not respond to warning messages (Perry, 1987). The point made by Auf der Heide may have been exemplified during the first seconds at Manchester when the belief there had been a tyre burst seemed to hold sway amongst the crew but then the severity of the crisis became so great that no-one was able to doubt for long that the aircraft was on fire.

Although the severity of the Manchester fire gave very little scope for denial, support for Perry's denial argument has been found in other situations, including fires. In a case study looking at responses to a major fire at a large underground mining operation in western Pennsylvania Mallett, Vaught and Brnich (1993) reported 'actual communication failures. . . . [which]

included technological malfunction and human error'. They described:

> workers who consistently reported they were not concerned by the first warning of fire ... [who] attempted to define the warning within a normal and non-threatening context';
> miners who 'even after encountering smoke, ... attempted to define the situation as fairly routine';
> miners who 'until presented with overwhelming evidence to the contrary, ... generally equated their present state with past instances when they had seen smoke in the mine'. (Mallett, Vaught and Brnich, 1993, pp. 721–2)

Communication Within and Between Teams

So far this section has concentrated on individual senders and receivers, but in organizational settings very many communications take place within and between groups. With the increased complexity of pathways and multiplication of processing points these bring comes a sharp rise in the opportunities for communication breakdowns, overload, misunderstandings and so on. In a typical organization it cannot be assumed that each individual has direct access to information from primary sources. As March and Simon (1958) point out:

> The vast bulk of our knowledge of fact is not gained through direct perception but through the second-hand, third-hand, and nth-hand reports of the perceptions of others, transmitted through the channels of social communication. Since these perceptions have already been filtered by one or more communicators, most of whom have frames of reference similar to our own, the reports are generally consonant with the filtered reports of our own perceptions, and serve to reinforce the latter ... perceptions of the environment are biased even before they experience the filtering action of the frame of reference of the perceiver. Salesmen live in an environment of customers; company treasurers in an environment of bankers; each sees a quite distinct part of the world. (March and Simon, 1958, p. 152–3)

Figure 6.14 shows the generally accepted view of communication networks within groups. These forms have, however, been shown by Stewart (1993) to be gross over-simplifications. Using a method based on sociometry together with a software package called 'Netmap' he has modelled actual patterns of communication within and between work-based teams. Using

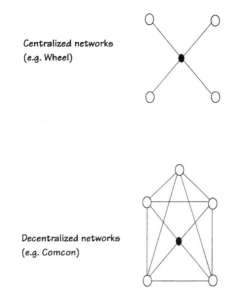

Centralized networks
(e.g. Wheel)

Decentralized networks
(e.g. Comcon)

Figure 6.14   *Communication networks within groups*

information from questionnaires he was able to provide pictures of interactions in terms of who communicates with whom, how often, and on what subjects. These pictures, or maps, captured formal and informal communication networks and were also able to show how important the content of the communications were felt to be by the participants.

Figure 6.15 is a picture of communication in an organization with several departments. The central circle illustrates communications between individuals in different departments (inter-departmental links) and the outer circle shows communications within departments (intra-departmental links).

One potentially important finding from these detailed analyses concerns 'agreed/disagreed communications'. (This picks up the point made by Lucas that there may be agreement or disagreement over the nature, frequency and importance of a communication.) Questionnaire responses can be used to look at each communicating pair to see whether the perception of the sender accords with that of the recipient. Stewart suggests that disagreement may indicate 'that inappropriate information is being sent, important information is being disregarded, the

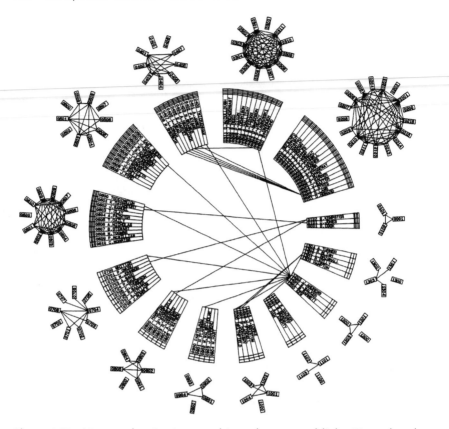

Figure 6.15   *Netmap showing inter- and intra-departmental links. (Reproduced by permission of Active Analysis Ltd, courtesy R. Stewart)*

format is incorrect i.e. too much–too little, or indeed that there is a difference in personal regard between the individuals'. Figure 6.16 shows communications taking place within a team and separates out the agreed and disagreed communications. The high level of disagreement is a clear pointer to communication failures.

Stewart also uses the maps to make comparisons between how the communication links within an organization are structured, what is thought to happen in practice (as reflected by information gathered from questionnaires), what does happen (as captured using audio or video recordings) and what conceptually should happen. (The last of these can be generated via the use of a variant of Checkland's Soft Systems Analysis which

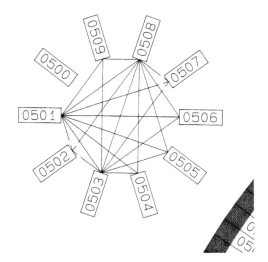

Figure 6.16 *Netmap showing (a) agreed and (b) disagreed communications. Within team communication—agreed communications are indicated by solid lines and disagreed by broken lines. (Reproduced by permission of Active Analysis Ltd, courtesy R. Stewart)*

enables a conceptual communication model to be built.) The distinction between formal and informal communication channels can be an important one where the study of failure is concerned. Formal links can tend to become the focus of analysis because they are easier to define and identify, but they do not necessarily represent an accurate picture of the communication processes that were actually taking place, especially during a crisis.

Perhaps detailed mapping could shed light on the breakdown of communication concerning the rendezvous point (RVP) for the external emergency services at Manchester. Four weeks before the fire a meeting between the Head of Airport Services, the Airport Fire Officer and a Senior Fire Officer from the Greater Manchester Council (GMC) had agreed that the North RVP would be used in future instead of the West. The Police were not informed of the meeting and nor were they told of its decision to change the RVP. As a consequence: the GMC appliances waited for their police escort at the North RVP; the escort sat waiting at the West; and at the same time the airport firemen at the scene struggled to overcome their water shortage problems. Who set up the meeting? Why was a police representative not invited? Why were the changes to the RVP not promulgated?

Such failures of communication involving complex communication networks are all too common so it is important to have the tools to investigate them. The application of Stewart's recent work within the Failures Method has opened up the prospect of building case-specific models of the communication networks that should be in place if the system is to be capable of operating without failure. These theoretical ideals, which could be based upon the actual activities being undertaken or upon the activities implied by the need to affect the transformations required, can then be compared with reality in order to predict failure.

HUMAN ASPECTS OF THE PARADIGMS

The term 'human error' figures prominently in very many reports of accidents and disasters—sometimes, it must be said, with a degree of glibness that betokens an unwillingness to consider underlying causes. Thus at one level, failure to close the Herald of Free Enterprise's bow doors was 'human error', but at another level of analysis it was an outcome of a general lack of concern for safety procedures, and at yet a third level it triggered a capsize that was an emergent property of a certain type of roll-on-roll-off ferry design. Nevertheless, people, their decisions and activities, must be central to any investigation of failure. A study carried out in the nuclear power industry and reported by Embrey (1991), for example, indicated that human performance problems accounted for more than 50% of 'significant events' including those events that did not necessarily lead to severe accidents (see Figure 6.17).

FSM and all forms of the other paradigms thus far considered have human aspects built into them. For instance:

- FSM incorporates a decision-making subsystem. The higher-level decisions, at least, such as selecting transformations for implementation, must be carried out by people.
- The 'controller' in many control processes is a human, and even fully automated control processes often rely on manual

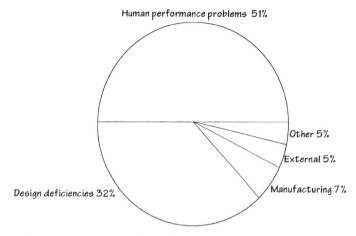

Figure 6.17   *Causes of 'significant events' (Embrey, 1991)*

over-ride to cope with exceptional circumstances or extreme input values.

• People are central to communication processes. All of the communication models which have ben discussed have emphasized the role of people as senders, receivers or interpreters of information.

Clearly, the psychological, sociological and physiological aspects of human performance at the organizational, the group and the individual level which could be taken on board during an application of the Systems Failures Method is vast. Even a cursory survey of this ground is not feasible here, so instead, an attempt has been made to draw out exemplars which illustrate the range of material available and which the authors and others have found useful when gaining understanding of failures via the Systems Failures Method. These are divided into three subsections: the first looks at human factors at the organizational level; the second at human factors at group level; and the third at human factors at the level of the individual.

Human Factors at the Organizational Level—The Concept of Cognitive Adequacy

The concept of cognitive adequacy is particularly useful when considering the relationship between a system and its environment within the framework of the FSM because it is concerned with an organization's ability to respond to observations of hazard. Westrum (1988) describes it as being concerned with the specification of:

1 Who is responsible for what kinds of actions;
2 What appropriate conduct for various positions is;
3 What information is communicable;
4 What is considered fixed or changeable;
5 How problems are to be solved.

Cognitive adequacy is shaped by the organization's culture and Westrum gives a number of examples of organizational cultures that have had negative impacts on safety. He links, for example, the Challenger tragedy (discussed in Chapter 1 of this book) to the culture at NASA where: 'budget cuts led to a willingness to cut back on safety measures; ignoring critical problems became routine; [and] eventually suppression of internal criticism began to take place' (Westrum, 1988, p. 11). A UK example can be found in Horlick-Jones (1990). Discussing the circumstances leading to the Clapham rail crash, he points out: 'The errors made in wiring the signals must be considered in the context of the excessive levels of overtime carried out by British Rail workers, one third of whom were working for more than 50 hours a week, and over 17% working more than 60 hours' (Horlick-Jones, 1990, p. 21).

So what is culture? Clearly it is a complex concept, open to a very wide variety of interpretations, and one which attracts large numbers of theorists. Martin and Siehl (1990) approach the subject by looking at what cultures do and claim to 'capture the essence of much of the recent organizational culture research' in just four sentences:

> First, cultures offer an interpretation of an institution's history that members can use to decipher how they will be expected to behave in the

future. Second, cultures can generate commitment to corporate values or management philosophy so that employees feel they are working for something they believe in. Third, cultures serve as organizational control mechanisms, informally approving or prohibiting some patterns of behavior. Finally, there is the possibility, as yet unsupported by conclusive evidence, that some types of organizational cultures are associated with greater productivity and profitability. (Martin and Siehl, 1990, p. 71).

In considering this distillation one should, however, be aware of the views of Schein (1985), one of the most prominent organizational theorists in this area. He argues that most definitions of culture 'reflect the organization's culture, but none of them is the essence of culture' and insists that 'the term should be reserved for the deeper level of basic assumptions and beliefs that are shared by members of an organization.' Schein also delivers the warning, important in the context of failure analysis, that observations of behaviour cannot be used to define culture because although behaviour is determined partly by culture, it is also affected by what is happening in the environment. This mixing of cultural and environmental influences can be seen in the Challenger example cited earlier where budget cuts were linked to changes in the prevailing culture. It can also be seen following the Manchester fire where discussion about whether smoke hoods would increase or decrease chances of survival was muddied by cost considerations. We can only hypothesize about why changes such as the introduction of smoke hoods were not made, but one possible hypothesis could be that there was a culture in the industry which fostered the belief that over-emphasis on safety devices might lead passengers to perceive flying as unduly risky.

In recent years many airlines have made marked changes to the way in which they introduce safety briefings for passengers. In the past the culture was rooted in a history which implied that safety explanations were an imposed requirement. More recently there appears to be an attempt to change the culture to one in which passengers are more aware of what to do in an emergency and many airlines now consider it an important part of their customer care obligations to ensure that passengers are well briefed.

Use of the concept becomes even more problematical when

level of analysis is taken into account. Some writers on culture appear to imply that it is a monolithic phenomenon, with a single culture being shared throughout an organization. The following quotation from Peters and Waterman (1982) is perhaps a typical illustration:

> Without exception, the dominance and coherence of culture proved to be an essential quality of excellent companies. . . . In these companies, people way down the line know what they are supposed to do in most situations because the handful of guiding values is crystal clear. . . . Everyone at Hewlett-Packard knows that he or she is supposed to be innovative. Everyone at Proctor & Gamble knows that product quality is the sine qua non. (Peters and Waterman, 1982, p. 76)

Martin and Siehl (1990) put forward the opposing view. They argue that 'cultures can [also] express conflicts and address needs for differentiation among organizational elements' and explore the relationships that might exist between the dominant culture and three different types of subculture: enhancing, orthoganal and countercultural. (One of the authors has experience of a situation where the effects of an enhancing subculture were evident. A manufacturer's quality strategy was in effect being undermined because the people carrying out final inspection were implementing their own, more rigorous, standards instead of those laid down by the company. The dominant culture accepted that it was important to meet quality standards. The enhancing subculture was to try to achieve perfection.)

As Hildebrandt, Kristensen, Kanji and Dahlgaard (1991) point out, Schein's view 'is a conception of culture which is rooted more in the theories of group development and group dynamics than in anthropologic theories of how cultures develop. . . . [It follows from it] that it is possible . . . to take advantage of learning theories and to develop a dynamic conception of corporate culture.' This view leads back to the question raised in Chapter 1 which is an underlying theme of this book. Can a learning organization that can benefit from the results of failure analyses be fostered, and if so, how?

The Safety Culture Paradigm

A term that has particular resonances with respect to failures is safety culture. In his report on the Kings Cross Disaster, for example, Lord Justice Fennell described the breakdown in corporate 'safety consciousness' at London Underground. Most organizations lay down sets of rules which are supposed to ensure safe working practices, but those rules are far more likely to be followed if a safety culture, i.e. a culture which encourages safe practices, exists. As the story of the chemical plant disaster at Bhopal in the next chapter shows, having the technology in place is no guarantee of safety unless the discipline required to follow prescribed procedures and good operating practices is also present. Similarly, at Manchester the permit to work procedure did not prevent the contractors from isolating the hydrants. At a less dramatic level the absence of a safety culture can be observed on building sites where workers choose not to wear hard hats or safety boots.

So in specifying the safety culture paradigm, what are the characteristics of an organization where such a culture can be said to exist? Although it is not practicable to pin-point and specify all of the characteristics, a number can be readily identified. These include:

1 an organization that takes a positive attitude towards criticism and other feedback from lower levels within it and from outside;
2 an organization that takes into account the boundaries and patterns of communication within it when designing processes, procedures and working practices;
3 an organization that promotes concern for the consequences of its activities and for the effects of individual actions;
4 an organization that encourages involvement and commitment and is able to resolve conflict without causing alienation.

This list can be used as a basis for assessing the extent to which a safety culture could be said to have been in place prior to, and at the time at which a failure was occurring.

Human Factors at Group Level—Team Behaviour Paradigms

Although it is not specifically stated, the Formal System Model implies a strong emphasis on group working with each of the main subsystems likely to comprise a number of teams. Stewart (1991) provides a method for investigating team behaviour within the Systems Failures Method. He uses concepts drawn from the disciplines of sociology, social psychology and organizational psychology to provide a set of social paradigms that 'address areas of less desirable emergent behaviour' at three different stages in a team's life cycle:

1 when the team is new;
2 when the team has developed as an entity and is performing normally;
3 when the team is well established and has been operating successfully for a period of time.

Each of the paradigms is a description of how a team that is less than fully effective might behave and the possible causes of the team's problems. If one of the descriptions appears to fit the behaviour of a team in the failure situation then the remainder of the paradigm—the possible causes of the group's problems—can provide a basis for further investigation.

The Anomic Reaction Paradigm

This paradigm takes its name from the concept of anomie which has been described by its originator, Durkheim, as the feeling of aimlessness or purposelessness provoked by rapid social change whereby traditional norms and standards become undermined without being replaced by new ones.

Description of team behaviour
The team has been formed with the members coming from different areas of the organization. There is a degree of uncertainty as to exactly what they are meant to be doing and the scope of their authority. This manifests itself in a continuous checking of work and decisions, both internally within the team and with other areas of the company. The

level of communication of team members with previous formal and informal networks is high, showing a propensity to discuss previous activities. There is a reluctance to let drop past 'favoured' activities and a possible low commitment to, or understanding of, the new tasks. There is not yet a full identification with the new team, nor an understanding of how this new appointment may serve individual member's long term needs. (Stewart, 1991)

Possible causes of the team's problems
People have been moved around in organizations since organizations were formed, however the fluidity now required in task based organizations is such that as soon as they have settled into one team, they can be moved. This has the effect that as one set of norms and relationships are stabilised, then a new set has to be formed. Hence change is continuous. The new responsibilities, goals and authority may not be crystal clear and the relationships to other people and teams are yet to be firmly established. The old networks of peer groups and informal networks has been disrupted. (Stewart, 1991)

This model of organizational life is, of course, different from the changing flight crew model where although individuals change from flight to flight the roles are well known and clearly established.

The Team Cult Paradigm

This paradigm is based on a number of concepts such as cognitive dissonance (the contradiction between behavioural patterns and belief systems) and groupthink (the process, discussed in Chapter 3, whereby individual members of a group suspend their ordinary critical faculties and instead join in with a group opinion which ignores or distorts reality).

Description of team behaviour
This paradigm examines the relationship of individuals to the team. Intra-team norms, work and social patterns have stabilised. A tightly knit society has developed with a 'clan' type of operation of close working ties and personal connections within the team and to other teams. A strong or charismatic leader may have arisen, with pressure on members to conform to the team. A team developed in this form can cause dissatisfaction and indeed some form of cognitive dissonance to some members. Other problems may surface as a result of the formation of a strong team. For example, 'deindividuation' may cause a lack of self-recognition, 'groupthink' and 'group polarization' may run counter to an individual member's strongly held attitudes and beliefs

all leading to disassociation from the team or indeed 'reactance' or rebellion. (Stewart, 1991)

Possible causes of the team's problems

The group has developed a strong culture whereby the team cohesiveness is more important than individual members. The emergence of a strong leader is driving the team in directions that are counter to members wishes. Authority and responsibility levels are being disregarded or abused. Team members are not being consulted or are overridden in decision taking processes and there is no place for minority views. The social and personal activities of the team are given undue importance. (Stewart, 1991)

The Team Primacy Paradigm

Concepts related to alienation lie at the heart of this paradigm. Three of the categories of alienation identified by Blauner (1973)—powerlessness, isolation and self estrangement—are combined with the concept of 'dependent participation alienation' as defined by Touraine (1971).

Description of team behaviour

This paradigm examines the relationship of the team to the organization. The team has developed a strong identity, self-belief and self-importance bordering upon arrogance. It is very clear on how to run its activities successfully, the resources it should have, how it should be structured and demands the authority to define its own boundaries of operation. It perceives as interference, hierarchical and lateral organization attempts to control its activities by setting detailed objectives, goals and budgetary limits in areas where the team believes it knows best. The team feels that it does not have the power to follow its own strategies and is not being given the support or recognition warranted. This leads to some stormy external relationships. The belief of the team is that its activities are of prime importance to the success of the organization, and hence a 'primacy' or pre-eminent status should be attributed. The result of not obtaining this status is an alienation of the team to the organization. This team alienation is demonstrated by a resentment of the way in which the team is forced to operate and frustration at the way in which they are required to apply their skills and knowledge without the discretion and autonomy they expect. The end product is an estrangement of the team to the organization and from the senior management's perspective, counter-productive behaviour. (Stewart, 1991)

Possible Causes of the Team's Problems

In the process of flattening the structure and the creation of task teams, too much emphasis is given to the importance of specific teams. Whilst this may be important in the motivation of the members, there is a danger of elitism. The devolving of tasks and functional responsibility to teams without the corresponding devolution of authority can cause either a high degree of annoyance or projection of responsibility. Similarly where a semi-autonomous unit has been set up, the nature of the performance control mechanisms is important. A problem arises if feedforward control is not given predominance over feedback. A lack of explanation of where in the overall strategy this team's activities contribute, with associated defined importance, can cause a focussing on the team not balanced by the overall picture. This causes a sense of isolation and exploitation of the team. (Stewart, 1991)

Human Factors at the Level of the Individual—Human Aspects of Control and Communication

As technology and the mechanisms used to control it has become more sophisticated, separation from the people using it has increased. This has led to even greater reliance on the displays via which information is received. Centralization has also increased. Control functions which were split between a number of work stations may now be combined into a single display with just one operator who may not even be aware of how the processes being controlled work and may have only been trained to respond to a series of predetermined emergencies. This can leave the operator exposed, unable to cope with rare, unexpected events. One way of providing operators with better understanding of processes is to incorporate predictive displays into control panels. Another option is to include models of the processes in the control systems so as to allow operators to input sample values of key parameters and see whether the values predicted by the models correspond with those measured by the instrumentation. A third approach is to design control systems so that they fit 'models' of the systems held by the operators.

Traditional dial displays have been replaced by computer screens or visual display units. These can present far more information in total but usually only a limited amount of the information is available at any one time because a hierarchical structure is adopted which means that the display is serial rather than simultaneous. Paradoxically, such displays can carry the danger of overloading the operator with unnecessary information or masking critical items, especially at times of stress such as when the system malfunctions.

In investigating a breakdown in control, guidelines for best practice can be used to check whether human aspects were taken account of in the design and use of visual display units. These guidelines include:

The Positioning of Information on the Screen

Research has shown that operators respond most rapidly to information carried in the upper left quarter of a screen so this area should be used for data that must be responded to quickly.

Grouping Items in the Display

Grouping similar items in the display together improves readability and can highlight relationships between different groups. Groups can be identified through the use of colour coding, graphic borders or highlighting.

Style of Text

Conventional upper- and lower-case text can be read about 13% more quickly than text that is all upper case. Text that is evenly spaced is easier to read than text with variable spaces between the words such as those that result from right-justification. The optimal spacing between lines is equal to or slightly greater than the height of the characters used.

Cognitive Load Reduction

Reliance on an operator's memory can be reduced by using menus and by using names rather than numbers to refer to objects and variables and by providing clear, concise system documentation. The amount of learning required can be minimized by selecting names and symbols that are meaningful and by using them consistently. The selection should also take account of the conventions used in similar systems with which the operator may be familiar.

There are, of course, many other aspects to the individuals' roles in communication and control. They need to be able to activate control mechanisms effectively, for example, by pressing buttons, say. They need the communication skills to listen and to tell. The three levels of individual, group, and organization provide the framework within which possible flaws in communication can be considered further; specialist knowledge and expertise in areas such as social psychology or human factors will often be needed to tease out the lessons.

ITERATION AND SYNTHESIS

As this chapter has explained, comparison within the Systems Failures Method begins with use of the Formal System Model to examine aspects of a situation at the 'system' level, perhaps making separate comparisons at different hierarchical levels. The control, communication and human aspects of these outcomes are then investigated further using a variety of paradigms.

Figure 6.18 shows the full version of the Systems Failures Method with its main iteration loop, but many more loops could be shown. At every stage of the method iteration may be required, both within stages and between them. For instance, the absence of a performance information feedback loop in Figure 6.4 should trigger further analysis and modelling. Gaps may appear in the analysis or it may become clear that choices, perhaps relatively minor ones such as placing a component in the environment rather than in the system, were inappropriate, thus making it necessary to revisit a particular stage in the Method. Because multiple viewpoints and perspectives are required it may even be necessary to make a number of passes through the entire method. In the extreme case a situation which was designed to match the model precisely, and which should thus be capable of operating without failure, could still be judged by some observers to be a failure because it relied on a high degree of coercion or encouraged self-exploitation. The

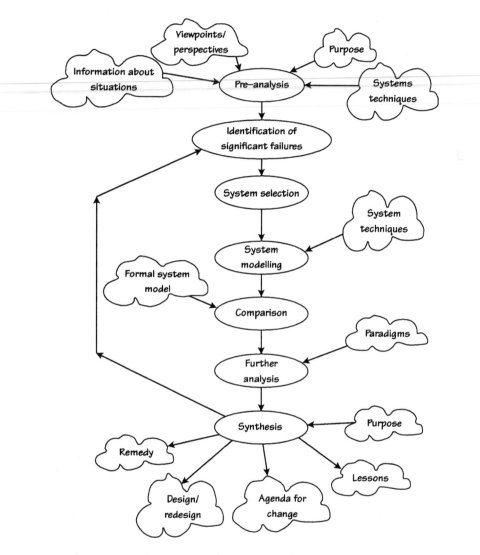

Figure 6.18   *The Systems Failures Method*

failure would not emerge until their perspectives were considered.

When the analysis starts to look complete it becomes necessary to draw the threads back together so as to build an understanding of the failure as a whole. In order to maintain the systemic nature of one's understanding the best way to begin the synthesis is to return once again to the Formal System Model and use the findings of all the comparisons to re-model the system at the various key levels.

Once that has been done the format of the remainder of the synthesis may well vary according to the purposes to which the results of the study will be put. As a first stage it may be helpful to prepare another version of the set of FSMs which emphasize the salient features. What is 'salient' is always a difficult question, with the answer depending upon the eye of the beholder. However, one three-way distinction which the authors have found helpful is between those factors which if they had not been as they were would have prevented the particular failure being studied, those which would have avoided similar failures and those which although significant did not contribute materially to the particular set of events. These distinctions are important because it is always the case that investigations discover some things which are thought worthy of change but which would not have made any difference in the particular case. For example, the Trident Papa-India air crash outlined in Chapter 1 resulted in the introduction of a compulsory incident reporting scheme, but all the previous incidents which would have had to be reported under the compulsory scheme had been reported voluntarily anyway. A small example at Manchester concerns therapeutic oxygen cylinders. Sensible recommendations about the compulsory fitting of pressure relief valves and their storage in thermally protected areas, preferably at low level, were made in the Accident Report on the grounds that they 'could have caused severe casualties amongst rescue personnel'.

It may be the case that the synthesis has to be reported to others and the final format may therefore be contingent on the features of this wider forum. As was stated earlier in this book, the process of understanding failure, learning from that understanding and taking action is paramount and so the synthesis has to be developed and presented in such a way as to support that process. The output may be a report to a client of some kind which may in turn be fed into the preparation of a training programme, an improvement programme or into the drafting of a policy document. For a situation that has not experienced irretrievable failure the findings may suggest that remedy is possible. (This is more likely to be the case if the consequences of the failure were systemic but its causes were simple.) On the other hand, in situations where the causes and the consequences were systemic, redesign may be indicated and the findings can be fed into a process for generating an agenda for change. This idea of feeding the results into a design process is picked up in the Chapter 8.

In an ideal world all the information about any failure situation would be available, but in practice, understanding is like all knowledge; it is tentative, provisional and incomplete, and limited by lack of time and shortage of creative imagination. Failure is an emotive subject; it causes people to hide things, even trivialities, but in studying past failures one does at least have the benefit of hindsight. In the next chapter we shall be looking at another case readers can analyse using the Systems Failure Method and then considering other frameworks for its understanding.

REFERENCES

Auf der Heide, E. (1989). *Disaster Response: Principles of Preparation and Coordination*, The CN Mosby Company, St Louis.

Blauner, R. (1973). *Alienation and Freedom: The Factory Worker and His Industry*, University of Chicago Press, Chicago.

Cameron, S. (1983). *Systems Approaches*, Open University Press, Milton Keynes.

Checkland, P. B. (1981). *Systems Thinking, Systems Practice*, Wiley, Chichester.

Churchman, C.W. (1971). *The Design of Inquiring Systems*, Basic Books, New York.

Embrey, D. (1991). 'Bringing organisational factors to the fore of human error management', *Nuclear Engineering International*, October, 50–2.

Fortune, J. (1993). *Systems Paradigms*, Open University Press, Milton Keynes.

Guetzkow, H. (1965). 'Communication in organizations', in March, J. G. (Ed.) *Handbook of Organizations*, Rand McNally, Chicago.

Hildenbrandt, S., Kristensen, K., Kanji, G. and Dahlgaard, J. (1991) 'Quality culture and TQM', *Total Quality Management*, 2, 1–16.

Horlick-Jones, T. (1990). *Acts of God? An Investigation Into Disasters*, EPI Centre, London.

Jenkins, G. M. (1969). 'The systems approach', *Journal of Systems Engineering*, **1**, 3–49.

Koester, R. and Luthans, F. (1979). 'The impact of the computer on the choice activity of decision makers', *Academy of Management Journal*, **22**, 416–22.

Kuhn, T. (1970). *The Structure of Scientific Revolutions*, University of Chicago Press, Chicago.

Lucas, H. C. (1986). *Information Systems Concepts for Management*, McGraw-Hill, New York.

Mallett, L., Vaught, C. and Brnich, M. J. (1993). 'Sociotechnical communication in an underground mine fire: a study of warning messages during an emergency evacuation', *Safety Science*, **16**, 709–28.

March, J. G. and Simon H. A. (1958). *Organizations*, Wiley, New York.

Martin, J. and Siehl, C. (1990). 'Organizational culture and counterculture: an uneasy symbiosis', in Sypher, B. D. (Ed.) *Case Studies in Organizational Communication*, The Guilford Press, New York.

Mason, R. and Mitroff, I. (1973). 'A program for research in management information systems', *Management Science*, **19**, 475–87.

Perry, R. (1987). 'Disaster preparedness and response among minority citizens', in Dynes, R. R., De Marchi, B. and Pelanda, C. (Eds), *Sociology of Disasters: Contribution of Sociology to Disaster Research*, Franco Angeli, Milan, Italy, pp. 135–151.

Peters, G. and Fortune, J. (1992). 'Systemic methods for the analysis of failure', *Systems Practice*, **5**, 529–42.

Peters, T. J. and Waterman, R. H. (1982). *In Search of Excellence*, Harper & Row, New York.

Rogers, E. M. and Agarwala-Rogers, R. (1976). *Communication in Organizations*, The Free Press, New York.

Sage, A. P. (1981). 'Behavioral and organizational considerations in the design of information systems and processes for planning and decision support', *IEEE Transactions on Systems, Man and Cybernetics*, **11**, 640–78.

Schein, E. H. (1985). *Organizational Culture and Leadership*, Jossey-Bass, San Francisco.

Shannon, C. and Weaver, W. (1949). *The Mathematical Theory of Communication*, University of Illinois Press, Urbana.

Stewart, R. (1991). 'The use of social paradigms in the analysis of team behaviour during organizational change', in Jackson, M. C. *et al.* (Eds) *Systems Thinking in Europe*, Plenum Press, New York.

Stewart, R. W. (1993). 'A surprising union?—soft systems analysis and sociometry', in Stowell, F. A., West, D. and Havell, J. G. (Eds), *Systems Science*, Plenum Press, New York.

Touraine, A. (1971). *The Post-Industrial Society,* Random House, New York.

Volta, G. (1988). 'Safety control and new paradigms in systems science', Position Paper for World Bank Workshop on Safety Control and Risk Management, October 18–20, Washington.

Westrum, R. (1988). 'Organizational and inter-organizational thought', paper presented to World Bank Workshop on Safety Control and Risk Management, October 18–20, Washington.

Young, O. R. (1964). *General Systems: Yearbook of the Society for General Systems Research,* **9**, 61.

7
Bhopal: An Accident Waiting to Happen

INTRODUCTION

During the early hours of 3 December 1984 a gas leak occurred at the Union Carbide of India pesticide production plant in the town of Bhopal in the state of Madhya Pradesh in India. The result was what soon became known as 'the worst industrial accident in history'. Although exact figures for fatalities and injuries have never been agreed, 3000 immediate deaths and 250 000 permanent disabilities as a direct result of the incident are generally accepted as reasonable estimates. The incident remained the subject of legal action for more than ten years after its occurrence and there is not, nor is there ever likely to be, a single reliable inquiry report of what happened.

The scale of the tragedy at Bhopal thankfully almost puts it in a class of its own. Table 7.1 shows the ten industrial accidents which had caused the most fatalities up to that time.

This account deliberately tries to avoid the distressing details of the impact on individuals. Socially and ethically it may be seen as irresponsible to dehumanize such a tragedy, but readers will need little imagination to appreciate the horror of the events for those who were involved. The sheer scale of the accident for the people of Bhopal is hard to comprehend. This version also tries to keep to the details which are commonly accepted and where necessary makes clear some of the differences of view or

Table 7.1   *Industrial accidents with highest number of fatalities up until 1984 (after Bogard, 1989, from Lagadec, 1982, Bowonder, Kasperson and Kasperson, 1985 and Shrivastava, 1987)*

Year	Accident	Location	Fatalities
1921	chemical plant exploded	Oppau, Germany	561
1942	coal dust exploded	China	1572
1947	fertilizer ship exploded	Texas City, US	562
1956	dynamite exploded	Call, Columbia	1100
1956	mercury discharge	Minimata, Japan	250
1975	mine exploded	Chasnala, India	431
1979	chem. warfare accident	Novosibisk, USSR	300
1984	petrol exploded	Cubaloa, Brazil	508
1984	natural gas exploded	Ixuatapec, Mexico	452
1984	poison gas leak	Bhopal, India	approx 3000

interpretation that exist. Its purpose is to provide a case study which could provide the opportunity for readers to enhance their own capabilities in the application of the techniques and Method described in Chapters 5 and 6. It is not the intention to produce a comprehensive and exhaustive survey; what happened is described only in sufficient detail to allow readers to conduct their own analyses and to look critically at the work of others who have sought to explain it.

The work of others forms the topic for the second part of this chapter. It looks at other approaches which have been used to analyse the Bhopal disaster and examines the outcomes of the analyses. These analyses are particularly relevant to the use of the concepts of perception, appreciation, *Weltanschauung* and holism which were introduced in Chapter 3.

OVERVIEW

The Bhopal plant was owned and run by Union Carbide of India Limited (UCIL) which in turn was 50.9% owned by the US-based Union Carbide Corporation (UCC). In Bhopal UCIL made a widely used pesticide which is generically called carbaryl and which was marketed internationally by UCC as Sevin. The method which was used in the plant involved the production and subsequent storage of an intermediary chemical called methyl isocyanate (MIC). It was this chemical which leaked into the atmosphere from one of the partially underground storage tanks.

MIC Tank

If a chemical engineer was given the task of describing the method of production of carbaryl used by UCIL at Bhopal she or he would be likely to treat a storage tank as a small and peripheral component in the process. However, where an analysis of this particular tragedy is concerned, the MIC storage tank, and the two others like it, were not peripheral; they were central.

Essentially, refined MIC was stored in tanks after it had been produced and until such times as it was needed for the production of other products. (In this case Sevin.) The three stainless steel tanks were each about 12 m long, 2.5 m in diameter and with a capacity of about 57 000 l. The tanks were horizontal, partially below ground level, with concrete-covered earth mounded above. One of the tanks was reserved for emergency use. Because MIC has a boiling point of about 39°C, the tanks were refrigerated. The tank from which the leak emanated was referred to as tank 610.

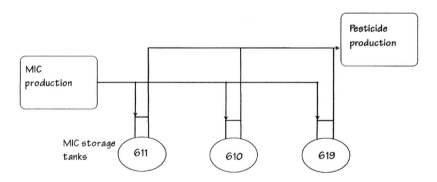

Figure 7.1 *MIC production and storage*

MIC

The gas which escaped from the Union Carbide pesticide production plant in the early hours of 3 December 1984 was an isocyanate. Three isocyanates are in common commercial use. Two of these, toluene di-isocyanate (TDI) and 4,4'-diphenylmethane di-isocyanate (MDI), are used in the manufacture of urethane and isocyanate polymers which in turn are widely used in the making of foams and insulation materials. Methyl isocyanate (MIC) is, however, used almost entirely in the manufacture of carbamate pesticides, although a small amount is used in the production of pharmaceuticals and certain other chemicals.

Isocyanates are known to be strongly reactive. They react with a variety of compounds which contain active hydrogen atoms, including water. (Chemists will know that in this respect they are like the more common ketones and aldehydes.) Furthermore, isocyanates are also examples of 'cumulated unsaturated systems', a feature which makes them even more reactive, so in general isocyanate reactions tend to be particularly vigorous. This ability to be strongly reactive is an important strength, for although it causes them to be more difficult to handle it also means they can serve as useful chemical intermediates which act as staging posts in the manufacture of other compounds.

As well as being strongly reactive, all three isocyanates in common commercial use are flammable and highly toxic. Their toxicity can be gauged by the very low levels of their concentration in the air which safety bodies permit. At the time of the Bhopal leak, the United States Occupational Safety and Health Administration had set maximum allowable average 8 hour concentrations of 0.002 parts per million (ppm) for MIC and MDI and 0.005 ppm for TDI.

MIC is different from the other two commercial isocyanates in that it is also highly volatile. It has a boiling point at normal atmospheric pressure of about 39°C. As a liquid it is slightly less dense than water, but as a gas it is twice as dense as air. It therefore follows that in a hot climate the liquid needs to be kept cool. If it is released into the air the gas tends to stay close to the ground rather than rising and being dispersed quickly.

Both of these features turned out to be important in the development and outcome of the disaster at Bhopal.

As has already been pointed out, MIC is highly reactive with a wide variety of substances. It can self condense in any state and can actually react with itself. What is more, the reactions can often be violent and produce heat which can in turn speed up the reactions still further. Everest (1986) quotes a UCC internal publication: 'Water reacts [with MIC] . . . to produce heat and carbon dioxide. This reaction may begin slowly, but it will become violent.' In addition to reacting with water, MIC also reacts with many metals. UCC's own leaflet on MIC storage states:

> Iron, copper, tin and zinc must be excluded from contact with MIC. They catalyse a dangerously rapid trimerization [formation of a substance containing three molecules]. The induction period varies from several hours to several days. The heat evolved can generate a reaction of explosive violence.

Because of the possibility of the stored chemical reacting with its storage tanks, the tanks at Bhopal were made out of a special type of stainless steel and specific precautions were taken to ensure that rust or other contamination could not enter them.

The next subsection of this chapter explains a little more of the chemistry of the production process. For those who wish to skip over the detail the two most important points to note are:

1 Chloroform is used in the production of MIC and some of it can remain in the MIC during storage in the tank and when it is fed into the Sevin production process.
2 Phosgene, a toxic gas, also has a role in MIC production. In the immediate aftermath of the leak some thought the gas which was released into the air might have been phosgene.

MORE DETAILED DESCRIPTION OF THE PROCESS

The same chemical end point can often be reached via a variety of routes so different chemical plants producing the same finished product may not necessarily use the same manufacturing process. Plants can also be designed to start the process at different stages. At the time of the incident, UCIL brought chlorine and another raw material called monomethylamine (MMA) into the plant at Bhopal from other parts of India. They were both stored in tanks until needed. Chloroform was also produced elsewhere and then used as a solvent during the process.

Carbon monoxide was produced on the Bhopal site and then allowed to react with the chlorine to produce phosgene. (Phosgene is a highly toxic gas which has been used in chemical warfare; you may have heard of its use in World War I.) The phosgene was then reacted with MMA to produce methylcarbamyl which when heated gave off MIC. The design of the plant was such that excess phosgene had to be introduced deliberately in order to ensure that all the MMA was used up in the reaction. Next chloroform was used as a solvent to provide a solution from which the excess phosgene could be readily separated in a phosgene-stripping still prior to reuse. The main solution then passed through a condenser to separate out another waste product, hydrogen chloride (HCl). Finally, a refining unit split off most of the chloroform from the MIC before the MIC was piped to one of the storage tanks. The subsequent use of MIC to produce carbamate is not relevant to the leak and so will not be amplified here.

THE ACCIDENT ON 2 DECEMBER 1984

There will always be some dispute about exactly what happened at the Bhopal plant on 2 and 3 December 1984, and about the events which led up to the gas leak. What is certain is that gas escaped from a MIC storage tank, tank number 610, as a result of chemical reactions which went partially undetected and which were not fully contained by accident prevention and mitigation devices. Because MIC is very reactive almost any contamination might have had dramatic consequences. It is generally agreed that in this incident water somehow became mixed with the MIC in the storage tank, but there is less agreement about how much water or how it entered the tank.

Shortly after the gas escaped, a team from UCC conducted an investigation on the site of the accident. They took samples from different locations at the plant, and from the residue in tank 610. From a series of calculations, computer simulations, and laboratory tests, they were able to estimate the volume and content of residue in the storage tank and produce an hypothesis about how the incident happened. They concluded that the leak resulted from the introduction of a large amount of water and the presence of higher than normal quantities of chloroform and some iron. In the team's view, the iron probably resulted from corrosion of the tank walls during the early stages of the reaction when the temperature rose. The chloroform content of MIC reaching the tank should have been no more than 0.5%, and any batches with abnormally high levels should ideally have been sent to the reserve tank (619) for recycling. However records showed that some MIC with high concentrations of chloroform had earlier been sent to tank 610 instead of tank 619, and that in October the MIC refining still, which fed the storage tank, had been operating at a higher than normal operating temperature. A computer simulation suggested that this would have resulted in higher concentrations of chloroform. An analysis of the MIC in the next stage of the process also showed 2–2.5% chloroform whereas the MIC in the other storage tanks was close to the 0.5% maximum. UCC concluded therefore that the higher chloroform levels were associated with tank 610. The UCC investigators inferred that there was a real possibility that chloroform was present in sufficient quantities to influence the course of the reactions and to partially explain the residue found after the reaction and gas escape.

UCC's laboratory tests showed that chloroform alone would not have produced the reaction, but when they conducted simulations using water and chloroform together the resultant residue was similar to the samples they extracted from the tank after the event. The UCC team estimated that between 500 and 900 kg of water would have been needed to produce a residue of similar composition. Without any chloroform present the reaction could still have occurred but more than 1000 kg of water would have been necessary.

There is disagreement about how the water entered the tank and about the exact form of the reaction and its chemistry. The water may, as some believe, have been introduced when an inexperienced technician flushed out an adjoining pipe without fully isolating the storage tank, or it may have been, as UCC posited in 1985, a deliberate act of sabotage. The most commonly held view implicates the inexperienced technician. According to this version at about 2215 hours the supervisor on duty asked the technician to wash out a length of piping which adjoined the MIC reactor. This was a long process, and although there were safety valves to isolate one part of the complex from another it was also standard procedure to insert a metal sheet called a 'slip bind' to fully isolate the pipe from the rest of the plant. It is believed that this slip bind was not inserted and the water was left running until possibly 0130 in the morning.

SAFETY DEVICES

A chemical plant such as the one at Bhopal would always contain mechanisms to alert operators to any variation in the chemicals used. If a chemical such as MIC became contaminated to such an extent that it became dangerous or unstable it should have been destroyed or reprocessed so whatever the chemical origin of the reaction in the storage tank, several safety mechanisms in the plant design should have been triggered so as to contain it, reduce its consequences, or alert the operators to the impending emergency. However, for a number of reasons which will be explained next, several of these mechanisms did not come into play fully.

In general, the speed of chemical reactions is greater at higher temperatures than it is at lower temperatures. For this reason the MIC storage tanks were equipped with a refrigeration unit to enable the contents to be kept at a temperature of around 0°C. Because lower temperatures result in slower reactions they either avoid unwanted incidents occurring completely or, at the very least, provide extended warning periods during which avoiding action can be taken out. However, the refrigeration unit for tank 610 had not been operational since June 1984. The temperature of the stored material must therefore have been close to the average air temperature which the UCC investigators estimated as being in the range 15–20°C.

Once the reaction had started the temperature would have risen and should have triggered a high temperature warning alarm. But in the case of tank 610, the alarm had not been reset to a temperature above the ambient temperature after the refrigeration unit was disabled, so on the night of the leak it was not triggered by a further rise in temperature.

The reaction would also have produced a change in pressure. The UCC team report that the pressure gauge for the tank had been at a low value of 14 kPa (2 lb/in^2 (psig)) on 1 December and was reportedly still at that level at 2220 on the next day. At 2245 on 2 December a new shift of staff came on duty and at 2300 the pressure was evidently 70 kPa (10 psig). Since the normal range was 14–175 kPa (2–25 psig) a value of 10 psig would only seem worthy of note if the control room operator knew that it had been at the much lower value of 14 kPa (2 psig) only 40 minutes beforehand. UCC was unable to discover whether this information had been passed between shifts. At 2300 a leak was reported but its source was not discovered, and at 0015 a different leak in the MIC process area was detected and the control operator noted a pressure of 200 kPa (30 psig). Moments later the pressure gauge went off the top of the scale at 380 kPa (55 psig).

Although the handling of contaminated material interferes with the smooth running of a chemical plant, it is not unusual. Such plants are designed to cope with contamination at various stages in the production cycle. Ways in which it is dealt with are best understood in the context of normal production.

For the plant at Bhopal there were four standard ways of handling MIC which had been contaminated. All of them could have been brought into play if the status of the MIC in the storage tank had been appreciated earlier. They were as follows:

1 It could have been pumped back to an earlier stage in the MIC production cycle and reprocessed.
2 Of the three tanks, two were used for storage and the third was reserved for MIC which was unfit for production, so the MIC could have been pumped to this storage tank (tank 619) until such times as it had cooled down, or until it could be dealt with in one of the other three ways.
3 Non-recyclable MIC could be sent to a vent gas scrubber (VGS).

4 It could be burnt off and discharged into the atmosphere via a flare tower.

The first two of these options would have been most appropriate had the state of the MIC been detected earlier, which it was not. However, even if it had been recognized in time, they were both unavailable. The first route, pumping the MIC back into the production cycle, was not an option at the time because the MIC production plant had been closed down. By October 1984 there was more than sufficient MIC in storage to meet the needs of pesticide production, and so the MIC production facilities had been closed since October and were undergoing maintenance. The second option of diverting the MIC to the reserve storage tank was closed because this tank was already full of MIC.

The VGS consisted of a circulating solution of caustic soda which was contained in a 1.7 m (5.6 ft) diameter tower. It took in gases or liquid MIC from the normal processes and from the safety valves. These were then passed through the caustic soda solution and neutralized. After neutralization the gases could be directed either to the atmosphere or to the flare tower.

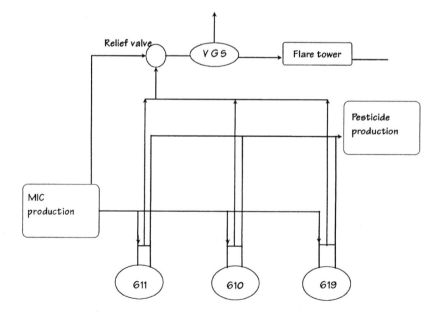

Figure 7.2   *The UCIL storage facility*

The VGS was an integral part of the MIC production process. It had been switched from operating mode to standby mode on 23 October 1984 following the suspension of production, and so on the night in question it had to be operated manually. When the operator who noted the rise in pressure to 380 kPa (55 psig) ran outside he heard rumbling noises and saw that the concrete above the tank was cracking. He returned to the control room and turned on the VGS circulating pump. The flow meter did not indicate that the circulation of caustic soda had started and he did not enter the unit to check whether the pump was running and the flow had started. However after the event there was some evidence that the pump had been in operation. The temperature in the tower the following morning was 60°C and a later inspection by UCC/UCIL staff showed it to be operational. There were some verbal reports that the flow meter was subsequently cleaned and thereafter worked properly.

The flare unit was a 30 m (100 ft) high pipe which was used to burn off waste gases high in the air. Normally a pilot flame would have been alight so that the flare tower could be activated quickly. However, a part of the piping leading to the tower had corroded and so at the time of the incident the flare unit had already been removed from service for maintenance.

Other safety devices apparently did work. When the pressure in the tank rose above 280 kPa (40 psig) a pressure safety valve was designed to open to allow gases to go either to the VGS or to the flare tower. It did open, although exactly when and at what pressure is not known precisely. Between 0130 and 0230 the pressure safety valve reseated and it must be assumed that the gas escape from the tank stopped.

Staff at the plant took various other actions in the course of the night. At 0100 the toxic gas alarm was sounded and water was hosed on to the stack and the MIC process area.

OUTSIDE THE PLANT

The exact length of time during which the gas escaped is uncertain, but it is suggested that it was greater than 30 min and less than 2 h, with about 1 h as the most likely figure.

By Indian standards it was a cool, still and misty night. The gas cloud moved slowly across the nearby shanty towns of Jiaprakash and Chhola towards the railway station. In its path it left many hundreds of people who had died in their sleep, together with their cattle. Thousands more were awakened and tried to flee to safety. The first signs of the poisonous gas were an acrid smell, often described as being like chillies thrown into a hot pan, painful smarting eyes, and choking caused by a build up of fluid in the lungs.

On the first day about 20 000 people tried to attend the local Hamidia hospital. About 8000–10 000 were treated for eye disorders whilst others suffered from gastric problems, vomiting and diarrhoea. Initially the doctors were unsure about which gas was causing the distress and so were unable to do little more than provide general treatment for the symptoms.

The efficacy of the treatment administered to the victims is another aspect of this awful saga about which there is still dispute. At the time there was uncertainty about which gases had leaked into the atmosphere. There were rumours of cyanide and phosgene, the second of which had a history of use as a chemical weapon. In addition there was no local case history of how to treat MIC poisoning. The local doctors, although inundated, acted with great skill and very quickly devised treatment regimes which saved many lives and mitigated some of the effects.

The largest dispute about the treatment given centres on whether there was evidence of cyanide poisoning. Although he later claimed that he was responding to rumours, Dr Avashia, the Medical Director at UCC's carbamate plant in Institute Virginia, sent a telex which advised:

> Urgent pass this info to doctors in Bhopal.
> 1 treat patients with respiratory problems from MIC by intravenous injection of hydrocortisone or prednisone 1gm immediately and 24 hours after. Also give oxygen and supportive treatment.
> 2 If cyanide poisoning is present administer sodium nitrite and sodium thiosulphate: if the patient does not respond to the amyl nitrite administration or if severe exposure is suspected, administer intravenously 0.3 gm sodium nitrite at the rate of 2.5 gm to 5 ml/minute, followed by injection of 12.5 gm sodium thiosulphate at the same rate and via the same needle and vein.
> 3 Observe patient: the blood levels of methemoglobin should be moni-

tored and not allowed to exceed 40%. The patient should be kept under observation for 24 to 48 hours. If signs of intoxication persist or reappear, the injection of nitrite and thiosulfate should be repeated in one half the above dose. Even if the patient appears well, this second injection may be given two hours after the first for prophylactic purposes.

The Head of the Gandhi Medical College Department of Forensic Medicine and Toxicology, Dr Heeresh Chandra, led a team which conducted 155 autopsies within the first 24 h. By 1500 on 3 December they had reported to the medical authorities in Bhopal that there were classic signs of cyanide poisoning. However, despite Dr Heeresh Chandra's findings, and their subsequent endorsement by an eminent German toxicologist Max Daunderer, the cyanide theory was rejected on all sides. Those who came out against it included: UCC who issued a press release on 4 December; Dr N P Misra, the Dean of the College of Medicine at Gandhi medical college; and the medical superintendent for Hamidia, Dr R M Bhandare.

Three months after the leak researchers at the Indian Medical Research Council conducted experiments in which they injected half of a sample of victims with thiosulphate and half with a harmless placebo. The experimental group showed signs of increased secretion of thiocyanate. Such a result would be consistent with cyanide poisoning and may well have implied that the methyl isocyanate had been broken down in the body to yield cyanide in some form. The researchers did however leave open the possibility that cyanide had been inhaled.

THE WIDER CONTEXT

The brief description above covers the basic details concerning the plant, its processes and the events in early December 1984, but information about other parts of the surrounding hinterland is needed in order to appreciate the analyses which others have conducted and the conclusions which they have reached.

Indian Technology

India is particularly strong in engineering and technological expertise and knowledge. It has a high proportion of engineering graduates amongst its population and its Institutes of Technology have an international reputation. The plant manager at UCIL, Jaganathan Mukund, had an engineering degree from Cambridge and as a postgraduate had studied at Massachusetts Institute of Technology. At the same time, however, India has, by western standards, high illiteracy rates. To visitors to India from more developed countries it might look as though India was at that time trying to jump from the 19th century to the 21st century. It had high levels of competence and expertise in the newer information technologies and yet in many villages there was heavy reliance on animal and human power for transport and production.

It had long been a part of Indian Government policy that it would try to develop its own expertise in technology and engineering. India was deliberately restrictive in the extent to which it allowed overseas companies the opportunity to operate in India. It was the view of UCC that it would have made more sense financially to import finished pesticides into India than to manufacture them locally. However, the production process was gradually transferred as a result of pressure from the Indian Government. UCIL had been in existence for 50 years when the accident occurred, but the first pesticides had only been formulated in Bhopal in 1969. Even then only the very last stages of production, packaging and distribution were undertaken there. Later MIC was transported to Bhopal by train, and it was not until 1981 that the MIC production plant was commissioned. UCC stated that the last American personnel left in 1982 (Browning, 1985).

The UCC UCIL link

The pesticide production plant in Bhopal was owned and operated by Union Carbide India Limited (UCIL). UCIL was a sizable company; by 1984 it had 14 plants, five operating divisions, more than 9000 employees and sales of $174 million. The relationship between this company and its parent company, Union Carbide Corporation, was a strong one. UCC owned 50.9% of UCIL and had several members on its Board of Directors. In addition UCC provided design expertise and technical assistance. Initially the technology of the plant was provided by UCC. Staff visited India from the USA and vice versa. The precise extent of the control exercised by UCC over UCIL is difficult to discern and more difficult still to describe. In simple terms UCIL had control over its day to day operations, but referred large decisions to UCC. The annual budget of the company was referred to the American headquarters and the US parent had the right to intervene over serious matters concerning operational safety.

The History Of The Plant At Bhopal

When the site for the UCIL plant on the northern edge of Bhopal was selected in 1969 it was technically outside the city limits. Although it was two miles from the centre of the old town, the railway station and the bus station with their associated densely populated areas were much nearer. By the time of the leak in 1984 there were sizable population centres close to the plant. The nearest of these was J.P. Nagar colony. It was situated across the road from the plant perimeter and was about 100 m (110 yd) from the tower from which the gases escaped. This colony was only about 400 m ($^1/_4$ of a mile) wide and 55 m (60 yd) deep, but it contained about 500 single-storey shanty houses and a population of in the order of 3000 people. Next to it was the Kazi Camp which was already of a similar size when the 1975 town plan was drawn up. Shanty dwellings are insubstantial; they are built out of scrap wood, bamboo, plastic sheet and other readily available materials. They are usually found where there is infrastructure such as roads, electricity and water and where there is work or some other source of income nearby. In the case of J.P. Nagar colony the infrastructure, such as it was, comprised a road and an electricity cable. There was no running water or sewerage system, but there were local wells, and roadside ditches.

The town of Bhopal had a population of about 800 000, to

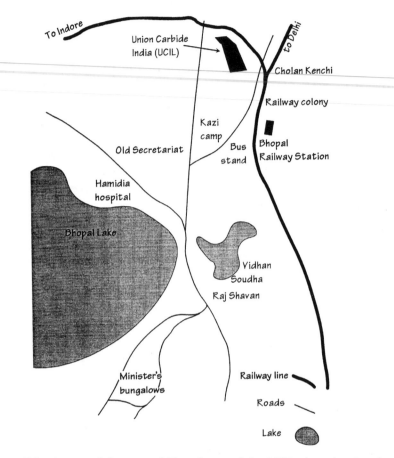

Figure 7.3   *A map of the area of Bhopal around the UCIL plant showing the approximate area affected by the gas leak (Adapted from Bowonder, Arvind and Miyake, 1991, by permission of John Wiley & Sons Ltd)*

which must be added an estimated 60 000 migrant workers. The latter did not even live in shanty houses; they slept either at the railway station or on the streets. The leaked gas from the UCIL plant drifted mainly to the south-east and east of the city rather than across it, but still an estimated 200 000 people required medical treatment.

Previous Incidents

One of the recurring themes which appears in the analysis of disasters and failures is the recognition of earlier relevant incidents. With hindsight some would argue that had these incidents been accorded the appropriate significance when they occurred the disaster under analysis could have been avoided. Whatever the acuity of hindsight these incidents can certainly provide additional insight into the circumstances which led to a particular event. In the case of the accident at Bhopal there had certainly been earlier significant incidents and warnings. In 1982 a journalist, Rajkumar Keswani, wrote several articles in which he criticized the safety standards at the UCIL plant, and in which he predicted disaster. At the end of September 1982 and in the first week of October he had articles published in a local Hindi paper and on 5 October 1982 a gas leak at the plant resulted in 18 workers being given medical treatment. By June 1984 he had published details of a highly critical report by a team from UCC who had surveyed plant safety in May 1982. He also revealed that the October 1982 incident had caused thousands of residents of the adjoining shanty towns to vacate their homes for several hours.

Pesticides And The Green Revolution

In the mid-1960s India and Pakistan suffered particularly badly from food shortages. Eventually, the weather conditions coupled with the poor state of the soil led to famine. Other countries were able to dispatch help, but although it saved many lives, imported food could only be a stop-gap solution to the problem of feeding large countries with growing populations. During the latter half of the 1960s and early 1970s the methods of food production were substantially altered. At the time the term 'Green Revolution' came to be applied primarily to the introduction of seeds with much higher yields, notably the 'miracle' wheats and rice strains developed by the Nobel prize winner Norman Boraug. These strains required more fertilizers and more water, and the importance of the crops meant that pesticides and herbicides also became much more critical in the overall food production regime. The success of the Green Revolution was such that by 1972 when India again faced potential famine conditions it did not need to import grain.

The demand for pesticides continued to rise over the subsequent years until by the time of the leak in 1984 consumption in India had risen to almost 100 000 tonnes. This was four times the 1970 level.

The Chemical Industry

Unsurprisingly, throughout this period the chemical industry world-wide had been expanding. In the ten years prior to 1978 the value of its international trade multiplied more than fivefold to almost $100 billion. Of that, the proportion which was exported to the developing countries increased even faster, so that by 1978 it was 25%. Pesticides are only one aspect of the chemical industry's total output which also includes pharmaceuticals, industrial chemicals and that other necessity of the Green Revolution, fertilizers. Pesticide imports by Third World countries in 1978 stood at about $1bn. The USA was one of the major countries involved in this export of pesticides to developing countries, but it had only 20% of the market. The other players were: Germany 25%; UK 15%; Switzerland 15%; and France 13%. The Third World represented just under 40% of total world demand for pesticides at this time (FAO, 1979).

Pesticides and Sevin

The pesticide which UCIL made at Bhopal was Sevin, a market leader which Union Carbide had developed in the 1950s. It was generically known as carbaryl (1-naphthyl-N-methyl-carbamate). Carbaryl is one of a set of carbamate pesticides which are made by Union Carbide and other chemical manufacturers.

When Union Carbide first produced carbaryl it used a process which did not involve the production of MIC. It started with the raw materials alpha-naphthol and phosgene, which were reacted together to give a chloroformate (1-naphthol chloroformate) and hydrogen chloride. Hydrogen chloride, which is a gas, was then separated in an absorber and the chloroformate reacted with another raw material, methylamine, to produce carbamate and more hydrogen chloride. This method of production was used by Union Carbide in the United States of America from 1958 until 1978, and is still used throughout the world by some other chemical companies.

The method of production used by Union Carbide in India and the USA after 1978 relied on the same raw materials but deployed them in a different order. As described earlier, in this process methylamine and phosgene were pumped into a reactor and heated to give off hydrogen chloride and methyl isocyanate. These products were then cooled and the liquid MIC was then separated from the gaseous hydrogen chloride by absorption of the latter. It was this methyl isocyanate (MIC) which escaped in large quantities into the air at Bhopal. To complete the process of carbaryl production the MIC was mixed with alpha naphthol to give a high yield of carbaryl and no by-products of any consequence.

Even with this method of production it was not necessary to store large quantities of MIC. Elsewhere, Du Pont, for example, in the USA had been developing a plant which had only 20 kg (44 lb) of MIC in the system at any one time, and Bayer in Germany and Belgium operated an ambient pressure process which used the MIC almost immediately it was produced.

The reasons Union Carbide had for using the production method they did were partially a matter of commercial judgement as to the efficiency and cost of their version of the process, but they did regard their process as superior. In the USA the reasons for adopting this method could probably be linked to UCC's wider activities. Sevin, although a popular product, was not the only carbamate-based pesticide which UCC produced, or might produce in the future. In addition they manufactured pesticides for other companies, including Nudrin for Shell, and supplied MIC itself as a raw material to other pesticide producers. Customers included Du Pont, who used it to produce Lannate. At the time of the Bhopal accident UCC was the only MIC producer in the United States.

In India, however, the situation was different. At Bhopal, MIC was only produced as an intermediate product in the production of Sevin. Whether UCIL intended to sell MIC at some later date or to diversify into other pesticides based upon MIC is not known. It has been suggested that UCIL intended to research and develop its own products in the future and would therefore need the flexibility that this method of production provided. It has even been alleged in some quarters that UCIL was researching and developing military products in Bhopal for which MIC might be a useful starting point (Bogard, 1989; Press Trust of India, 1985).

VIEWS OF THE BHOPAL ACCIDENT

Largely because of the enormity of the tragedy at Bhopal, a considerable number of books and articles have been written which have sought to explain what happened, determine its causes and examine how the disaster affected the inhabitants. Newspapers and other more technical publications were quick to report their own interpretations. UCC also produced a report, cited earlier in this chapter, which sought to probe the chemistry of the incident and provide possible explanations of its triggers. Clearly there were many facets to this incident and many lessons to be learned. The International Organization of Consumer Unions (1985) gave some indication of the range of viewpoints when they commented:

> The deadly cloud that wreaked havoc at Bhopal has, is, and will continue to rear its ugly head in many forms, in many sizes and in many places. Obviously there are many lessons to be learnt about occupational health and safety; about proper siting of production facilities; about science and technology; about access to information; about 'trade' secrecy; about 'cover-ups'; about 'double standards'; about medical and legal remedies; about the responsibilities of transnational corporations, governments, and international agencies; and most crucial of all, about what ordinary people can and must do to protect themselves from the plague of such deadly clouds. (International Organization of Consumer Unions, 1985)

On a more academic plane, Bogard (1989), having studied a variety of interpretations by different groups of people of the hazardous situation which led up to the catastrophe at Bhopal, said:

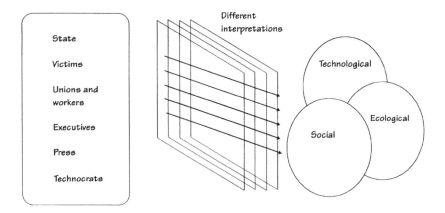

Figure 7.4 *Representation of the actors and perception networks through which the systems of interacting hazards at Bhopal are perceived (after Bogard, 1989)*

In no case is an ultimate, definitive or totally satisfactory causal explanation of the tragedy in Bhopal likely to be found. Instead, one is confronted with complex ecological social and technological systems of interacting hazards on the one hand and a similarly complex discursive network of conflicting and contradictory interpretations of this systems on the other—a discursive network that articulates the rationalisations and problemizations of corporate executives, technocrats, union officials and workers, the press, the State, and of course the actual victims of the tragedy. These groups rarely perceived the hazards systems surrounding Bhopal in the same way. (Bogard, 1989, p. 8)

Any description of what happened at Bhopal at the time of the incident, even one which sought to present the undisputed facts, would still have to be selective. It would therefore carry with it some implicit framework about what was important and what was less important. Earlier in this chapter there was no mention of many things which others might consider crucial to one's understanding of the incident and its effects. The whole of the production process was not recounted. The local building and land use planning procedures in Madhya Pradesh were not explained, and the different medical bodies and their relationships to each other were largely omitted. The appreciative system of each individual analyst gives rise to a different interpretation and a different set of salient features to which they attend. It is always impossible to achieve a completely holistic synthesis of all the events, but the process of striving for holism can nevertheless be enhanced by trying to view the situation from different standpoints. In the case of Bhopal that process is aided by the myriad studies which exist.

In the remaining sections of this chapter the reader will find examples of the frameworks and the methods of analysis that others have used in their consideration of the events at Bhopal.

Examples drawn from the range of standpoints others have used are presented. The selection of authors has been guided by the principle that it would be more instructive in the context of this book to consider the analyses which are more systemic and far reaching rather than look at technical details such as the chemical engineering or metallurgy of the plant.

INTERNATIONAL DIMENSIONS

There are those who see the incident at Bhopal as independent of its location; in other words, it could have happened any-where. A study by an international group of trade unionists (International Conference of Free Trade Unions, 1985) concluded that the underlying causes were, in their experience, common to other international chemical production plants (Table 7.2).

Table 7.2 *Features of the Bhopal accident which are common to other international chemical production plants (International Conference of Free Trade Unions, 1985, quoted in Jones, 1986)*

Insufficient attention to safety and process design
Dangerous operating procedures
Inadequate maintenance
Faulty equipment
Cutbacks in staffing
Inadequate training
Unresponsiveness by management and government to safety complaints
Siting of potentially dangerous plants in heavily populated areas
Lack of information
Lack of disaster planning

Others see the incident almost entirely in terms of the developing world's treatment by the developed world, or at least by the multinational companies that operate across the globe. At the extreme end of this spectrum are those who per-ceive the multinationals interfering in the political processes of their host countries too. Banerjee (1986), for example, says of Bhopal:

> ... it was a well planned experiment in chemical war amidst the 8th general elections in India in order to destabilise the foundation of democracy, immediately after the tragic assassination of Indira Gandhi ...
> The killer gas leaked out of the U.S. multinational Union Carbide plant was one more in a long list of outrages perpetuated by the multinational against the peoples of developing companies. (Banerjee, 1986)

Banerjee goes on to quote the United Nations Environment Programme's claim that '22 000 people die each year in the developing countries from the use of multinational produced pesticides no longer manufactured in the West.'

In systems terms Banerjee has drawn his boundaries internationally and included within his description not just the producers of agri-chemicals, but all those companies which operate across the divide which he perceives between the developed and the developing nations. Multinationals have some freedom to make international decisions about where they produce and market products, how they price transactions between their various subsidiaries and which technologies they use in which localities. They are also subject to local regulation regarding subjects such as safety standards, employment law and the movement of capital. The relationship between First World multinational companies and developing countries is a complex one. On the one hand the companies present themselves as only responding to legitimate demands to improve food production, health and prosperity in poor countries whilst some of their critics accuse them of dumping products which would not necessarily be approved as safe elsewhere. For example, in the mid-1980s, 30% of United States exports of pesticides were not approved by the US Environmental Protection Agency, and some of the products had been de-registered because they had been banned in the USA (Rele, 1985). It has been suggested that a similar trend can be seen in the export of hazardous production facilities (Castleman, 1979). However, it should be noted that Union Carbide manufactured the pesticide carbaryl in the USA using the same production methods as those in use at Bhopal and that the chemical was also produced elsewhere in the First World by other big corporations. An examination of the table of industrial accidents presented at the beginning of the chapter (Table 7.1) shows that in the year 1984 alone there had been two major industrial accidents in developing countries before Bhopal. (The countries were Mexico and Brazil.) However, as Jones (1986) has pointed out, the companies involved were 'state capital' ones rather than multinationals: Pemex in Mexico; and Petrobras in Brazil.

Besides concepts such as the international export of capital and the export of hazards (Castleman, 1979), there are several others which have been applied to this and other accidents and which reflect certain sorts of international perspectives. Examples include; 'double standards' (Castleman and Prabir, 1985), and 'differences in national regulation in some cases driven by nationalism' (Gladwin and Walter, 1985). A different but still international viewpoint sees Bhopal as a special case of the way in which the chemical industry operates world wide (Jones, 1986). As an illustration, Jones points to similarities between the Bhopal gas leak and another leak at UCC's plant at Institute, West Virginia. According to her these included: inadequate safety systems which were overwhelmed; UCC taking hours to reveal what chemicals had leaked at Institute and downplaying their hazards; inadequate information on the health effects of the leaked chemical (aldicarb oxine at Institute).

RELATIONSHIPS AND RESPONSIBILITIES

Analytical frameworks which are being applied by analysts to the Bhopal accident vary and are clearer at some times than others. Sufrin (1985) of MIT, for example, starts from the position that the accident was not an 'Act of God' but an event which could have been avoided. In his view avoidance hinged on what he terms the 'engaged people acting responsibly and in accordance with what was expected of them'. By engaged people he refers to those who have designated functions within an organization, so he includes not just the employees of UCIL but others employed as inspectors of factories, or government planners. By responsibility he primarily means social responsibility which he argues should also be reflected, albeit imperfectly, by legal responsibility. His is presumably not a generalized model of all accidents but one which arises from his understanding of this particular case.

Sufrin goes on to pose three general questions in order to develop his analysis, though at first glance they appear to be superficial attempts to apportion blame:

1 Who were the engaged, i.e. who were the relevant people who failed in their duties and obligations?
2 What would responsible action have been?
3 Who was responsible and what happened?

His use of this framework leads him not to individuals who were culpable, but to structures and processes which were inappropriate. For example, he highlights diffuse decision making which did not sit comfortably with long information pathways and chains of command stretching back to UCIL headquarters in India and UCC in the USA. He considers that this diffuse decision making was aggravated by an environment in which rules and procedures were not followed.

He goes on to argue that once a government encourages or decides to allow an external company such as a multinational to build a plant like the one at Bhopal on its territory an ongoing partnership and mutual set of interconnected responsibilities is established and that those responsibilities are both moral and legal.

Sufrin identifies three areas for further analysis: Government policy; policy of large firms; and protection of individuals. Like others, he considers success or failure to be dependent upon perception and context. So, for example, the success of governmental policy in meeting its purpose will depend on the economic and political context. He argues that in a private market economy the ultimate criterion of success might be the satisfaction of the owners of an organization, but he acknowledges that this is only a partial measure and that even in a market economy there are other stakeholders such as the tax office, creditors, work force, buyers and even competitors who have interests. India is, of course, a more planned economy than some, and so governmental interest, and therefore in Sufrin's view responsibility, rested particularly heavily upon the governmental organizations.

SIMPLE SYSTEMIC ANALYSIS

The most elementary analysis of a situation in systems terms is to view the situation as interacting social and technical sub-systems within an environment. This is the approach adopted by Bowonder, Arvind and Miyake (1991) in a paper which is interesting even though it is unfortunately riddled with drafting errors (Figure 7.5).

Having established a system-based model, Bowonder *et al.* developed their analysis further by assembling six parameters of socio-technical systems into a framework for considering generic reasons for failure in hazardous situations. The six parameters chosen were drawn from Schoderbek (1971). They were: goals; structure; function; information flow; linkages; and decision making. Table 7.3 shows for each parameter the failures types which they identified and gives in each case a Bhopal-related example.

Subsequently they utilized the same parameters to search for inter-system errors rather than intra-system ones. They concluded, for example, that there were goal conflicts between a social agency such as health and an industrial firm. Although

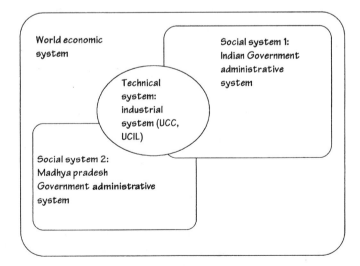

Figure 7.5 *Social technical system description of Bhopal incident (after Bowonder, Arvind and Miyake, 1991)*

Table 7.3 *Generic system failure types and examples from Bhopal (After Bowonder, Arvind and Miyake, 1991, by permission of John Wiley & Sons Ltd)*

Parameter	Reasons for hazardous failure	Failure example
Goals	Goal conflict	Maximization of safety and profit simultaneously are conflicting
	Goal setting	Goals are in purely monetary terms, neglect intangible goals
Structure	Structural defect	Safety manager reports to works manager
	Procedural defect	Treating non-hazardous as well as hazardous facilities at par
	Procedure not defined	How to handle unusual events in plant not specified
Function	Absence of a functionary	No designated safety manager in a hazardous facility
	Lack of coordination	No safety improvements even after serious accidents
Information flow	Absence of efficient channels	Plant and plant manager had no direct links
	Absence of effective utilization	Enquiry report of the Oct 83 accident was not followed up
	Absence of information collection	Increasing failures not monitored
	Absence of feedback and review	Safety audit carried out in 1981 was not followed up
Linkages	Inadequacy of linkages	Safety managers conferences
	Absence of linkages	No emergency coordination
Decision making	Styles	UCC has centralized decision-making
	Biases	Considering phosgene as more toxic than MIC
	Errors	Supervisor ordering washing of MIC lines
	Delays	Delays in informing public and civil authorities

the approach used is not as structured as the Formal System Model advocated in this book and does not deploy the set of further paradigms which are also explained in Chapter 6, Bowonder, Arvind and Miyake have in effect adopted a similar approach by utilizing a simple system model with which they have made comparisons.

SYSTEMIC COMPARISONS

As well as those who apply systems concepts to explore one particular failure, there are others who have developed more general models of failure aspects of systems and then used them to reveal exemplars from different case histories. Wahlström (1992) has placed particular emphasis on layers of control in complex technological systems. Drawing upon the Bhopal accident alongside the nuclear incidents at Three Mile Island and Chernobyl, he has developed a model of complexity within which he has identified layers of control which at each stage have the potential for failure. Amongst his examples he has identified 'persistent risk pathogens' which make a system vulnerable to what otherwise might have been harmless events or changes (Table 7.4).

Table 7.4 *Risk pathogens in the control structures of technological systems (after Wahlström, 1992)*

Generic control level	Example of persistent risk pathogens
Inherent controls	Handling of methyl isocyanate and water in nearby systems (Bhopal)
	Threat of small break, loss of coolant accidents (Three Mile Island-2)
	Positive void coefficient in the reactor (Chernobyl)
Engineered controls	Unavailable safety systems at the plant (Bhopal)
	Misleading indication of pressure relief valve position (TMI-2)
	Possibility of disconnecting crucial safety systems (Chernobyl)
Personnel controls	Lax attitudes among management regarding obvious deficiencies in safety (Bhopal)
	Operators at the plant not aware of problems with failed open pressure relief valve (TMI-2)
	Major plant tests initiated without reactor safety clearance (Chernobyl)
Societal controls	Inefficient regulations for hazardous technical installations (Bhopal)
	Deficiencies in the feedback of operational experiences (TMI-2)
	Acceptability of plants with possible runaway reactions (Chernobyl)

This chapter has provided an example of a very large-scale accident which can be viewed from very different standpoints. Those who have analysed it from a systems perspective have compared it with a simple system model and paid particular attention to aspects of control and communications. These analysts have not used the FSM, but perhaps unsurprisingly they have still found these two areas to be particularly fruitful avenues for detailed exploration.

In the next chapter the change of scene is dramatic. It moves from death and suffering in India to the high tech future of modern Western health care. Instead of looking backwards and being concerned with a disaster which has already occurred, the next chapter looks forward. The Systems Failures Method is applied with a view to preventing failure.

REFERENCES

Banerjee, B. N. (1986). *Bhopal Gas Tragedy, Accident or Experiment*, Paribus Publishers, New Delhi.

Bogard, W. (1989). *The Bhopal Tragedy*, Westview Press, Boulder.

Bowonder, B., Arvind, S. S. and Miyake, T. (1991). 'Low probability—high consequence accidents: application of systems theory for preventing hazardous failures', *Systems Research*, **9**(2), 5–58.

Bowonder, B., Kasperson, R. E. and Kasperson, J. X. (1985). 'Avoiding future Bhopals', *Environment*, **27**(7), 6–27.

Browning, J. B. (1985). 'After Bhopal', in IBC Technical Services, *The Chemical Industry After Bhopal*, Proceedings of an International Symposium, IBC, London.

Castleman, B. (1979). 'The export of hazardous facilities to developing nations', *International Journal of Health Studies*, **9**, 596–606.

Castleman, B. and Prabir, P. (1985). 'The Bhopal disaster as a case study in double standards', in Ives, J.H. (Ed.), *The Export of Hazard*, Routledge and Kegan Paul, Boston.

Everest, L. (1986). *Behind the Poison Cloud, Union Carbide's Bhopal Massacre*, Banner Press, Chicago.

FAO (Food and Agriculture Organisation) (1979). *1979 Trade Year Book*, p. 33, Rome, FAO-UN.

Gladwin, T. N. and Walter, I. (1985). 'Bhopal and the multinationals', *Wall Street Journal Europe*, 21 January, p. 6.

International Conference of Free Trade Unions (1985). *The Trade Union*

Report on Bhopal, International Conference of Free Trade Unions, Geneva.

International Organization of Consumer Unions (1985). *The Lessons of Bhopal—A Community Action Resources Manual on Hazardous Technologies*, Penang, Malaysia.

Jones, T. (1986) 'Hazards for export: double standards?', *Radical Science*, **20**, 11–138.

Lagadec, P. (1982). *Major Technological Risk*, Pergamon, New York.

Press Trust of India (1985). 'Carbide's war gas tests right under DST's nose!', in *Bhopal, Industrial Genocide?*, Arena Press, Hong Kong.

Rele, S. J. (1985). 'Dumping ground for pesticides', in *Bhopal, Industrial Genocide?*, Arena Press, Hong Kong.

Schoderbek, P. P. (1971). 'Systems a viewpoint', in Schoderbek, P. P. (Ed.), *Management Systems*, Wiley, New York.

Shrivastava, P. (1987). *Bhopal: Anatomy of a Crisis*, Ballinger, Cambridge.

Sufrin, S. C. (1985). *Bhopal, its Setting, Responsibility and Challenge*, Ajanta Publications, Delhi.

Wahlström, B. (1992). 'Avoiding technological risks: the dilemma of complexity', *Technological Forecasting and Social Change*, **42**, 351–65.

8
Using the Method: Looking Forward to an Electronic Patient Record

INTRODUCTION

A 1993 paper on electronic patient records had a very revealing title; it used a semantic nicety which many of us in the academic world have employed when our research hasn't taken us quite as far as we hoped it would. It was entitled 'Toward an electronic patient record'. And yet information technology was by then already well established in the health care field. In the US and Canada alone, millions of dollars had been spent on electronic patient record systems. What had gone wrong? Why were electronic patient records not well established in acute hospitals? This chapter describes a study carried out for the Department of Health which sought to answer those questions.

The main purpose of the chapter is to illustrate the process of using the Systems Failures Method, but in so doing it covers two topics of growing significance: the design and implementation of information systems and the systemic nature of modern health care management.

MEDICAL RECORDS

The medical record lies at the very heart of health care and its management. Wrenn *et al.* (1993), for example, make its importance plain:

> It is the primary way health professionals communicate with one another, allows information to be preserved, and facilitates continuity of care. It is the source document when questions of medical negligence or malpractice arise. Under the new relative value resource based system reimbursement scheme [in use in the US], documentation affects physician reimbursement. It often is the only information used in quality assurance activities. Finally, the record can serve as a source of data for clinical research as well as research into 'process of care' for purposes of planning strategies to impact on the overall cost of health care delivery locally and nationally. (Wrenn *et al.* (1993), p. 809)

Despite their importance there is strong evidence that many medical records are incomplete and/or inaccurate. For example, Patel, Mould and Webb (1993) report the findings of a study which looked at the extent to which hospital records conformed to the *Guidelines for Medical Records and Notes* produced by the Royal College of Surgeons of England in 1990. Analysis of notes of 100 consecutive discharges from two surgical units at different hospitals showed that, overall, only about 66% of the entries specified by College Guidelines were both present and correct, with 'regular update of notes, post-operative instructions, comments about post-operative recovery, the record of advice given to relatives and incorrect consent' all identified as 'substandard categories'.

Even where individual records are well kept the formats and methods of storage used do not allow equivalent information from large numbers of records to be extracted easily, thus eroding the value of the information as a research resource.

The gains that would be derived from an electronic system have been recognized for some time. In 1988, for example, McDonald and Tierney identified three kinds of benefits:

1 improved logistics and organization of the medical record to speed care and improve care givers' efficiency;
2 automatic computer review of the medical record to limit errors and control costs;

3 systematic analysis of past clinical experience to guide future practices and policies. (McDonald and Tierney, 1988, p. 3433).

THE EPR PROJECT

In the UK in the early 1990s several strands started to come together which convinced people that the time was right to put major effort into getting computer-based patient record systems up and running. Recent changes in information technology meant that processing had become faster and cheaper and user-friendly graphical interfaces could also be provided relatively inexpensively. A surge of interest in the US which resulted in a series of papers on the topic being presented at the American Medical Informatics Association fired the interest of UK delegates from the Department of Health and the Medical Royal Colleges. They recognized that the integrated NHS organization and structure meant it might be easier to carry out the development work which could lead to generic, integrated systems. This work would also be able to feed off a Clinical Terms Project which was already under way to produce a thesaurus of terms used in health care through which clinicians could communicate.

In the light of all these good omens the Department of Health in the UK decided in the spring of 1993 to give the go-ahead to the 'electronic patient record (EPR) project', a large, three-year strategic research and development programme. It was launched under the management of a Programme Board made up of clinicians and representatives of the Department of Health, NHS management and suppliers at the beginning of 1994.

The mission statement adopted by the Programme Board was as follows:

> The Project will help doctors, nurses and other health care professionals [henceforth collectively referred to as clinicians] to give better care to patients through the use of Electronic Patient Record systems. It will show the potential benefits of EPR systems by working in acute hospitals with clinicians, managers, suppliers and the Department of Health to produce working demonstrations and by supporting a programme of research into the EPR and related problems.

The following objectives were set for the project:

1 To improve patient care through Electronic Patient Record systems and to explore the use of and value to clinicians of generic, integrated EPR systems in acute hospitals.
2 To build two demonstrator systems in acute hospitals using a prototyping approach to explore the issues relating to the EPR with a view to:
   (a) capturing the interest of the clinical professions;
   (b) convincing managers of the benefits of EPR systems;
   (c) influencing suppliers to develop the next generation of hospital information technology;
   (d) learning lessons of wider relevance to other person-based programmes.
3 To identify potential benefits of EPR, both tangible and intangible, to quantify their cost and to develop a methodology to ensure realization of cost-effective benefits.
4 To understand the cultural issues relating to the EPR within and between departments in acute hospitals, between acute hospitals, and between acute hospitals and the long-stay and community services, including general practice, at national level.
5 To examine the issues concerning communication in an EPR system within an acute hospital and between it and other related systems.
6 To investigate the technical issues involved in building and implementing EPR systems.
7 To undertake a programme of research and development work to underpin the development of the EPR demonstrators.
8 To ensure that the EPR Project makes maximum use of the lessons learned from other Information Management Group (IMG) initiated projects and other initiatives that relate to the EPR.
9 To ensure appropriate confidentiality and security safeguards are built in and the necessary data protection and medico-legal lessons learnt.

THE BRIEF

In line with many other large-scale contemporary IS projects, particularly those being carried out in the public sector, it was decided to use the PRINCE methodology to manage the EPR project. PRINCE (PRojects IN Controlled Environments) is a systematic approach which aims to ensure that a project is well defined and executed. It emphasizes the following:

- *Organization*—with the setting up of a management structure comprising a project executive, a project board (called a programme board for the EPR project), a project manager, a project assurance team and a project team.
- *Planning*—which covers the activities of estimating, collating, sequencing, scheduling and assigning resources.
- *Controls*—of quality, progress and exceptions, all with their own reporting procedures.

When PRINCE is being used, initiation, leading to the creation of a formal project initiation document, is the first stage in the project life cycle. As part of initiation the EPR Programme Board refined its objectives and began to identify the potential benefits of the EPR Project itself and of the effective EPR system it was intended to produce. At the same time, it started to consider the risks associated with the Project, identifying a number of hurdles at which the Project itself might fall, such as inability to find two appropriate demonstrator sites. It also recognized that important lessons might be learnt from looking at previous attempts to introduce electronic patient record systems. Accordingly it commissioned the authors to conduct a study using the Systems Failures Method. The formal brief for this was to identify the factors which are critical in ensuring the successful implementation of an electronic patient record (EPR) system in hospitals providing care to acutely ill patients.

It was agreed that the study would concentrate on the functions of the proposed system, the people who would use it and the environment in which it would be developed and used and would assume that the EPR project itself would be well managed and would not of itself constitute a failure. It was also assumed that the EPR system, as designed, would carry out its intended functions and be robust and reliable and that sufficient funding/resources would be available for design and implementation and for the future running of the system.

THE STUDY

The study had two parts:

1 Systems failures analyses were made using published accounts of attempts to introduce clinical information systems.
2 The findings of the analyses and information gained from interviews with interested parties were used to look forward to the development and introduction of the EPR system with a view to predicting the risks associated with it.

A literature search revealed a number of accounts that were suitable for inclusion in the first part of the study. The criteria for inclusion were:

1 hospital, as opposed to General Practice, setting;
2 sufficient detail to allow analysis;
3 the system being introduced was complex and had wide-ranging consequences.

The third of these posed the most problems. In terms of scope and sophistication the EPR system envisaged by the Programme Board was at the top of the range covered by the published accounts available.

THE ACCOUNTS USED

Eight accounts were chosen:

1 The COSTAR V system at the Internal Medicine Department of Nebraska College of Medicine (Campbell *et al.*, 1989)
2 The mini-medical record system at the University of North Carolina Hospitals (Carey *et al.*, 1992)

3 The clinical information system at Columbia Presbyterian Medical Center (Clayton, Pulver and Hill, 1994)
4 The medical information system at the University of Virginia Medical Center (Massaro, 1993)
5 The Regenstrief MRS at 30 hospitals and clinics in the Indianapolis area (McDonald *et al.*, 1992)
6 The outpatient medical record system at Beth Israel Hospital (Rind and Safran, 1994)
7 OSCAR at Foothills Hospital, Calgary (Sears Williams, 1992)
8 COSTAR in the Outpatients Department of a 100 bed acute general hospital in the UK (Young, 1994).

Just a couple will be summarized here as examples. The first is Massaro's account of the introduction of a medical information system into a 700-bed teaching hospital at the University of Virginia, USA.

In 1981 a firm of management consultants recommended a programme of IT expansion at the hospital. This began with the successful introduction of a financial and accounting system and was to be followed by the installation of a medical information system (MIS) which would bring cost savings of $26.3 million over five years with a payback period of less than two years. From 1985 to 1987 basic administrative functions such as admission, discharge and transfer were computerized 'with no discernible impact on clinical practice'.

Between 1988 and 1991 the following were added in turn: on-line dietary and radiology orders; laboratory ordering and results retrieval; pharmacy; and major ancillaries and nursing procedure orders. But their introduction did not go smoothly. Delays built up and costs rose to almost three times the original estimates. Working relationships were also damaged: 'the project provoked a major confrontation between the medical staff and the hospital administration.' Cultural and behavioural problems emerged: 'the new system challenged basic institutional assumptions; it disturbed traditional patterns of conduct and forced people to modify established practice routines.' Valid criticisms of the quality and user-friendliness of the IT equipment were also often used as a 'surrogate for other agenda items related to the challenging of basic institutional assumptions and beliefs.'

The second account to be summarized is by Rind and Safran and looks at the outpatient medical record (OMR) system for outpatient care at Beth Israel Hospital in the US. The system forms part of the hospital's large integrated clinical information system (there were more than 1400 terminals in total when the account was written) and was first used in 1989. It has been further developed since then (for example the facility to write electronic notes was added towards the end of 1990) but four years after the initial introduction paper records were still being kept alongside the electronic system. 'We currently print every note written in OMR and have it placed in the paper chart ... significant handwritten charting continues ...' This has led to significant printing problems, including finding sufficient space to house all the printers required.

Events surrounding the introduction of OMR were clearly far less dramatic than those described by Massaro but, nevertheless, barriers have been placed in its way. Indeed, Rind and Safran entitled their account 'Real and imagined barriers to an electronic medical record'.

OMR relies mainly on direct entry of data by clinicians. This proved to be less of a problem than expected: 'Clinicians are willing to keep extensive online problem lists and medication lists, and seem far more willing to type than had been predicted.' Data security and privacy provoked far more concern than was predicted and attempts to find solutions only led in turn to concerns that necessary access to information was being denied.

ANALYSIS

The Formal System Model

Each of the eight accounts formed the basis for a comparison with the Formal System Model. It was recognized that each of the accounts was only partial, but as with many studies which are undertaken after the event it was not practicable to flesh out the information with first-hand research. Nevertheless, by considering the results across eight different comparisons instead of relying on the results of individual comparisons a powerful approach could be adopted which would enable the recurring themes to be identified.

By its inclusion in the selection that had been made, each of the accounts had been labelled a failure for the purposes of the study, with the extent and nature of the failure varying from case to case. For example, the COSTAR system described by Young had been introduced with the backing of seven consultants. One of them ceased to use it after his second clinic and another gave up part way through the first year. Several of its features were discontinued not long after introduction and although the remainder of the system ran for seven years until the hospital closed only three of the consultants ever described it as useful and none of them asked for it to continue at the replacement hospital. The more sophisticated COSTAR V system described by Campbell *et al.* met with mixed reactions from physicians but was well received by nurses and clerical staff. However, although it was said to offer 'complete medical records features' and to have brought benefits such as greater efficiency for some aspects of patient care and improvements in physician performance with protocol care, Campbell *et al.* felt 'our results may point to a decrease in efficiency among the residents using COSTAR' and 'data from our time study suggest that . . . benefits may not translate into faster or more efficient use of scheduled clinic time.'

In representing each account as a system which could be compared with the FSM the perspective was that of an outsider with a brief to draw out lessons which could be applied elsewhere. For convenience, the FSM which was introduced in Chapter 6 is reproduced again as Figure 8.1.

Comparison between the FSM and each of the eight systems representations produced sets of discrepancies and deficiencies which are summarized in Table 8.1.

Drawing together the results across the range of eight comparisons revealed five themes which were each common to a number of the accounts.

1 The subsystems which carried out the transformations tended not to have good links to the remainder of the systems nor to the wider systems.

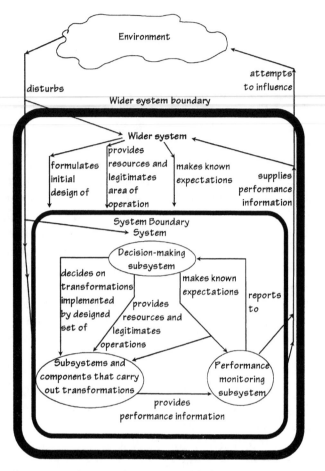

Figure 8.1 *The Formal System Model (from Fortune, 1993)*

2 Ability to influence the environment appeared to be low whilst the disturbances, such as pressures for change, were high.
3 Decision-making subsystems tended to operate in isolation from the subsystems that carry out the transformations and in some cases were isolated from the wider system.
4 Expectations were not made known (at all levels).
5 Some resource problems existed.

Since one of the assumptions of the study was that the project would be properly resourced, the last of these themes was not

Table 8.1 *Comparison between accounts and FSM*

Account	Discrepancies and deficiencies
Campbell *et al.* (1989)	The decision-making subsystem within the system was deficient. For example, the effectiveness of reminder systems was limited by the sophistication of the decision rules that generated reminders.
Carey *et al.* (1992)	The wider system failed to provide sufficient resources; cost was seen as one of main barriers to a fully computerized system.
Clayton *et al.* (1994)	The design of the subsystems and components that carry out transformations within the system was deficient, resulting in low utilization by some physicians.
Massaro (1993)	All three of the necessary links from the wider system to the system were deficient. For some considerable time there was no decision-making subsystem. A team from the Computing Services Group devised the computer system and put it in place but had no decision-making authority.
McDonald *et al.* (1992)	The subsystems and components that carry out transformations were deficient, leading to data input problems.
Rind and Safran, 1994	There were problems with the formulation of the initial design of the system which presumably led to poor decision-making. Examples included printing difficulties and security and privacy problems.
Sears Williams, 1992	The link 'formulates initial design of' between the wider system and the system and that of 'makes known expectations' within the system were deficient leading to the emergence of unexpected consequences from the design.
Young, 1994	The seven consultants who tried this system were never really part of the subsystem that carries out the transformations even though they were, theoretically, the key users. In a sense these key people could not make their expectations known because they did not really have any. In the words of Young, 'They could not see much in the way of benefits.'

considered further. All of the other main problem areas were characterized by lack of involvement of key players and poor communication so two paradigms were chosen to explore the accounts further. These were communication and team behaviour.

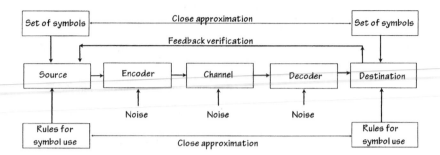

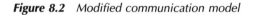

Figure 8.2 *Modified communication model*

Communication

The communication model introduced in Chapter 6 as Figure 6.12 and repeated here as Figure 8.2 was used to identify the following:

- *Mismatch in symbols*—where there are differences of format, coding structures or attributable meaning in the data or information between the sender and receivers.
- *Channel problems*—where the channel of communication has not been agreed or properly defined or has been inappropriately used or breaks down.
- *Noise*—where external factors adversely affect the encoding, transmission, or decoding of communications.
- *Mismatch of rules*—where a shared understanding of the use of data or information does not exist or is not adhered to.
- *Feedback verification*—where there is no process to acknowledge receipt of communication.

As before, each account was analysed separately and the results then brought together to draw out general findings as follows:

1 There were many communication channel problems. These were mainly due to incorrect or ill-defined or non-defined channels.
2 User interfaces were too complex or otherwise inadequate.
3 There was a lack of standard interfaces for communication.

4 Rules of information use were not clearly defined or had not been agreed.

Team Behaviour

Turning to human factors at group level, the team behaviour paradigm as set out in Chapter 6 was used to look at involvement and working relationships. Across the accounts as a whole the problems experienced appeared to be related to the following concepts:

- *In-group/out-group*—demonstrated as own group bias, prejudice against other groups, the stereotyping of other groups and individuals and the attribution of characteristics that do not exist to other groups.
- *Anomic reaction*—as found in new groups and characterized by uncertainty about group and individual roles, responsibilities and power.
- *Team primacy*—found when a well-established group, successful in its own domain, and with strong identity, believes it knows better than any other groups what is best for the organization and resents what it perceives as interference from outside groups.
- *Conflict*—related especially to unresolved conflict within or between groups.

Considering again the account published by Massaro (1993) as an example, specific instances of each could be seen.

- in-group/out-group in the alteration of existing practices;
- anomic reaction in the failure of the clinicians and the IT people to form a team capable of consensus decision making;
- team primacy implicit in the view that the new system was a managerial initiative imposed from outside and with no real sponsorship from the medical community;
- conflict between the medics and the administrators.

Over the accounts as a whole there was obvious and widespread evidence of in-group (management/admin) versus out-group (everyone else) problems and of team primacy amongst clinicians, managers and administrators and IT personnel. There was little evidence of interdisciplinary teams being set up, and no evidence of them working. (The term interdisciplinary team is being used here to denote a team with a common purpose rather than a group which merely provides a forum for consultation and discussion.) There were plenty of examples of conflict being allowed to grow, with some groups remaining unable or unwilling to buy into the systems, and very few instances in which conflict was ever really resolved.

CONCEPTUALIZING AN EPR SYSTEM— MODELLING THE FUTURE

The second part of the study involved using the findings of the analyses of the published accounts, together with information gained from interviews with the project director and other interested parties, to look forward. First, an attempt was made to construct a systems map of the proposed EPR system and to use this to check understanding of the nature of the system. The final version, achieved after a number of iterations, is shown in Figure 8.3.

Formal System Models were then built at three different levels:

1 the highest level, i.e. the system level—a patient care system (see Figure 8.4)
2 the middle level, i.e. the subsystem level—a message system (see Figure 8.5)
3 the lowest level, i.e. the sub-subsystem level—a computer system (see Figure 8.6)

It was necessary to iterate between the three nested systems so as to check that the connections that would be necessary if the EPR system as a whole was to be capable of operating without failure had been considered.

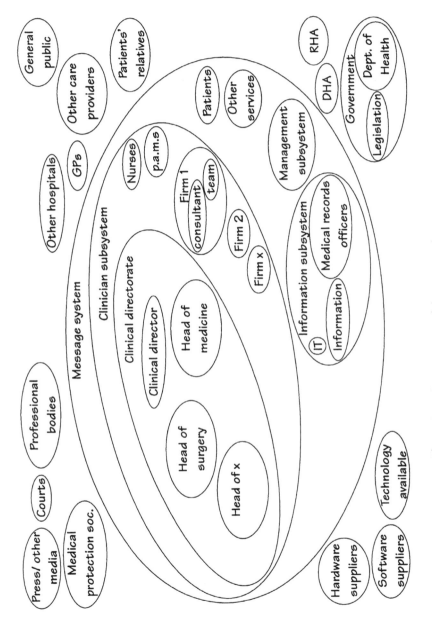

Figure 8.3 Systems map of the proposed EPR system

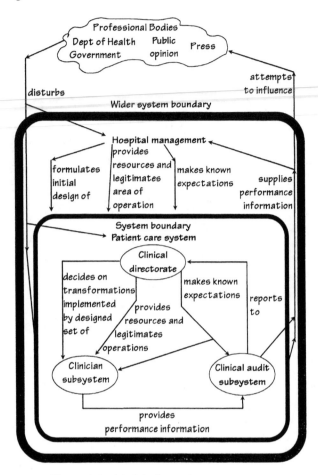

Figure 8.4 *Model of a patient-care system*

FINDINGS AND SUGGESTIONS

The results from the study as a whole were brought together
and reported to the Programme Board as a series of lessons. For
ease of access these were grouped under eight subject headings
as follows:

1 reaction to change
2 climate
3 ownership
4 threat or opportunity?

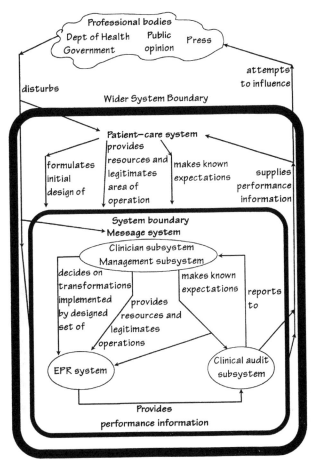

Figure 8.5 *Model of a message system*

5 system and record design
6 user involvement in design and implementation
7 choice of technology
8 implementation.

Taking the lessons related to system and record design as an example, the analysis of the published accounts showed that false assumptions had frequently been made about how people worked, what their information needs were and what links were needed within the systems. For example, custom and practice for routine tasks such as ordering tests was often different from

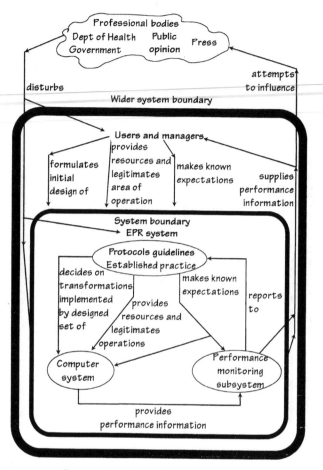

Figure 8.6   *Model of a computer system*

the official procedures that had been laid down, but this 'flexibility', essential to the smooth operation of care procedures had frequently not been built into the design of the computerized system.

The important issues for the EPR system picked out under the heading 'system and record design' included:

- how the records will be used;
- the level of detail required for different purposes;
- the extent to which it will be necessary to be able to pick up patterns emerging over time;

- information needed temporarily versus information required to be stored permanently and whether there is always a clear distinction between the two;
- the needs and preferences of individual clinicians;
- team style;
- the needs of different specialisms;
- information needed for care of the patient as opposed to the treatment of disease;
- treatment of patients with multiple problems if specialism-specific records are used.

It was pointed out that an effective design was likely to be one that would allow the data set or parts of it to be presented to different users in different forms, thus allowing for flexibility in the initial design and for different sets of expectations. For example, some users might regard it as essential to be able to view information by source, whilst others wish to view it by problem or by protocol.

The analysis showed that the question of standardization was an important one with the balance of research evidence appearing to support the idea that standardization would improve the quality of records. Arguments in favour of standardization are that: it allows exchange of information; it prevents information overload by restricting the volume of information whilst not under-reporting; and it can reflect best practice. The problems which tend to be associated with standardization are that it requires the variations in terminology between individuals, between departments, between hospitals and so on to be ironed out and guide-lines and protocols, standard definitions, structures and codes to be agreed before proformas can be designed. Such agreements were not reached in many of the situations described in the accounts, and in some cases agreement had not even been sought.

Confidentiality, data security, and privacy were also important issues. In the UK the legal implications of the Data Protection Act 1984, the Access to Health Records Act 1990 and the guidelines issued by various bodies were important environmental influences, especially since medical negligence case law would hold an individual or group of clinicians responsible, rather than the system that provided the information. However, although it is an important area, the accounts tended to indicate that confidentiality, data security, and privacy were not as big obstacles as many perceive them to be.

In presenting the lessons, recommendations were made, where appropriate, to try to help to carry the project forward successfully. For instance, it was suggested that criteria for assessing the 'rightness' of the climate should be established before the demonstrator sites were chosen. Evidence from the published accounts suggested that lack of involvement, commitment and integration by key players, especially clinicians, had been an important feature in the failure of many electronic patient record systems but there was a danger that demonstrator site selection would be largely determined by technical factors such as the computer systems already in place and the level of IT expertise available.

CONCLUSION

The client for the work described here felt that the report provided valuable criteria to help identify two suitable hospitals to develop the demonstrators. The report was given to the project managers at each of the selected hospitals to use in project planning and the insights carried forward to contribute towards the selection of the criteria to be used to monitor the project.

However, as was said in the introduction, the main purpose of this chapter has been to illustrate the process of using the Systems Failures Method.

Information about the situation has only been included in sufficient detail to allow the nature of the study to be understood. In this regard the next chapter is a complete contrast. It provides very detailed background information about a situation and leaves the analysis to others.

REFERENCES

Campbell, J. R., Giver, N., Seelig, C. B., Greer, A. L., Patil, K., Wigton, R. S. and Tape, T. (1989). 'Computerized medical records and clinic function', *M.D. Computing*, **6**, 282–7.

Carey, T. S., Thomas, D., Woolsey, A., Procter, R., Philbeck, M., Bower, G., Blish, C. and Fletcher, S. (1992). 'Half a loaf is better than waiting for the bread truck', *Archives of Internal Medicine*, **152**, 1845–9.

Clayton, P. D., Pulver, G. E. and Hill, C. L. (1994). 'Physician use of computers: is age or value the predominant factor?', *AMIA*, 301–5.

Fortune, J. (1993). *Systems Paradigms*, Open University Press, Milton Keynes.

McDonald, C.J. and Tierney, W.M. (1988). 'Computer-stored medical records', *JAMA*, **259**, 3433–40.

McDonald, C. J., Tierney, W. M., Overhage, J. M., Martin, D. K. and Wilson, G. A. (1992). 'The Regenstrief Medical Record System: 20 years of experience in hospitals, clinics, and neighbourhood health centers', *M.D. Computing*, **9**, 206–17.

Massaro, T. A. (1993). 'Introducing physician order entry at a major academic medical center', *Academic Medicine*, **68**, 20–30.

Patel, A. G., Mould, T. and Webb, P. J. (1993). 'Inadequacies of hospital medical records', *Annals of the Royal College of Surgeons of England*, **75**, 7–9.

Rind, D. M. and Safran, C. (1994). 'Real and imagined barriers to an electronic medical record', *AMIA*, 74–8.

Royal College of Surgeons (1990). *Guidelines for Clinicians on Medical Records and Notes*, Royal College of Surgeons, London.

Sears Williams, L. (1992). 'Microchips versus stethoscopes: Calgary hospital, MDs face off over controversial computer system', *Canadian Medical Association Journal*, **147**, 1534–47.

Wrenn, K., Rodewald, L., Lumb, E. and Slovis, C. (1993). 'The use of structured, complaint-specific patient encounter forms in the emergency department', *Annals of Emergency Medicine*, **22**, 805–12.

Young, D. (1994). 'Consultants' views on their use of a computer-based medical record system', *Proceedings of Healthcare Computing 1994*, 217–22.

9
Safety in the Channel Tunnel

The main purpose of the previous chapter was to illustrate the process of using the Systems Failures Method. This chapter contrasts sharply with it in the sense that it sets out detailed information about a situation but leaves the analysis up to the reader. The two chapters do have one thing in common, however: they both describe situations where the future is the main concern and the purpose of looking at past events and decisions is not to just understand what has already gone wrong but also to predict where and how failures might occur.

TWO CENTURIES OF FAILURE

To anyone interested in failures the construction of the Channel Tunnel and the history of earlier attempts to construct a fixed link make fascinating reading. The first detailed scheme, for a tunnel, was put forward almost two centuries ago and was commended to Charles Fox by Napoleon during the signing of the Treaty of Amiens, the treaty which brought a brief halt to the war between Britain and France. From the 1830s onwards, with peace well established, many more proposals followed, often inspired by that great new phenomenon: the railway.

The proposals were numerous and various, as were the proposers. However, if there was a prize for persistence and ingenuity it would have to be awarded to Aime Thome de Gamond.

The suggestions he made during the years 1834 to 1865 included:

- levelling the sea bed with a shipboard rake and then laying a brick-lined cast iron tube;
- a submerged arch with a shield that would move across the sea bed;
- a number of different bridge designs;
- an 8 km rail track built out from each coast with a steam ferry running in between;
- a causeway with three gaps to allow shipping to pass;
- a port on the Varne sandbank with tunnels connecting it to the mainlands.

On 2 August 1875 a Channel Tunnel Bill and similar French legislation were passed and the following May both countries signed a protocol agreeing the treaty terms under which the tunnel would be built. A French study ordered by the Geological Commission began and drew up a geological map of the route. All later schemes, including the tunnel now in operation, would be based upon this work.

The French began tunnelling, followed, some time later, by the British, but British opinion started to move against the scheme, with many perceiving it to be a threat to national security. After some arguments the project was stopped in 1883 after over a mile of progress had been made on each side. It was to be over a hundred years before anyone would tunnel as far under the Channel again but proponents still continued to put forward plans and suggest various schemes. Government support waxed and waned, but it was to be many decades and two world wars later before it began to look as though a tunnel might be constructed at long last when in the 1960s The Channel Study Group, a consortium of companies and consultants, put forward their plan for a tunnel. Hopes of the attempt succeeding were, however, finally dashed in January 1975, soon after the tunnelling machine on the English side had been about to start work. The Secretary of State, Anthony Crosland, announced in the House of Commons that 'the project [to build the Channel Tunnel] will be run down as soon as possible.'

A good account of the two hundred years of failure can be

found in Hamer (1987). Morris and Hough (1987) provide a useful analysis of the attempt which came to grief in 1975 and provide it with a fitting epitaph: 'The Channel Tunnel was a political project. Born of political will, it died of political indifference.' (Morris and Hough, 1987, p. 37)

RENEWED INTEREST

Although Crosland's announcement marked the end of one set of hopes he made it clear that he at least was committed to the tunnel's revival at some not too distant date. He told the House: 'the studies, plans and works will be preserved in the best possible state so far as practicable in case the tunnel should be revived when circumstances are more propitious. Nothing will be done which might prejudice this possibility.' Amongst his senior political colleagues, however, the will to keep the project alive was missing. In France, however, their sentiments were not echoed; there was little serious opposition to a link.

It was not long before support for the pro-tunnelling view began to grow again in the UK. A 1979 report to the European Commission helped to raise the level of interest. This report was prepared jointly by the accountants Coopers & Lybrand and Setec Economie and suggested that private financing for a link would be feasible. In March 1980 the Secretary of State for Transport, Norman Fowler, invited anyone interested in promoting a privately financed link to submit proposals. A year later the Minister was telling the Commons Select Committee on Transport that a 'group of British merchant banks' were interested in financing a Channel link and that he himself would be 'enthusiastically in favour' of the project if it were viable (House of Commons, 1981).

Construction of a link was raised at the first meeting between the UK Prime Minister, Margaret Thatcher, and the newly elected French President, François Mitterand, in London in September 1981. They committed themselves to agree on a scheme and to embark upon it by 1984, though this target was later put back more than once. The meeting was followed up by the formation of an Anglo-French study group which reported in 1982 (Department of Transport, 1982). It was less enthusiastic than the pro-tunnellers had hoped, and for the next couple of years it began to look as though nothing might happen after all. For example, when the Prime Minister made an electioneering visit to the Dover Harbour Board on 24 May 1983 she told them that construction of a tunnel was 'not a live issue'. But at the same time, others, including the UK construction industry and its suppliers who were suffering from the effects of recession, were lobbying hard and behind-the-scenes negotiations were taking place.

Finally, in November 1984 the UK and French governments decided to proceed on the strict condition that the link would be funded entirely by the private sector with Government guarantees only covering cancellation on political grounds. They also agreed that a competition should be held to decide which scheme should be accepted and on 2 April 1985 issued a formal 'invitation to promoters'. Amongst other requirements covering financial matters, construction plans and timetables, environmental assessment and so on, the invitation laid down certain safety-related stipulations. These were concerned with:

- plans for dealing with accidents and emergencies;
- the risk to shipping from any bridge piers or artificial islands;
- precautions against rabies, plant disease, terrorism and sabotage.

CHOOSING A SCHEME

Ten submissions were received by the closing date of 31 October 1985, including one for a suspension bridge to be held in place by heavy-lift airships. Four went forward for formal assessment:

1 Channel Tunnel Group–Franche-Manche SA's scheme for twin rail tunnels of 7.3 m (24 ft) diameter to be bored underground.
2 Euroroute's plan for bridges from each coast, joined by a 21 km (13 mi) long undersea road tunnel, with an underground small diameter rail tunnel to be built in stages.
3 Eurobridge's scheme for a motorway to be constructed in an enclosed tube, suspended from piers 4.5 km (2.8 mi) apart.

An optional rail link on the bridge or in a tunnel was also suggested.

4 Channel Expressway's scheme for twin tunnels of 11.3 m (37 ft) diameter which would carry rail and road traffic. This proposal was later modified to suggest separate rail tunnels.

All four front-runners were judged on their financial and technical viability (results unpublished) and on their environmental impact (Department of Transport, 1986a). The House of Commons Transport Committee conducted its own separate appraisal (House of Commons, 1985), taking oral and written evidence from the promoters and from 'Flexilink', a pressure group formed from interested parties such as ferry, Hovercraft and port operators opposed to a fixed link.

Competition was fierce, with first one and then another scheme appearing to be the favourite. In Lille, on 20 January, 1986, President Mitterand and Prime Minister Thatcher announced the winner: the Channel Tunnel Group and Franche-Manche SA had been awarded the concession to construct a twin rail tunnel and to operate it until 2020 (now extended to 2052) and had given an undertaking to submit plans for a drive-through link by 2000. Justification for this choice, as set out in a White Paper published on 4 February, included:

- it is the safest project from the traveller's point of view;
- it presents no problems to maritime traffic in the Channel;
- it is the one that is least vulnerable to sabotage and terrorist action. (HMSO, 1986a, p. 4)

Two days after the announcement the French Government launched a regional development programme to cover Nord/Pas-de-Calais, Picardie and Haute Normandie, part of which would involve connection of the tunnel with the autoroute network.

SCRUTINY AND LEGISLATION

A draft Anglo-French treaty (HMSO, 1986b) was signed in Canterbury in February 1986 and the Concession Agreement (Department of Transport, 1986b) between the British and

French Governments and the two Anglo-French consortia, Channel Tunnel Group and Franche-Manche SA was signed on 14 March. This agreement set out the general characteristics of the link and specified the standards to which its construction and operation must conform. After it had been signed the consortia became subsidiaries of Eurotunnel PLC and Eurotunnel SA respectively.

Following legislation in both countries, the Treaty of Canterbury was ratified in Paris in July 1987. In France the legislative process was straightforward and was completed on 15 June 1986; in Britain it was complex with The Channel Tunnel Act not receiving Royal Assent until 23 July. An excellent account and assessment of the many stages required to get the Channel Tunnel Bill through the British Parliament can be found in Comfort (1987, pp. 68–90). These stages are shown in Table 9.1.

Table 9.1   *The stages of the Channel Tunnel Bill*

Commons	
Standing Orders' Committee	6/5/86–21/5/86
Second Reading	3/6/86 (passed 283 to 87)
Select Committee	19/6/86–23/11/86
Standing Committee	2/12/86–22/1/87
Report Stage/Third Reading	3/2/87–4/2/87 (passed 94 to 22)
Lords	
Second Reading	16/2/87 (unopposed)
Select Committee	2/3/87–30/4/87
Standing Committee	

Report Stage/Third Reading

Comfort's account draws attention to the impact the capsize of the Herald of Free Enterprise had on the Lords Select Committee hearings:

> The Lords Select Committee hearings had completed their first week when on 6 March [1987] the Herald of Free Enterprise went down off Zeebrugge, with the loss of almost 200 lives. When the committee next met, Lord Ampthill called for a minute's silence, but it was some time before the impact of the disaster affected the proceedings. At first the cause of the disaster was not known, the death toll was heavily underestimated and it took a little while to ascertain that drivers were still in

their cabs and that some lorries had been carrying chemicals barred from passenger ferries. The atmosphere when seamen's representatives from Dover testified a few days later was heavy with emotion, but it was [some time] before anyone sought to draw lessons for the Tunnel from the disaster. On 1 April, Dr Philip Goodwin of Oxford University's Transport Studies Unit, author of an early sceptical report on the Tunnel, told the committee: 'My judgement is that the fate of the Herald of Free Enterprise and its crew and passengers will raise the general standard of safety and attention to detailed procedures, but will very substantially alter the relative economics of ferries and Tunnel' [*Lords Minutes of Evidence*, 1 April 1987, p. 7]. The committee went ahead with all thoroughness, however, in questioning the fire risk in the Tunnel posed by passengers staying with their cars. And while Mr Drinkwater [John Drinkwater, QC, for Eurotunnel and counsel for the Government] was to complain of the 'virulent campaign' being waged by ferry operators to prevent Eurotunnel raising its share capital, there was a sympathetic hearing for the ferries' argument that they should receive some form of compensation once the link was operating. (Comfort, 1987, p. 88)

Ratification of the Treaty of Canterbury allowed Eurotunnel to purchase the land and works abandoned at the start of 1975 and to begin their own undertaking.

Because the Channel Tunnel Group and Franche-Manche SA were largely made up of construction companies whose primary interest was to secure the contract to build the tunnel it was necessary to carry out a certain amount of restructuring in order to separate the interests of Eurotunnel (as client) from those of its contractors. Further joint venture companies were therefore established by the same participants. Translink was set up in the UK and GIE Transmanche Construction in France and the two brought together to form an Anglo-French joint venture, Transmanche Link. Eurotunnel then contracted Transmanche Link (TML) to design, build and commission the tunnel and its associated works. The tunnelling work was to be carried out under a target cost form of contract and the fitting out and the construction of the terminals were to be the subject of a lump sum agreement.

THE TUNNEL AND ITS TRAINS

Work began on the site on 1 September 1987, with tunnelling starting on 1 December. This was considerably in advance of the timetable set out in the Concession Agreement which required 'the preliminary studies and preparatory work . . . be carried out within 3 years' and the 'construction of the works . . . be completed within 10 years' with both requirements being measured from the date of ratification in July 1987.

Progress on the English side was initially very slow—less than 5 km of the service tunnel was dug in 1988—due to a variety of problems including:

- poor ground conditions;
- technical problems with the overhead construction railway;
- the effect of salt water which seeped through tiny fissures in the rock and interfered with the controls of the boring machines;
- shorting-out of the construction locomotives.

Gradually the rate of progress improved; 15.8 km (9.8 mi) was completed in 1989, and 16.9 km (10.5 mi) in 1990. At peak production, 2000 tonnes of chalk marl were being brought out of the English end to be deposited at the base of Shakespeare Cliff, Dover. Overall, the amount of spoil was such that it added 180 ha (73 acres) to Britain's land mass.

The first breakthrough came on 1 December 1990 when the two halves of the service tunnel were joined. By June 1991 the last of the three parallel tunnels was joined beneath the sea. By the summer of 1993 tracklaying and most of the infrastructure was complete. The formal handover of the site from TML to Eurotunnel came on 10 December 1993. But the delays were not quite over yet.

The Channel Tunnel is the world's largest undersea tunnel. It joins Cheriton, near Folkestone, England to Coquelles in the Pas de Calais, France, 50 km (31 mi) away, and for 37 km (23 mi) it lies between 25 and 40 m (80 and 130 ft) below the seabed. Although the total length of the three adjoining tunnels is approximately 150 km (93 mi), its rail track extends for a total of over 200 km (120 mi). The service tunnel is linked to the rail tunnels by cross-passages every 375 m (1230 ft). These 3.3 m (10.8 ft) diameter passages are intended for maintenance use and for evacuation in case of emergency and are normally closed off by airtight doors. 2 m (6.6 ft) diameter piston relief ducts to equalize air pressure in the running tunnels occur at 250 m (820 ft) intervals. There are also two undersea rail crossovers: the UK crossover 7.75 km (4.82 mi) from Shakespeare Cliff; and the French crossover 12.5 km (7.8 mi) from Sangatte.

Construction, fitting out and commissioning took over a year longer than expected and starting dates for the various services which would run through it were postponed again and again. With investment in the project being put at more than £11 bn, it had cost more than twice its original estimate of £4.7 bn. In October 1994 the debt to various banks stood at £9.3 bn. Ten men died building it. Each of these statements indicates clearly that there were problems—some of which were undoubtedly significant failures—along the way. However, when they are set alongside the outcomes of other mega-projects the picture that emerges is somewhat less dark. For example, the single-bore Seikan rail tunnel between the mainland of northern Japan and Hokkaido took 24 years (the estimate had been 10) and had a much greater budget overshoot. The Humber Bridge took more than twice as long as was originally intended (nine years instead of four), cost £91 m in construction costs against an estimate of £24 m, and had already accrued interest charges of £54 m by the time it was completed.

The Tunnel was inaugurated by the Queen and President Mitterand on 6 May 1994, though it was another six months before passenger services began. It carries four different types of traffic: freight shuttles; tourist shuttles; through freight trains and Eurostar passengers-only services. The last two of these are capable of operating on three different power systems and four signalling systems.

Diagrammatic representations of the shuttle trains are shown in Figure 9.1. Each train has a locomotive at each end but either locomotive must be capable of restarting the train working on its own. A freight shuttle is approximately 730 m (2400 ft) long and is able to take 28 44–tonne trucks in its lattice-sided carriers and 52 drivers and passengers in a club car. A tourist shuttle train is about 775 m (2540 ft) long and carries a maximum of 120 cars in 12 enclosed double-deck wagons and either 60 more cars or 12 coaches and 12 cars with caravans or motor homes in 12 enclosed single-deck wagons. The tourist shuttle is organized in units of three wagons so that in an

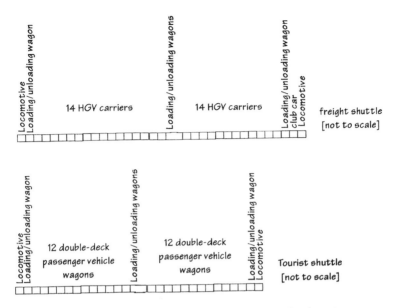

Figure 9.1 *Diagrammatic representations of the shuttle trains*

emergency the affected portion can be abandoned with the remaining wagons moving away in opposite directions.

Through freight trains are hauled using Special Type 92 locomotives. They have direct access to 240 000 km (150 000 miles) of European track and a network of terminals in places such as Glasgow, Middlesborough, Cardiff, Avignon and Perpignan have been set up, with the main French terminal being located at Frethun. Certain journey times have been guaranteed such as London to Milan in 28 hours.

Eurostar passengers-only services run between London and Paris and London and Brussels at present. These trains are based on the French TGV but are lower and narrower so as to fit the UK network. They run through the Tunnel at 160 km/h (100 mi/h) and have six first class coaches with 210 seats, 10 standard class coaches with 584 seats and two bars.

LOOKING FORWARD: SUCCESS OR FAILURE IN OPERATION?

So that is the background. What now of the future? Clearly one area of interest might be the future success or failure of the Tunnel itself or of Eurotunnel in financial terms. Will the Tunnel attract enough customers? Will the company be able to satisfy the banks and the shareholders? A second area of prime concern, and the one which will be explored here, is the safety of the Tunnel now that it is in operation.

Writing in 1989, David Black quoted a very pessimistic view of Tunnel safety from John Adams of the Department of Geography at University College, London:

> defiant optimism appears to be the only answer the proponents of the tunnel have to the security and safety problems. There is no prospect of the tunnel even achieving airport standards of security. To settle for less is to court catastrophe. To accept this is not cowardly or defeatist, but realistic, because if the tunnel cannot be made safe and secure then the economic and social case for it cannot be sound.

Although this is perhaps an extreme view of the level of hazard posed by the Tunnel it has been echoed, albeit in gentler form, by many others. Some of the fears expressed can clearly be put down to the journalist's desire for a good story and have ranged from the xenophobic (see, for example, Follain, 1992) to the sensational. An excellent example of the latter is a story from the *Sunday Times* of 21 November 1993 (Alderson and Harlow, 1993) which claimed:

> ... a heat ball from an electrical fault left a 750-metre section of the 10 bn pounds project severely damaged. A stretch of the tunnel 10 miles from the English entrance at Folkestone is reported to have been left a tangled and twisted wreck. Cabling and fittings melted. Employees of Transmanche Link ... claimed there would have been a disaster if a train had been in the tunnel.

On 9 December, however, the paper published a 'correction' admitting the seriousness of the event had been overstated and accepting that 'even if a train had been in the tunnel at the time, the passengers would not have been endangered.' (*The Times*, 1993)

Others, however, have written in more measured tones and

provided careful analyses of what they have perceived as real threats. One of the greatest difficulties in trying to assess their work and, indeed, in putting together the material for this case study is the high level of secrecy surrounding decisions made about safety measures.

SAFETY DECISIONS

The players who were privy to safety decisions have been represented as a decision-making system in the map shown in Figure 9.2.

The Maître d'Oeuvre (MdO) is a standard feature of French projects involving concessions, such as the construction of an autoroute. The Concession Agreement for the fixed link specified that:

> The Concessionaires shall at their own expense appoint one or more independent project managers (together the 'Maître d'Oeuvre') ... to review whether the works carried out conform to the relevant specifications, to the relevant construction and other codes, regulations and standards, to the relevant construction contracts and to the timetable and the relevant cost projections (Department of Transport, 1986b, p. 6).

The role of the Maître d'Oeuvre ended when the Tunnel was brought into full operation, the final function being to produce the safety report that enabled the Operating Certificates to be issued.

The Intergovernmental Commission (IGC) is a group of senior French and British civil servants, established under the terms of the Treaty of Canterbury (HMSO, 1986b) 'to supervise, in the name and on behalf of the two Governments, all matters concerning the construction and operation of the Fixed Link'. Its expenses are met by the concessionaires. Of its seven functions as specified in the Treaty, three are specifically related to safety:

- approving proposals made by the Safety Authority;
- drawing up, or participating in the preparation of, regulations applicable to the Fixed Link, including regulations

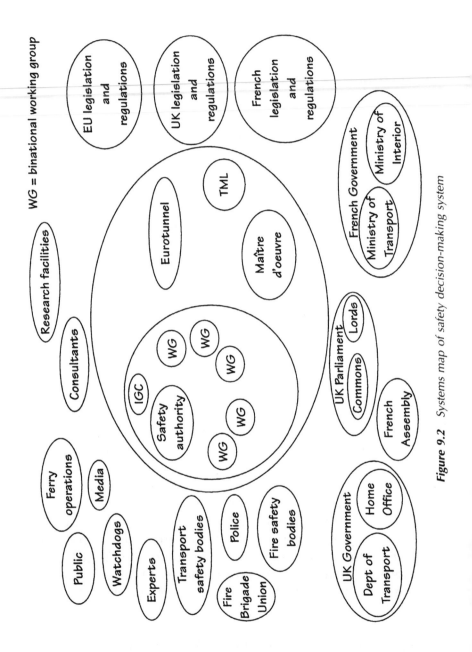

WG = binational working group

Research facilities

EU legislation and regulations

UK legislation and regulations

French legislation and regulations

Consultants

Eurotunnel

TML

Maître d'oeuvre

IGC

Safety authority

WG WG WG WG WG WG

Ferry operations

Media

Public

Watchdogs

Experts

Transport safety bodies

Fire Brigade Union

Police

Fire safety bodies

UK Parliament

Commons Lords

French Assembly

French Government

Ministry of Transport Ministry of Interior

UK Government

Dept of Transport Home Office

Figure 9.2 Systems map of safety decision-making system

relating to maritime matters and the environment, and monitoring their subsequent implementation;

- considering any matter referred to it by the Governments or the Safety Authority or any other matter which appears to it to be necessary to consider. (HMSO, 1986b, p. 6.)

The Safety Authority, set up in 1987 under the same Treaty as 'an independent bi-national body', advises and assists the IGC on all safety-related matters. It has a very wide remit on safety matters and in its five French and five UK members brings together expertise in health and safety, transport inspection and safety and fire safety/fighting. It can, for example, undertake inspections and investigations, bring in outside bodies and experts, and make reports direct to the French and UK governments at the same time as its reports to the IGC.

The formal specification of the role of the Safety Authority is set out fully in Article 11 of the Treaty. Adams (1988) appears to suggest, however, that its role is more circumscribed:

> The Safety Authority is already on record as defining its job as 'balancing' the conflicting requirements of profitability and safety. . . . according to Major C. F. Rose, the British co-chairman of the Safety Authority, 'matters of security are not within the competence of the Safety Authority'. (Adams, 1988, p. 11.)

Throughout the project Eurotunnel had to submit formal proposals, called Avant Projets (APs), for each individual part of the design, and similar submissions for each type of through train, so that taken together the APs would cover all aspects of the Tunnel project. The list of APs as published in 1993 (Channel Tunnel Safety Authority, 1993b) are summarized below.

- AP01 Tunnel civil engineering (9 separate APs)
- AP02 Tunnel drainage and pumping system
- AP03 Tunnel aerodynamics and ventilation
- AP04 Tunnel cooling system
- AP05 Electric power supply
- AP06 Control and communication
- AP07 Railway signalling and safety
- AP08 Fire protection and detection
- AP09 Railway layout and track

- AP10 Catenary
- AP11 Shuttle trains (3 separate APs)
- AP12 Service tunnel transport system
- AP13–AP22 UK and French terminals: layout; earthworks; drainage; civil engineering; roads; buildings; environment (10 separate APs)
- AP23 Permanent works in UK and France (2 separate APs)
- AP25 Ashford inland customs depot.

The purpose of the APs was to define the characteristics and objectives of the proposed works and to describe how they would conform to safety rules. Theoretically, each aspect of the works could only proceed if the IGC raised no objections to its AP. However, this did not happen in practice. In its report for 1988–89 the Safety Authority revealed the following:

> The Authority recognised early on that, to meet the timescale laid down by the Concessionaires, Eurotunnel would be obliged to design and construct some parts of the Project at its own risk before completing the relevant APs. After discussion with Eurotunnel and the Maître d'Oeuvre, it was therefore agreed that Eurotunnel should submit the relevant component parts of APs for informal clearance by the Safety Authority in advance of the preparation of formal APs . . . The Authority however restricted its informal clearances to matters on which they were satisfied on the fundamental design and safety issues. (Channel Tunnel Safety Authority, 1990a, p. 2)

As fitting out continued, the commissioning process began, with the MdO acting as an independent observer. As installation of individual items of equipment was completed, TML issued Installation Release Notices confirming testing could begin. Tests were carried out first at 'group of equipment' level (over 900 separate lots) and then at 'system' level (over 50 different systems such as the tunnel cooling system, the overhead catenary system and so on). Finally, Tests of Completion were used 'to ensure all the separate systems will perform coherently together'.

This proving process took significantly more than twice as long as the six months which had been allowed for it, but no longer than many technical experts had predicted it would take. Only after it was complete could the IGC issue the Operating Certificate to Eurotunnel. At one time it was assumed that the initial Certificate would cover all of the different services running through the Tunnel but because they were not all ready at once it has been necessary to look at each service individually and to grant amended Operating Certificates on satisfactory completion of its tests. The first service to be given a certificate was the freight shuttles, and then in August 1994 the IGC gave clearance to promotional operations involving the passenger services. The certification process was not completed until 1995.

Five bi-national working groups were set up as reports to the Safety Authority. These were concerned with: the transport of dangerous goods; health and safety; civil engineering and general equipment; rail safety and technology; and rescue and public safety. The Rescue and Public Safety Working Group was responsible for drawing up the Bi-National emergency plan for dealing with

> ... any incident—actual or potential—which causes death, injury or endangers life within the Channel Tunnel System or which causes or threatens disruption within or beyond the system and which requires or may require action by the Emergency Response Organisations of the United Kingdom and the French Republic. (Bi-National Emergency Planning Group (1993)).

This plan later became a requirement under the Sangatte Protocol (HMSO, 1993).

A description of the organizational structures and lines of liaison set up under the plan can be found in Charlwood and Pearce (1993). They are careful to point out, however, that

> the Bi-National Plan, is not itself a specific plan, but rather a generic or interface document which allows for the individual service plans of the emergency response organisations of each nation, and the operating plans of Eurotunnel, to work together in a co-ordinated fashion, to deal with major incidents occurring within the Channel Tunnel. (Charlwood and Pearce, 1993)

Although the Safety Authority has published annual reports on its activities and a special report on the non-segregation of drivers and passengers from their vehicles, much of the information used by the IGC and the Safety Authority has not been made public. Details of their decision-making processes are also outside the public domain, with research establishments and universities that have carried out investigations for Eurotunnel and TML bound by their contracts not to reveal the results of their work. In a long article in the *New Scientist*, Watts (1989) drew attention to this secrecy and built up a powerful argument against it. She finished by quoting Desmond Fennell QC in his report on the enquiry into the fire at King's Cross underground station in London in 1987 where 31 died:

> I view with some dismay the suggestion that information gained by a statutory authority which has a bearing on the safety of the public using a system for mass transportation should not be made publicly available. The travelling public has a right to know about the safety arrangements made by transport operators . . . (HMSO, 1988)

The Consumers Association (1994) is also critical of the secrecy surrounding the Safety Authority's decisions. In an issue of *Which?* (May) it said 'The Safety Authority is the watchdog for public safety in the Tunnel. But the public can't have confidence in safety decisions made in secret.'

Undoubtedly the identification of potential safety problems has been a live issue with awareness of risks growing and strategies for dealing with them evolving as the project progressed. For example, the IGC required modifications to be made to the tourist shuttles to widen the fire doors between the wagons by 10 cm and the addition of transverse bulkheads between every wagon on the shuttles. The many changes, large and small, have combined to cause delay and significant cost increases. (The *Independent on Sunday*, 1992, suggested a figure of at least £100 m for the cost of additional safety requirements.)

ASSESSING RISK

The Safety Authority required Eurotunnel to carry out a comprehensive risk analysis of the project as part of the safety case. Presentation of this case was an essential part of the evidence required before an operating certificate could be granted. Detailed information about the methodology and the results of the analysis, which according to a report by Watts (1990) were predicted to cost over a million pounds, have not been published. However, some clues to its form and the philosophy behind it are available. A paper by Kersley of the Channel

Tunnel Safety Authority and Dumolo and Whittingham of Electrowatt Engineering Services (1992) (Electrowatt, Electricité de France and the Institut National de Recherche sur l'Environnement Industrielle et la Sécurité were employed by the Safety Authority to advise on risk analysis) 'set out the principles behind the development of a Safety Case for Major Undertakings for any hazardous, industrial or public facility'. Although the paper begins by taking a wide view of what is meant by 'major undertakings' it soon begins to focus on 'mass transit systems' and sets out the purpose of a safety case as being 'to demonstrate that the design is itself inherently robust and provides adequate defence against potential faults'. They further specify that

> the Safety Case must examine all hypothetical system faults and externally imposed hazards, both in operating systems and engineered protection and mitigation systems to show that the design is able to cope with faults which might lead to intolerable levels of residual risk.

This specification raises a very important question: when does the level of risk become intolerable? In discussing this question Kersley, Dumolo and Whittingham (1992) quote the UK Health and Safety Executive (1988): 'The maximum level (i.e. risk of death) that we should be prepared to tolerate for any individual member of the public from any large-scale industrial hazard should be 1 in 10 000 per annum.' They go on to point out that 'this level of risk approximates to the average risk of death in a traffic accident in the UK'. Their figures thus tie in very nicely with a statement by the Safety Authority that 'a journey through the Tunnel, whether by through train or shuttle, should be at least as safe as a train journey of the same length on the line between London and Folkestone or between Paris and Coquelles.' (Channel Tunnel Safety Authority, 1993a). Batchelor (1994) quotes the following figures:

> Eurotunnel initially set itself a risk factor for foot passengers of no more than 4.7 deaths per 100 million journeys, while for passengers with their cars the risk of death should not exceed 5.6 per million journeys. But the risk to passengers without cars is 50 times lower than the criteria set, and for those with cars 30 times lower because of the safety measures adopted. (Batchelor, 1994)

In discussing the first stage of the safety case, the Preliminary Safety Case Report, *The Safety Authority Report 1992–93* identified a number of issues which would need to be included or developed further in interim and final reports that were to follow. These were:

- the transport of dangerous goods
- shuttle operations in high winds and the effect of wind fences
- the resilience of the pipework in the tunnels
- the need for additional quantitative data.
  (Channel Tunnel Safety Authority, 1993b, p. 20)

THE RISK FROM FIRE

A safety issue that attracted a lot of attention right from the start was the fire risk, with a particular focus being whether passengers should be allowed to remain with their cars. Eisner was one of the first to raise it in an article published in 1986 and it was made much of in an anti-Tunnel video put out by Sealink British Ferries in the same year. Drawing comparison with supposed ferry practice, the video attacked the idea of non-segregation of passengers and their cars. The late John Silkin, a prominent Labour politician and founder of an all-party anti-Tunnel group in the House of Commons, is said to have been prompted to remark that the Tunnel could become the longest crematorium in the world (Hughes, 1987).

The issue was also raised before the House of Commons Select Committee during its hearings in the second half of 1986. As Comfort (1987) points out in his description of the passage of the Bill:

> it was the ferry operators . . . who first raised the issue of fire safety in the tunnel [at the hearings]; if they could oblige passengers and cars to be segregated in tunnel 'shuttles', they could adversely affect the relative economics of tunnel and ferry travel.

He also notes:

> At the time, prior to the Zeebrugge disaster and the ensuing disclosures that lorry drivers often stayed with their vehicles, the ferry operators'

evidence that segregation always took place at sea was accepted. (Comfort, 1987, p. 79)

The need for the segregation of passengers and their cars was debated again in January 1987 when the Bill was being examined by the House of Commons Standing Committee. A proposal was put forward that the planned Safety Authority should require it as part of its regulations. Evidence from the Fire Brigades Union and the ferry operators was cited in support of segregation, with the Alpine-tunnel experience of the Swiss— no fires in 34 years of transporting passengers in their cars by train—being used to argue against it. When the matter was voted upon the segregationalists lost by eight votes to nine.

During 1987 when it was the turn of the Lords to consider the matter, Dr Herbert Eisner, a former director of the Health and Safety Executive, told the Lords Select Committee that any fire would:

spread from vehicle to vehicle, wagon to wagon, fanned by the ventilation. There can be little doubt that the fire would spread in a series of explosions of increasing violence. These could become so violent as to blow out the cross passage doors between the running tunnel and the service tunnel through which any escape would have to be organized. (House of Lords, 1987)

The greatest argument for non-segregation was that it would be logistically much simpler, and hence cheaper, and less likely to cause delays to travellers. Another argument put forward for non-segregation was that it would deter terrorists, though the proposition that all terrorists are unwilling to blow themselves up does not, of course, tend to stand up to interrogation.

The final decision, agreed by the IGC on the advice of the Safety Authority in 1989, was that car and coach passengers would travel with their vehicles unless they were carrying or using liquefied petroleum gas, but people would be separated from freight traffic. (See Channel Tunnel Safety Authority, 1990b.)

The Tunnel project led to a number of fire-modelling studies, in Britain and in France, which pushed forward knowledge in this area to a considerable extent. For example, the Fire Research Station was asked to look at the thermal content of cars with a view to assessing the amounts of heat, smoke and gases given off as a result of different types of fire. The results from these were used in the design and assessment of fire-fighting capability and ventilation.

The shuttles themselves are made from stainless steel with a particularly high nickel content. This not only makes them resistant to corrosion but also allows them to remain intact for a relatively long time in a fire because of the steel's high melting point (about 1420°C (2590°F) compared with 650°C (1200°F) for aluminium, say) and low heat conductivity. For tourist shuttles a 30 min resistance to fire and smoke has been specified for barriers between wagons and for the divisions between upper and lower decks. Of course, none of this would protect wagons if overheated petrol tanks of the vehicles within them exploded.

The plan for action should a fire break out has three key features:

1 Find it and suppress it quickly.
2 Keep the train moving and carry out the within-train evacuation procedures.
3 As a last resort, get the passengers off the train and into the service tunnel where they can be picked up by another train.

Clause AI.52 of the Concession Agreement specifies the requirement that 'all passengers, including those from the stranded train can reach open air within a period not exceeding 90 minutes.'

The First Report of the Home Affairs Committee on fire safety and policing of the Channel Tunnel (House of Commons, 1991) listed the principal features to minimize fire risk as:

1 uni-directional, one-track tunnels
2 advanced control and signalling systems
3 tunnel and walkway design which should ensure that a derailed train remains upright
4 fire detection systems in the rail tunnels
5 low flammability materials
6 automatic train protection to override driver error
7 high grade track to minimise derailment risk
8 detectors for overheated wheel bearings that could cause derailment

9 two control centres each able to control the system
10 electricity sub-stations fed from the power grids in each country, either able to feed the entire system, together with a back-up emergency standby generator
11 train to track, train to control centre and on-board communications systems
(House of Commons, 1991, p. xviii).

The fire detection and suppression systems that have been installed are more comprehensive than those originally planned. In addition, there are clearly plenty of human watch-dogs around in the shape of fellow-passengers which should help to ensure that by-laws forbidding smoking, vehicle repairs and refuelling during the crossing are observed.

In the running tunnels a fire-fighting water main supplied by four reservoirs has been installed with outlets every 125 m (410 ft).

Water sprinklers are fitted in the shuttle trains, together with extinguishers containing halogenated hydrocarbons (halons). There is some controversy over the use of halons. Although the gas is extremely effective in putting out fires, halons are toxic. At concentrations above 20% they cause asphyxiation and it is claimed that at just 6% (the approximate level at which they would be used in the tunnel) a person with a weak heart may lose consciousness. Production of the halon concerned, Halon 1301, is due to be phased out under the Montreal Protocol on Substances that Deplete the Ozone Layer, so a substitute will have to be found as stocks become depleted. Such substitution will require the submission of a revised Tourist Shuttles AP.

The ventilation system within the tunnels, vital in an emergency where smoke and fumes are being generated, is very sophisticated, comprising a normal ventilation system (NVS) and a supplementary ventilation system (SVS) that has ability to deal with a smoke plug as one of its design objectives. Fans ensure that the flow of air is always from the service tunnel, where the pressure is higher, to the rail tunnels so that the service tunnel can fulfil its 'safe haven' role.

In June 1994, before the Tunnel opened, a full-scale evacuation test involving hundreds of volunteers was carried out, but of course such tests can never really replicate the conditions which would be experienced in a real emergency. The first genuine evacuation took place in June 1994 and was the result of a false alarm which indicated that the props used during the loading of a freight shuttle had engaged. All the HGV drivers on board were led to safety through the service tunnel to the other line, but there were only ten of them.

THE TERRORIST THREAT

As might be expected, hard information about the threat posed by terrorism and the steps taken against it is in very short supply. Perhaps more surprisingly, speculation about it has been somewhat muted. For example a 25 column-inches long article published in the *Financial Times* on inauguration day, 'On guard against accidents and terror' (Burns, 1994), confined itself to just two short paragraphs about terrorism:

> A recent risk assessment commissioned by the London based Research Institute for the Study of Conflict and Terrorism concluded that the Channel Tunnel was probably the least vulnerable to major damage of any under-sea tunnel in the world.
> However, several experts believe that the biggest threat to the Tunnel stems from its being a prestige target for terrorists. (Burns, 1994)

A *Kent Messenger Group* (1994) supplement's attempt was at least fuller even though it was not necessarily more informative, nor, in places, especially convincing. It claimed Eurotunnel had made the following points in relation to its anti-terrorist measures:

> There are about 40 metres (130 ft) of rock cover above the tunnel, which is lined with concrete stronger than that used in the pressure vessels of a nuclear reactor. This makes the tunnel, designed to have at least a 120–year life, 'completely bomb proof'.
> Passengers have to stay with their cars on a shuttle. This means planting a bomb in a car would be a suicide mission.
> Eurotunnel has had the advantage, that other existing transport systems have not, of including terrorist and other safety precautions in their fundamental design—rather than simply tacking them on afterwards.
> One of the six reasons given for the choice of the Eurotunnel scheme in the government's 1986 white paper was that it was the one 'least vulnerable to sabotage and terrorist action'.
> The House of Commons Home Affairs Select Committee in 1992

declared itself 'fully satisfied' on the Chunnel security precautions after hearing evidence in camera from Eurotunnel, the security services and Kent police.
The Tunnel developers have had to satisfy the government of France as well as the UK of their precautions. (Kent Messenger Group, 1994)

Although the general tone is reassuring, a less positive picture emerges in parts of an article by Wyatt (1994) aimed at the private security industry. Writing about site security he says:

There would seem to be great reliance on both the Police and Fire Brigade. With such professional organizations this is understandable, but such dependency may be unwise. The training in particular seems simplistic in concept, with limited aims. When the risks are relatively low with Police support at hand, this may be acceptable, but in a high risk situation it is a gamble. (Wyatt, 1994, p. 150)

A more serious treatment of the subject has been attempted by Clutterbuck (1994). His study, which appears to have been Burns' source in the *Financial Times* article referred to above, concluded:

The Channel Tunnel is probably the least vulnerable under-sea tunnel in the world ... Security is easier than on the ferries ... [but] the tunnel [is] more vulnerable to a total blockage. While it is still a novelty, therefore, there will be an incentive for terrorists and other malicious persons to grab the headlines by blocking it, either by a terrorist act, or by sabotage or by a hoax call. When that novelty has worn off, the main concern will be the threat ... from internationally organised crime, ... drug trafficking and the flow of illegal immigrants. (Clutterbuck, 1994, p. 21)

Clutterbuck, a renowned expert on security, does describe some of the precautions in place and speculates on some of the others which may be in place, pointing out the need to 'balance ... desire for unimpeded traffic flow against security'. He mentions, for example, the 'Euroscan' building (a building so prominent on the Cheriton site it would be difficult to miss it) which a sample of HGVs are routed through and which, amongst other equipment, houses a large, very powerful X-ray machine. Clutterbuck describes it as providing 'whatever degrees of search are judged to be necessary in the light of the threat assessment.' (p. 6)

POWER SUPPLY

The power supply to the Tunnel was designed to provide a high level of redundancy. Martin (1990) provides a useful summary of the arrangements that have been made and their likely implications:

> Power for the tunnel will come from two 240 MVA main intakes at the terminals at Coquelles in France and Cheriton near Folkestone. Under normal operation Electricité de France and Seeboard will each provide the power for half the tunnel. But [. . .] if the power fails on one side of the channel, the intake on the other side will provide sufficient power to evacuate the tunnel safely and maintain essential services. [. . . It] can also cope with disruptions within the tunnel. If the 25 kV catenary becomes damaged at one point, that section can be isolated and power can be supplied by an alternative route. All substations in the service tunnel are connected to both ends of the tunnel by two 20 kV cable routes, making four routes in total. Two separate circuits from each substation power the lighting in each train tunnel. (Martin, 1990, p. 14)

But the same author also pin-points some potential dangers:

> 1 The French [electricity] supply and the British supply are not synchronised. If they became connected therefore, there would be a massive in-rush of current, with the stronger of the two systems trying to force the other into synchronization.

In connection with this point he quotes the Project Manager for the installation of the tunnel's electrical systems as saying this cannot happen because the switching system is designed to be electrically and mechanically foolproof.

> 2 Despite the pressure relief ducts, possible structural damage to cables, catenaries and their supports due to the massive air pressures generated by the passing trains.
> 3 Corrosion accelerated by dampness introduced into the tunnels by the trains.

EARTHQUAKES

In its 1988–89 Report, the Safety Authority described seismic risk as being of 'considerable concern' to them and reported their decision to commission a study by two independent experts, Professor N. N. Ambrayses, Professor of Engineering

Seismology at Imperial College and M. Vogt, Docteur en Géographie, Ingénieur Seismologue au Bureau de Recherches Géologue et Minières. The Concession Agreement had specified that the Tunnel works should be able to 'withstand the effects of natural events predicted to happen once in 120 years' and this had been equated on the basis of statistical analysis to an earthquake with a horizontal ground acceleration of 0.05g. However, the new study was to take on board the maximum historical earthquake in the Kent/Pas-de-Calais region. This had an estimated horizontal ground acceleration of 0.2g and occurred in 1580. The likelihood of seismic disturbance and the effects seismic activity might have on the tunnel and other structures and on vital equipment such as electricity supply, pumping, ventilation and communications were examined. Again, the detailed findings were not published though some information was made available. The Safety Authority Report for 1991–92 revealed the standby generators were to be relocated because the new seismic studies had shown an earthquake could cause rock falls at Shakespeare cliff and the site previously chosen would place them in the likely path of any falling rock. The 1992–93 Report implied no dramatic findings were expected from the study, noting that of the formal objections to APs that had been raised due to concern about the effects of earthquakes only one (to AP01.4 Auxiliary works underland) was still in place 'pending completion of the last studies on seismicity'.

Writing in 1992, Eisner and Stoop expressed surprise that so much time had elapsed from the start of that project before the possible effects of earthquakes on the tunnel's design had been investigated and, at the same time, raised an important question:

> ... by September 1991, well after the boring and lining of the three tunnels that make up the Channel Tunnel system had been successfully completed, it had not been established whether the design would safely stand an earthquake 'equivalent to the most serious one historically known at Dover and Calais'. Whether or not this problem has since been resolved, the very existence of such a state of affairs cannot fail to evoke interest in the way other hazards may have fared in the design process. (Eisner and Stoop, 1992, p. 120)

COLLISIONS AND DERAILMENTS

A major safety feature to prevent collisions is the 4 km (2.5 mi) separation between a freight shuttle (whether moving or stationary) and the following shuttle.

Control centres at each end of the Tunnel, either of which can take over sole responsibility for operation, are linked to computerized communications equipment on board the trains (shuttle and TGV) to provide trackside signalling and monitoring and safety systems and are able to activate the brakes in an emergency. Each train driver gets signalling information inside the cab, which he would not receive from traditional trackside systems. The orders required to operate the train appear on the driver's console in the form of illuminated indications. The communication link is provided by fibre-optic cable that is capable of carrying 700 million pieces of data per second. Under the system of automatic train protection (ATP) that is being used, the actual speed of a train is monitored continually and compared with the cab-signal permitted speed. If the actual speed is too great the emergency braking system is activated automatically.

The signalling systems could be threatened if excess water gathers inside the tunnel. A problem of this nature was experienced shortly before the full public opening of the tunnel and was blamed on the drainage pipes which have been installed to gather water which seeps through the walls.

THE VERDICT?

So that, at the time of writing, is the story in so far as we can ascertain it. Where would you put the Channel Tunnel on the continuum between the safest transport system in the world and an accident waiting to happen? In Chapter 8 we used information about the past to look forward to a project about to start and to anticipate how and why its outcomes may fail to meet expectations. This time we are leaving you to conduct your own analysis and to draw your own conclusions.

REFERENCES

Adams, J. G. U. (1988). 'The Channel Tunnel—the risks in perspective', *Disaster Management*, **1**, 9–14.

Alderson, A. and Harlow, J. (1993). 'High voltage inferno triggers Channel tunnel safety fears', *The Sunday Times*, 21 November.

Batchelor, C. (1994). 'Eurotunnel safety assessed', *The Financial Times*, 4 May.

Bi-National Emergency Planning Group (1993). *The Channel Tunnel Bi-National Emergency Plan*.

Black, D. (1989). 'The human element at the core of disaster', *The Independent*, 20 March.

Burns, J. (1994). 'On guard against accidents and terror', *Financial Times*, 6 May.

Channel Tunnel Safety Authority (1990a). *Annual Report 1988–89*, HMSO, London.

Channel Tunnel Safety Authority (1990b). Special Report, Non-segregation of Drivers and Passengers from their Vehicles (available from the Safety Authority).

Channel Tunnel Safety Authority (1993a). *Annual Report 1991–92*, HMSO, London.

Channel Tunnel Safety Authority (1993b). *Annual Report 1992–93*, HMSO, London.

Charlwood, F. J. and Pearce, T. W. (1993). 'The organisation of the response to a bi-national emergency within the Channel Tunnel system', in Cox, R.F. and Watson, I.A. (Eds) *Engineers and Risk Issues*, SARS Ltd., Manchester.

Clutterbuck, R. (1994). 'The Channel Tunnel security threats and safety measures', *Conflict Studies*, 269.

Comfort, N. (1987). 'Politics, lobbying and diplomacy', in Jones, B. (Ed.), *The Tunnel The Channel and Beyond*, Ellis Horwood Limited, Chichester.

The Consumers Association (1994). 'Is the Channel Tunnel safe?', *Which?*, May.

Department of Transport (1982). *Fixed Channel Link: Report of UK/French Study Group*, Cmnd 8561, HMSO, London.

Department of Transport (1986a). *Channel Fixed Link: Environmental Assessment of Alternative Proposals*, Prepared by Land Use Consultants, Department of Transport, London.

Department of Transport (1986b). *The Channel Fixed Link: Concession Agreement*, Cmnd 9769, HMSO, London.

Eisner, H. S. (1986). 'Channel Tunnel fuels fire safety debate', *Tunnels and Tunnelling*, September, 49.

Eisner, H. S. and Stoop, J. A. A. M. (1992). 'Incorporating fire safety in the Channel Tunnel design', *Safety Science*, **15**, 119–36.

Follain, M. (1992). 'Tunnel safety system in disarray', *Independent on Sunday*, 17 May.

Hamer, M. (1987). 'La reve de Napoleon.. et al!', in Jones, B. (Ed.), *The Tunnel The Channel and Beyond*, Ellis Horwood, Chichester.

Health and Safety Executive (1988). *The Tolerability of Risk from Nuclear Power Stations*, HMSO, London.

HMSO (1986a). *The Channel Fixed Link*, Cmnd 9735, HMSO, London.

HMSO (1986b). *Treaty between the UK and the French Republic concerning the Construction and Operation by Private Concessionaires of a Channel Fixed Link with Exchange of Notes*, Canterbury, 12 February, 1986, Cmnd 9745, HMSO, London.

HMSO (1988). *Investigation into the King's Cross Underground Fire*, presented to Parliament by the Secretary of State for Transport, [Desmond Fennell], HMSO, London.

HMSO (1993). *Protocol between the Government of the United Kingdom of Great Britain and Northern Ireland and the Government of the French Republic Concerning Frontier Controls and Policing, Co-operation in Criminal Justice, Public Safety and Mutual Assistance Relating to the Channel Fixed Link* (signed in Sangatte, 25 November 1991; entered into force 2 August 1993) Cm 2366, HMSO, London.

House of Commons (1981). *The Channel Link, Second Report of the Transport Committee*, Session 1980/81, HC-155, HMSO, London.

House of Commons (1985). *The Channel Link, First Report of the Transport Committee*, Session 1985/86, HC-50, HMSO, London.

House of Commons (1991). *Fire Safety and Policing of the Channel Tunnel*, First Report of the Home Affairs Committee, Session 1991–92, HMSO, London.

House of Lords (1987). 'Special Report from the Select Committee on the Channel Tunnel Bill', Session 1986–87, Minutes of Evidence, Vol. 11.

Hughes, M. (1987). 'Railway of the century', in Jones, B. (Ed.), *The Tunnel The Channel and Beyond*, Ellis Horwood Limited, Chichester.

Independent on Sunday, 'Eurotunnel threatens to sue for £1bn', 2 February 1992.

Kent Messenger Group (1994). *The Tunnel Story*, Kent Messenger Group.

Kersley, M. J., Dumolo, R. N. and Whittingham, R. B. (1992). 'Developing safety cases for major undertakings', in Vardy, A. E. (Ed.), *Safety in Road and Rail Tunnels*, University of Dundee and Independent Technical Conferences Ltd., Bedford.

Martin, D. (1990). '20,000 volts under the sea', *Electrical Review*, **223**(16), 14–15.

Morris, P. W. G. and Hough, G. H. (1987). *The Anatomy of Major Projects*, Wiley, Chichester.

The Times (1993). 'Channel tunnel incident on November 13; correction', *The Times*, 9 December.

Watts, S. (1989). 'How safe will the Channel Tunnel be?', *New Scientist*, 25 November, 42–7.

Watts, S. (1990). 'New hitches may cut Channel Tunnel's capacity', *New Scientist*, 17 February, 21.

Wyatt, J. (1994). 'EuroTunnel—a perceived security nightmare?', *Intersec*, **4**, 148–52.

10
Where Next?

This book has been structured so that it can be read from cover to cover and then the specific chapters used individually to enhance the reader's familiarity with the application of the Method. Subsequently the reader's capability will be further enhanced by examining the published examples of applications by others. It is both inevitable and desirable that some practitioners will wish to develop and extend the Method to suit their own experience, types of application and personal preferences. This final chapter aims to give some further pointers to the use of the Method and to show how some related subjects such as quality can interplay with the Method to help avoid future failures.

The first point to make is that the application of a method can be very different from its initial description and its first utilization. In a book it is very difficult to avoid explaining the stages in a linear fashion, but in reality the process of using it is much more fluid and requires the rapid movement from stage to stage and back again according to how a particular application is developing. Time and again the comparison of the situation conceptualized as a system with the Formal System Model only makes clear that the situation is not sufficiently well understood to continue or that the system delineated is not a salient one. The use of the Method has to be both flexible and a part of a long term 'learning by doing' process. When they are first described systems methods, and indeed other non-systemic methods, can easily appear to be recipe book approaches: follow the instructions and all will be well. It is certainly the case that in a subject like chemistry a procedure requires that the same method is adopted in the same order each time. If the same conditions prevail the result should be identical. Some people, including one of the authors, approach cooking in this way, but this rigid mode of execution is inappropriate to the application of this systems method. Before the authors of cookery books rise up and demand that this slight on their works is halted, it is worth explaining that in the main, cookery books do not guarantee success. They may include recipes which in the controlled conditions of the kitchen should produce reliable results, but most are intended to describe an approach which contains some over-arching elements, maybe a theme like the cuisine of a region, some concepts like colour and balance, and some proven techniques like marinading or choux pastry making. Elizabeth David (1951) may go too far when she says, 'I should be surprised to hear that anyone had ever followed any cookery book menu in every detail; all that is needed to design a perfectly good meal is a little common sense and the fundamental understanding of the composition of a menu' but Anton Mossiman's comments are highly appropriate: 'The good cook tries, samples and tries again rather like a composer searching for themes at the keyboard and then combining them and elaborating on them. The good cook is the eternal apprentice.' (Mossiman, 1983)

Reflective systems practitioners will be eternal apprentices too, so where are the obvious places to try to increase one's repertoire? In what ways might the Systems Failures Method evolve further? The first place to start is with the wider systems movement. The content of this book has been determined by those ideas that the authors have found particularly valuable in the context of failures investigations; in no sense have we set out to try to write the definitive text book on systems ideas, methods and techniques. It might be useful, however, to draw attention to some additional concepts which may prove useful in certain settings.

CONCEPTS

Individual systems concepts can be exceptionally powerful. Whole nations can be transformed by ideas such as freedom, equality or human rights, and individuals' behaviour can be altered radically by notions such as evil or justice. The same impact can be achieved by systems concepts which can help the development of a set of tools for thought and generate insight when applied. Experience suggests that even the few that have already been included in this book such as system, holism, boundary, environment, feedback, open, closed, input, output, communication and control will unlock many scenarios. Alongside communication and control Checkland (1979) places emergence and hierarchy as being the four concepts at the heart of systems thinking. He defines hierarchy as 'the principle according to which entities meaningfully treated as wholes are built up of smaller entities which are themselves wholes . . . and so on. In a hierarchy emergent properties denote the levels.' (Checkland, 1981)

The concept of hierarchy is most apparent in the Method used here when one moves between different levels of comparison with the Formal System Model.

Ackoff (1971) identifies a larger group of 32 concepts and terms which he organizes into 'a system of systems concepts' and groups under headings such as system changes, behavioural classification of systems, and adaptation and learning (Table 10.1).

In effect this is an alternative way of organizing much the same material as that mapped by Young (1964) and incorporated in Chapter 6.

Most of Ackoff's and Young's collections of systems concepts are incorporated implicitly or explicitly within the Formal System Model and some are apparent in the other paradigms presented earlier in this book, but users may in the future wish to experiment with the balance or sequence of use in order to try to enhance and refine the potential of the Method.

For example, it might be that during the study of a failure in a part of an organization, the initial conceptualization of a system suggested that there might be explanatory advantage in considering what type of system it could be deemed to be. There

Table 10.1 A system of systems concepts (after Ackoff, 1971)

Concept group	Concepts					
Systems	Abstract system	Concrete system	System state	System environment	State of system	
	Closed system	Open system	System event	Static (one-state) system	Dynamic (multi-state)	Homeostatic system
System changes	Reaction	Response	Act	Behaviour		
Behavioural classification of systems	State-maintaining system	Goal-seeking system	Process	Multi-goal-seeking	Purposive system	Purposeful system
	Relative value of an outcome	Goal	Objective	Ideal	Ideal-seeking	
System relationship concepts	Variety					
Adaptation and learning	Function	Efficiency	Learn			
Organizations	Control(s)	Organization				

might be a prima facie case for deciding whether it could be considered to be a state maintaining system and thus so fixed in its ways that it could only return to its previous state, or a multi-goalseeking system which thus had the freedom to yield different outcomes in response to changes in its environment. Distinctions such as this might appear to provide a useful way of exploring system behaviour in some circumstances, but an important question arises as to whether there is anything to be gained beyond the attribution of a concept in terms of explanation or understanding of the failure, especially when the terms are being applied to the system which has been conceptualized rather than to the situation itself. In the authors' experience little additional interpretation or explanation is gained beyond the acquisition of a label. What is more, Ackoff's definitions of these particular concepts, which at first glance look relevant, cannot be applied to any systems which have the ability to learn and adapt. Ackoff's multi-goalseeking systems are in fact restricted to a particular type of response to changes in their environment; they can vary the actions which they take, but the outcomes of those different actions are predetermined by the environmental change. Of all the many systems classified by Ackoff it is only in those labelled 'purposeful' that people play a part in determining behaviour and outcome.

Vulnerability

Particularly when it comes to examining disasters, there is further scope for applying the concept of 'state' (both of a system and its environment). Ackoff's definition of state is not enormously helpful: 'The state of a system at a moment in time is the set of relevant properties which that system has at that time.' (Ackoff, 1971). However, the concept of state appears to embody considerably more potential when it is linked to the notion of vulnerability.

In Chapter 2 it was asserted that disasters occur when a complex set of internal and external interactions result in a human activity system being (sometimes increasingly) vulnerable, and therefore more susceptible to disturbance by relatively minor events. (See also Horlick-Jones, Fortune and Peters, 1993).

We also quoted Susman, O'Keefe and Wisner: 'Disasters are at the interface between an extreme physical event and a vulnerable human population.' (Susman, O'Keefe and Wisner, 1983).

The disasters which Susman, O'Keefe and Wisner were considering were natural disasters, usually in the developing world, where it is relatively easy to see how a natural phenomenon like a flood may be more or less serious depending upon the preparedness of the population. Figure 10.1 shows this relationship.

This conception of vulnerability, if expressed in systems terms, amounts to the view that a population is vulnerable because of the state of its environment. This idea can be developed further by considering other more statistical views of vulnerability. Solway (1994) defines vulnerability as the probability of an area being damaged by a hazardous event. It is not the population which has a vulnerability in this context but a location. By implication the vulnerability of the population and the local economy results in part from their location. Solway gives an example of the informal area of a city, sometimes comprising 35% of the population, who may be living in slums or shacks, or in well-established settlements, but where the common feature is that the residents have no land rights and therefore no incentive or opportunity to improve their living conditions. Although viewed from the standpoint of the citizen the vulnerability might result from the state of the environment, Solway's focus is the city, so in systems terms it is the vulnerability of the system which he wishes to quantify.

Horlick-Jones, Fortune and Peters have drawn links between the vulnerability expressed in a development world context

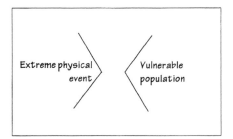

Figure 10.1 *Vulnerability and disaster*

with a number of UK disasters in order to pose the idea of a 'third world analogy' for disasters in any location which are characterized by:

- large numbers of people involved and overcrowding;
- out-of-date and poorly maintained equipment;
- poorly trained workers;
- inadequate preparations for emergencies.

(Again, see Horlick-Jones, Fortune and Peters, 1993.)

These ideas lead on to a vulnerable system model of disasters where both the environment and the system have states which have degrees of vulnerability. A system is conceptualized and one of its properties is taken to be its level of vulnerability to some initial trigger event. In a particular context like Bhopal the vulnerability level will depend on factors such as the extent to which the technology is operational and the staff have been trained for emergencies. The vulnerability of the system is the obverse of its ability to absorb disturbances, which in turn can be considered to be an indication of its resilience. Figure 10.2 shows this aspect of system vulnerability.

Since it is only disasters which are being considered here, population is the key aspect which must be focused upon. Figure 10.3 shows a vulnerable system model of disasters. The system represented in Figure 10.2 has been placed in the context of a vulnerable population.

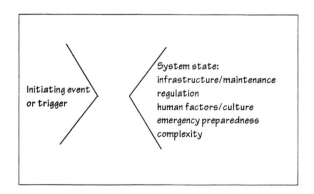

Figure 10.2   *System vulnerability*

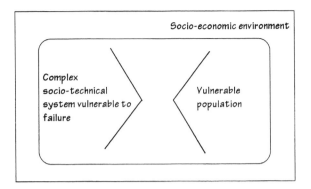

Figure 10.3 *Vulnerable system model of disasters (after Horlick-Jones, Fortune and Peters, 1993)*

In theory the concept of system and environmental vulnerability have the potential to not only facilitate the understanding of failures and disasters, but also to aid in their anticipation. But although the authors would expect that they can be used to describe states they are unlikely to allow quantification. For example, taking the case of the Bhopal gas leak again, it would seem reasonable to say *a priori* that there existed a particularly vulnerable population in the shanty areas around the plant and that at the time of the accident the state of the plant safety systems were at an increased level of vulnerability (or their resilience was reduced). Although knowing this at the time would not enable the day and the time or the precise trigger event for the accident to be predicted, it would seem reasonable, at least with hindsight, to say that there was an increased likelihood of a disaster at Bhopal compared with the similar plant operated by Union Carbide in Institute, Virginia.

Weltanschauung

Besides vulnerability there are other concepts which may prove to be suitable additions to the armoury deployed by those conducting analyses of failure. Indication of one such concept arose from an exercise by the authors to look for ways in which the Method could be improved further. It was decided to check whether it was appropriate to continue to use the Formal System Model as set out in Chapter 6. As was mentioned there, this particular form of a model of an ideal system is based on one used by Checkland (1981), drawing on ideas from Jenkins (1969) and Churchman (1971). Checkland's use of the model arose from a completely different context. He and his colleagues at Lancaster University had been utilizing the concept of a formal system and 'other systems thinking' to check on the robustness of the conceptual models of the systems they were formulating within the applications of their Soft Systems Methodology (SSM). However, subsequent experience led them to the view that the other main check which they employed was sufficient for their purposes; they only needed to know that there was total consistency between a conceptual model of a relevant system and the verbal description of it. (They refer to the verbal description as a root definition (Checkland and Scholes, 1990).) An analysis (Smyth and Checkland, 1976) of the characteristics of a set of root definitions led to the identification of a set of six elements which they felt provided 'a useful checklist against which a root definition can be tested.' (Wilson, 1984). These elements are known by the acronym CATWOE (standing for customer, actor, transformation, *Weltanschauung*, ownership and environment). The present authors have explored the possibility of using this much simpler set of characteristics of a system as a basis for comparison instead of the more complex, and cumbersome, Formal System Model. The general conclusion was that, even collectively, they provided too loose a framework to show up anything but the most glaring discrepancies. However, there was one possible exception to this generalization: the concept of *Weltanschauung*. With the current formulation of the Formal System Model any differences between the *Weltanschauungen* of those operating within a system or its wider system are most likely to be revealed by the absence of a fully disclosed set of expectations. (This was certainly the case in the application described in Chapter 8.) However, there is some merit in practitioners being aware that one of the explanations of why these expectations may not have been made clear is that they are implicit in the *Weltanschauungen* of the different parties. In other words mismatches in expectations may arise from differences in *Weltanschauungen* but because each party takes their own assumptions as 'given' and assumes they are shared by others the differences may not emerge in advance of the failure being perceived. Indeed, without specific attempts to apply the concept of *Weltanschauung* they may never be revealed.

VIABLE SYSTEM MODEL

The examination of CATWOE above is a part of an ongoing programme of re-examination of the models and paradigms recommended for use within the Method. Another alternative to the Formal System Model which offers some potential for further exploration is the Viable System Model (VSM). The application of systems concepts to organizations has been an interest of both engineers and social scientists, with the use of concepts derived from cybernetics being particularly prevalent. Cybernetics is the study of control and communication in living beings and machines. It is closely allied to systems and many regard it as part and parcel of the same subject. One strong advocate of models of organizations which rely heavily on bio-logical analogy and cybernetic principles is Stafford Beer. (See, for example, Beer, 1972 and 1979.) The core of his work is that an organization can be said to act as a series of interacting levels of systems and that these taken together form a Viable System Model (VSM) of the organization.

Beer's own definition of cybernetics as 'the science of effective organization' (Beer, 1973) reflects his belief that organizations designed to his guidelines will be successful. So VSM could be looked upon as an additional feature of the Formal System Model. Each level contains systems which fulfil different pur-poses. These clusters of systems are replicated again and again. So rather than a simple hierarchical model he conceives of systems which consist of patterns of recursive subsystems. Any deficiencies in the capability or functioning of the organization can then in theory be traced back to inappropriate or inadequate subsystems or linkages.

It is possible here to present only a simple version of VSM, but hopefully it will be sufficient to enable its potential as a way of exploring the sources of organizational malfunction to be appreciated. As has been mentioned already VSM is intended as a model of an organization, and like the Formal System Model it operates at several levels with each system containing within it other systems. In VSM, however, the five interrelated systems are functional. They are specified as follows:

- *System 1* parts are concerned with implementation of the activity. The various parts will each be autonomous and therefore to comply with VSM they must in turn each contain within them all of systems 1 to 5. These system parts are also connected to their local environment.
- *System 2* is concerned with the coordination of the various parts of system 1's activity and ironing out any uncontrolled variations in activity amongst parts.
- *System 3* maintains internal stability and ensures that policy is implemented by interpreting policy, auditing, and in particular controlling, for example through the allocation of resources.
- *System 4* gathers intelligence, models the environment and transmits the results.
- *System 5* sets policy and represents the system as a whole to any wider system. It also arbitrates between the internal and external demand on the organization.

Table 10.2 lists the common features which are said by Beer

Table 10.2   *Comparison of VSM with actual organizations*

- Mistakes in articulating different levels of recursion
- Not all system 1 parts are treated as important and therefore are not supported by the local management necessary to discharge their functions
- Additional and irrelevant features which inhibit effective functioning are found
- System 2, 3, 4 or 5 seeks to become viable in its own right. In other words a part of the organization develops an existence which is independent of its role in the whole organization
- System 2 is not fully established because managers of system 1 resent the interference
- System 3 managers interfere in the management processes at system 1 level
- System 4 is weak because it is regarded as a staff function
- System 5 collapses into system 3 because system 4 is weak
- System 5 is not creating an identity and is not representing the essential qualities of the whole system to the wider system and to the environment

to be observed when the Viable System Model is compared with organizations in order to identify deficiencies.

Beer's focus was improvement of the performance of organizations, as can be seen from his selection of the three indices for levels of achievement:

1 Actuality—the current achievement using existing resources and constraints.
2 Capability—the possible achievement with existing resources and within existing constraints.
3 Potentiality—what could be achieved by developing resources and removing constraints.

It appears, therefore, that in so far as examination of failures is also concerned with improving organizational performance there may be potential advantage in going on to examine the levels of VSM after using the Formal System Model. However, the authors have in their work so far found the Formal System Model powerful enough to yield understanding and have therefore not yet felt the need to apply VSM except as an academic exercise.

SYSTEM ACCIDENTS

A second way of developing the Method might be to add further failure paradigms. One model which in theory should be applicable is based upon the notion of a 'system accident'. Within the realm of human activity systems, and in particular high risk technologies, considerable attention has been focused on the design or engineering of plant which contains sophisticated safety features. Some of these concepts such as fail-safe and fail-soft and techniques for designing reliability into a piece of machinery have a very wide applicability. However, when these modern complicated technologies go awry the impact can be spectacular. Perrow (1984) has argued that these high-risk technologies often display two features which make them prone to failure: interactive complexity and tight coupling.

Interactive complexity is, as its name suggests, an aspect of a designed system which means that failures and events are not independent, but related, and that the more complex the system the more chance there is that sequences and patterns of events will be unforeseeable, and unexpected. Attempts to subsequently engineer warnings or the like only in turn increase the complexity still further, thereby introducing new potential configurations of events.

Tight coupling refers to the speed of interaction, and the extent to which parts of the system can be isolated. Taken together, interactive complexity and tight coupling, will, in Perrow's view, lead to what he terms system accidents, or normal accidents. Perrow's ideas have been much cited by those interested in the study of failures. For example Bowonder, Arvind and Miyake (1991) extended the analysis reported in Chapter 7 to include the use of Perrow's ideas alongside other socio-technical system concepts. They concluded that 'technical personnel in hazardous facilities neglect and discount the mode and speed of social interactive processes, resulting in neglect of social aspects of accidents as well as emergencies.' They also made a number of generalized recommendations about how to prevent hazardous failures by strengthening capabilities in a number of areas such as scanning trigger events and rehearsing for emergencies. However, despite considering this and similar work very carefully the authors of this book have yet to find sufficient evidence that the incorporation of these ideas within the Method would increase its power. It seems likely to them that the full value of the concepts Perrow deploys will only become apparent if it is possible to move beyond the concept stage to some way of measuring or evaluating the degree to which interactive complexity and tight coupling are present in a particular situation. There must also be a question mark over whether there is merit in considering the two component concepts of interactive complexity and tight coupling as separate. It is the view of the authors that tight coupling is an aspect of complexity. Like Casti (1979), the authors consider that complexity has two facets: the structure of the irreducible subsystem components; and the manner in which the components are connected. The connectivity and structure, when taken together, provide the static complexity, but there is also a dynamic complexity which results from the time behaviour of the system.

Reason (1990) refers to models like Perrow's normal or

system accident model as resident pathogen metaphors. His argument, in effect, is that many failures are not easy to predict and do not result from a simple cause or factor; instead they arise from a set of events which need to occur together. He argues that this is similar to a multiple-cause illness like cancer where 'resident pathogens' in the human body are potentially destructive and weaken the body's defensive mechanisms. If this metaphor provided additional insights into particular failures it would add an additional dimension to the concept of vulnerability discussed earlier. However, Reason also raises some doubts about its potential. Again he draws on an analogy, this time with accident proneness. Accident proneness was a theory which was at one time offered as an explanation of the variation in accident rates amongst individuals. On subsequent examination it was found that the differing rates of accidents which individuals experienced were primarily explicable by statistical variation. Any remaining variation did not support the accident-proneness hypothesis since the group who were experiencing higher than expected numbers of accidents in a given period were a markedly different subset of the population from those looked at over a later period.

For the moment the concept of vulnerability seems to have more mileage than the concepts associated with complexity. Elderly people or babies may not be accident prone, but their physical state may make them more vulnerable to events. Similarly a chemical plant may be complex, but the state of its repair may be the factor which renders it vulnerable to failure.

AVOIDING FAILURE

Examining ways in which failures and disasters can be avoided is a further way in which the Method in this book can be tested and extended and provides a wider context within which it can operate. The potential for failure in a particular setting can be reduced in a number of ways. First it is possible to act in a defensive way and assume that disasters may occur and take action to reduce their impact. This is the whole area of emergency planning, contingency planning and disaster preparedness and disaster mitigation, and is not really the province of this book. It is worth noting, however, that these procedures and the plans which flow from them are also susceptible to failure and should therefore be treated in the same way as other parts of an organization's activity. Therefore, the Systems Failures Method can be applied to the study of these schemes; indeed, because they are, in the main, required to respond quickly to events which cannot be entirely anticipated they warrant particular attention. See, for example, the description of events at Manchester airport after the aircraft had come to a halt (Chapter 4) and the medical treatment of survivors in the days after the gas leak at Bhopal (Chapter 7).

The Reliability Approach to Failure Avoidance

A second way of reducing the potential for failure is to design plant and procedures in such a way that when something does go awry it does not have a devastating impact, or it has at least been anticipated and planned for. This is the reliability approach, and is used in engineering design, for example, with failure mode and effect analyses (FMEAs) being carried out. Typically, an FMEA is prepared at intervals during the design of a product or process. Its purpose is to answer the question: 'What could conceivably go wrong with the system as a whole as the result of the failure of a single part?'. It is not concerned with the overall reliability (in the numerical sense) of the whole but with individual components and the ways in which they might fail and is therefore essentially a 'bottom up' approach.

The steps taken in carrying out an FMEA are shown in Table 10.3.

The vast majority of engineering reliability approaches are concerned with achieving robust designs by incorporating good practice and by systematically considering the likelihood of component or subsystem failure and allowing for it. FMEA is one of the few approaches which starts from the potential for failure and then considers the many aspects of a designed system and its environment. Other even more basic techniques still contain an element that tries to take account of the potential for failure. For example in a planned system the decision about whether to include alternative pathways to a particular objective

Table 10.3 *Steps taken in carrying out an FMEA*

1 *Definition of the system.* Precise boundary of the analysis is defined, together with the mission or purpose of the system under consideration. Inputs from and outputs to other parts of the system and relationships with the environment are also specified.

2 *Description of system operation.* Behaviour of the system when it is operating properly and what happens to all the various inputs and outputs when one or more components fail or the inputs change are described.

3 *Description of environmental conditions.* The physical environment in which the system will operate is described.

4 *Listing of failure modes.* A mode of failure is the description of how a component behaves after it has failed. All significant modes, including both random and degradation failures, must be evaluated.

5 *Analysis of failure mechanisms.* At least one failure mechanism must be identified for each mode of failure.

6 *Analysis of failure effects.* The interaction of a failed component with the rest of the system is described.

7 *Failure detection.* The mechanisms within the system that reveal the occurrence of the failure modes are identified. For components that may fail without causing the system as a whole to cease operation, means such as periodic tests may be necessary.

8 *Compensation for failure.* The provision of mechanisms to compensate for the failure mode at the level being analysed are noted.

will be predicated upon an estimate of the potential probability of failure of a single route.

The Learning Approach to Failure Avoidance

A third method for reducing the likelihood of failure involves asking questions such as does this situation have the hallmarks of a potential failure or disaster? This is the reflective learning approach on which this book is founded and which is facilitated by serious analysis.

As was stated in Chapter 1, it is the authors' view that the study of failure is an essential element of learning. The approach which has been described in this book is primarily focused on the understanding of specific failures, but its repeated application leads both to the refinement of the Method and to general learning about the nature of failures. This section reports some of the authors' research findings in relation to this general learning and includes a short discussion on the work of others who have undertaken comparable studies.

The authors have found five recurring aspects of failures in the situations they have investigated (Fortune and Peters, 1994):

- Deficiencies in the apparent organizational structure such as a lack of a performance measuring subsystem or a control decision system.
- No clear statements of purpose supplied in comprehensible form from the wider system.
- Deficiency in the performance of one or more subsystems.
- Subsystems with ineffective means of communication.
- Inadequately designed subsystems.

Brearley (1991) used the Formal System Model to look at a series of case studies which were 'representative of three categories of disaster: transport, industrial and scientific, and crowd control.' In summarising the findings from her analyses she found that the failures and problems identified could be drawn together into the following common themes:

— Failure to manage change
— Communication failures
— Performance monitoring failures
— Failure to act on feedback information
— Failure to learn past lessons or to heed early warnings
— Complacency
— Maintenance failures
— Manpower failures
— Violations of procedures
— Multiple failings
— Factors external to the system
   (Brearley, 1991)

Studies by others have yielded different insights. Work in the USA has taken the concept of systems failures and applied it in a prescriptive rather than an analytical manner. van Gigch (1988) has developed a metasystem paradigm to diagnose systems failures. In essence he has taken the control model and used it to try to describe particular failures. As a result of this process he has produced a taxonomy which can then be used to identify the characteristics of systems failures in a way which can also provide warnings of impending failure. He has classified failure modes into the taxonomy of malfunctions given in Table 10.4.

Table 10.4 *Taxonomy of systems failures (after van Gigch, 1983)*

- Failures of structure and regulation which stem from ill-designed organizational designs which do not meet avowed goals
- Failures of technology which originate from problems of mis-design in the equipment as well as in the hardware and software utilized in the information systems of the organization
- Failures of decisional processes which are then related to the flows of information and to the rationality required for decision-making
- Failures of behaviour which are attributed to psychological dysfunctions of the human element in the organization
- Failures of evolution which are caused by problems of mal-adaptation of the organization to change in the turbulent environment in which it evolves

Both the above sets of results are very general, and although they are interesting they are not sufficiently specific to readily provide a useful litany for those anxious to see whether calamity is about to strike. A much more detailed catalogue is derived from the work of Turner already outlined in Chapter 3 (Peters and Turner, 1976). As well as identifying common features of the three disasters he examined, he also produced the following listing of common preconditions of failure. In this comprehensive itemization, Turner proposed 18 factors which may combine to produce a disaster (Turner, 1979). These are summarized in Table 10.5.

An additional and somewhat different aspect of the learning approach is concerned with what happens when a disaster occurs. In the earlier chapter which examined the Bhopal accident, one of the studies examined (by Wahlström, 1992) used Bhopal to provide examples to support his model for the understanding of failures. This approach, called 'exampling' by Glaser and Strauss (1968), contrasts with the alternative of trying to build up a model from the data. An explicit and Bhopal related example of this is displayed by Bowman and Kunreuther (1988). Although the research quoted in Chapter 7 was based upon the Bhopal accident itself, Bowman and Kunreuther were already conducting research in another chemical company in the USA when the disaster occurred. From this vantage point they were able, over a period of a year, to track the impact that the Bhopal accident had on the American company, which they gave the pseudonym Chemco. They saw, for example, that within two days of the accident Chemco had telexed all its plant managers throughout the world asking for the following information:

Table 10.5 *Factors which may combine to produce disaster (based on Turner, 1979)*

- An inter-organizational grouping involved in
  - a complex ill defined and prolonged task which gives rise to
  - a variety of information difficulties
- During the course of the project:
  - goals are likely to shift, and because of the prolonged nature of the task the administrative machinery concerned with the task changes, and some of the parties change roles in relation to the task
- In any case, because of the complex and ill-defined nature of the task:
  - there will be ambiguities associated with handling the task
  - regulations may become dated or be not fully enforced
  - individuals are preoccupied with major issues relating to the task and are reinforced in their preoccupation by organizational tradition and precedent.
- A characterized task for such a grouping is:
  - a design of a system which includes large or complex sites, to which employees of a number of organizations have access, and to which the public is also admitted.
- The members of the organizations concerned operate with
  - stereotyped views of the public and its likely behaviour.
  - non-expert complaints are treated in a cursory manner.
- Where signs of hazard emerge some of them are recognized and planned for, but others will be neglected;
  - because they are not recognized by those working with approved organizational stereotypes,
  - because of pressure of work,
  - because recognizing them and taking action would require the difficult to justify investment of resources; and
  - because most individuals believe that probably it won't happen anyway.

1 What is the nature of the volatile toxic and flammable chemicals in the plant that might cause a catastrophe?

2 What are the potential population exposures within various distances if the event occurs ?

3 Are there any specific evacuation plans that have been prepared for the community and for the plant for dealing with Bhopal-type vapour cloud events?

In general they found that the disaster had an enormous impact on the behaviour of the American chemical company. Their work led them to make six propositions which they felt were worthy of test in other situations in which companies were faced with the aftermath of low probability but high-risk events. Their six propositions were:

1 Following a catastrophic accident there is a tendency for decision makers to ignore objective data for specifying probabilities and rather to focus on ways of dealing with the direct impact of the event.
2 There is a linkage of activities undertaken prior to the incident with solutions applied afterwards.
3 Crises enable the organization to exert tighter hierarchical control to take rapid action.
4 There is a confounding between chronic and catastrophic risks following a low-probability high consequence accident.
5 There is a tendency to ignore costs when crisis situations appear.
6 With salient events there is a form of organizational learning which turns tacit knowledge into organizational policy.

The hallmarks of a learning approach are reflective investigation followed by action based upon that reflection. It does not provide a set of solutions, but is instead a process for considering the lessons to be drawn from experience.

Quality Approach to Failure Avoidance

The fourth approach to avoiding failure which will be looked at here can be called the quality approach. In theory it should be possible to avoid the potential for failure by adopting procedures which guarantee success, in other words by adopting a zero defect approach on a grand scale. Such an approach is of course never completely feasible since even if it were practicable a completely zero defects process would require limitless resources. However, even if the zero defects promise of a failure-free world is undeliverable there are other more realistic schemes like the meeting of appropriate quality standards which mean that there is still plenty of scope for forging stronger links between the failures area and work on quality.

Problem Analysis in Quality and in Failures

There has in recent years been a marked shift towards the use of integrated approaches to quality within organizations. These approaches have broadly speaking been based either on the teachings of so-called quality gurus (Crosby's zero defects (Crosby, 1980), Deming's 14 points (Deming, 1982), and so on), or on the need to be seen to conform to certain national, international, or customers' standards (e.g. BS5750, ISO 9000, Q-101), or, sometimes, on a combination of the two. Recognition of the need to set in place mechanisms for tackling quality problems is to be found within most of the approaches that are commonly used, though at the more detailed level of description, the mechanisms suggested vary. Crosby, for example, recommends the use of quality circles, or similar teams, whilst Juran (1964) puts forward a more complex arrangement whereby a group of people manage an improvement programme and 'employ' problem solving specialists to undertake it.

When a problem solving mechanism is in place, it usually provides an umbrella under which many problems can be tackled at the same time, and in similar ways, by different groups of people. In some companies an explicit problem solving method such as the PDCA (Plan, Do, Check, Act) cycle is used but it is more common for problems to be tackled on an *ad hoc* basis, with techniques such as brainstorming, Pareto analysis and cause-and-effect diagrams being brought into play as and when they are judged to be necessary. (Detailed descriptions of these and similar techniques can be found in many text books on quality, for example, Dale (1994), and are grouped together in Fortune (1992).)

One of the basic principles behind many of the problem solving mechanisms that are used is that participants are free to operate upon problems that they select themselves as being of greatest concern to them and their closest colleagues. This principle is adopted so as to secure commitment to the problem-solving process. One snag that is inherent in this approach, though, is that it leads to solutions being found to easily definable, lower-level problems, whilst higher-level, higher-consequence, over-arching problems are neglected. For example, once a statistical process control (SPC) scheme has been introduced and been seen to work well, investigations into future problems are likely to be confined to individual processes, even in cases where the roots of the problems lie within the control system itself. Because individuals experience different smaller aspects of the same larger problem a huge amount of evidence may have to pile up before the scheme itself is suspected, and even then the problem-solvers may lack the means or motivation to tackle complex, poorly defined problems.

Quality and Failures

Quality and the study of failures have traditionally been seen as two distinct subject areas, each with its own body of literature and research. There are, however, significant areas of overlap between them and it can be argued that they have much to learn from each other. They are both primarily concerned with performance and the problems they address are often remarkably similar. It is frequently the question of scale that causes observers to distinguish between a quality problem and a failure. To take an example within the narrow confines of a 'conformance to specification' definition of quality: weld defects in cars coming off a production line may share many common features with the weld problem that led to the collapse of the Alexander L. Kielland accommodation rig in the North Sea oil field in 1980, but the former would be treated as a quality problem and the latter as a failure.

When a broader, more modern, definition of quality that encompasses the quality of the design and production process as well as the fitness of the final product or service, is considered, the overlaps become even more noticeable. As noted in Chapter 3, Jenkins (1969) presents a list of 'disasters that could have been avoided with Systems Engineering'. Several of the examples he quotes would today be widely referred to as quality problems. For example, supply chain management is now regarded as an integral part of quality management (see, for example, Dale (1994), Chapter 13) yet the third and fourth examples in Jenkins' list were concerned with interruptions to incoming supplies.

One example that provides a good illustration of the use of the Failure Method in a context which others would judge to be a quality problem concerns science education in primary schools over the decade 1975 to 1985 (Fortune, Peters and Rawlinson-Winder, 1993). A study of this problem area began by representing relevant aspects of the situation in system form. A map of the resulting 'science education in primary schools system' is shown in Figure 10.4.

A comparison was then made between this system and the Formal System Model. This comparison, which is represented diagrammatically in Figure 10.5, revealed a number of interesting insights, some of which were explored further using other paradigms. It showed, for example, that the decision-making subsystem did not make its expectations known to the performance monitoring subsystem. The wider system had not made its expectations known either, and nor had it formulated the initial design of the system. The system as a whole was not cohesive and had little influence over its environment; indeed,

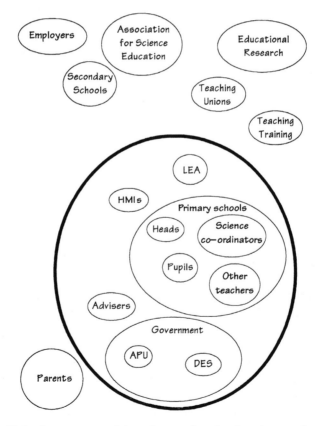

Figure 10.4 *Systems map of the science education in primary schools system*

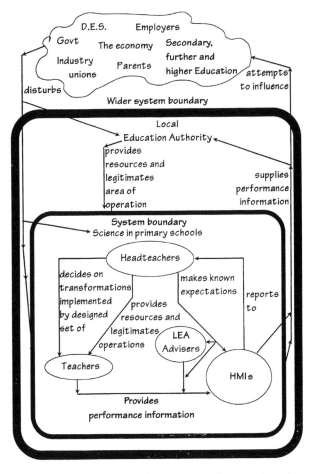

Figure 10.5 *Comparison between the science education in primary schools system and the Formal System Model (Fortune, Peters and Rawlinson-Winder, 1993)*

the performance monitoring subsystem was the only part of the system to have significant links with the environment.

By using the Systems Failures Method in the context of quality problems it is possible to tackle higher-level issues. This enables higher paybacks to be achieved and, in the longer term, should enable the total amount of resources spent on problem solving to be reduced.

CONCLUSION

The major part of this book has been an explanation of an approach to the analysis of failure which has been developed over a period of over twenty years. That the first example given of its application related to an air crash and the last to a non-technical area like the science curriculum is coincidental in a way, but it is also illustrative of the breadth of applicability of the Method and its strong affinity with modern conceptions of quality. It is the hope of the authors that readers will explore both avenues further. We believe that the reflective approach which is inherent in the study of failure has much to offer organizations facing increasing turbulent environments. It is our hope that this book will contribute to the wider understanding and analysis of failures, and that it will encourage others to be less reticent about admitting to failures and sharing the results of their experiences and analyses with others.

REFERENCES

Ackoff, R. L. (1971). 'Towards a system of systems concepts', *Management Science*, **17**, 661–71.

Beer, S. (1972). *Brain of the Firm*, Allen Lane, London.

Beer, S. (1973). *Designing Freedom*, Canadian Broadcasting Company, Toronto.

Beer, S. (1979). *The Heart of the Enterprise*, Wiley, Chichester.

Bowman, E. and Kunreuther, H. (1988). 'Post-Bhopal behaviour at a chemical company', *Journal of Management Studies*, **25**, 387–402.

Bowonder, B., Arvind, S. S. and Miyake, T. (1991). 'Low probability—high consequence accidents: application of systems theory for preventing hazardous failures', *Systems Research*, **9**(2), 5–58.

Brearley, S. A. (1991). 'High level management and disaster', in Keller, A. Z. and Wilson, H. C. (Eds), *Emergency Planning in the 1990s*, British Library/Technical Communications, Letchworth.

Casti, J. L. (1979). *Connectivity Complexity and Catastrophe in Large Scale Systems*, Wiley, Chichester.

Checkland, P. B. (1979). 'The shape of the systems movement', *Journal of Applied Systems Analysis*, **6**, 129–35.

Checkland, P. B. (1981). *Systems Thinking, Systems Practice*, Wiley, Chichester.

Checkland, P. B. and Scholes, J. (1990). *Soft Systems Methodology in Action*, Wiley, Chichester.

Churchman, C. W. (1971). *The Design of Inquiring Systems*, Basic Books, New York.

Crosby, P. B. (1980). *Quality is Free*, Mentor, New York.

Dale, B. G. (Ed.) (1994). *Managing Quality*, Prentice Hall, Hemel Hempstead.

David, E. (1951). *French Country Cooking*, John Lehmann, London.

Deming, W. E. (1982). *Out of the Crisis*, MIT, Cambridge, Massachusetts.

Fortune, J. (1992). *Quality Improvement*, Open University Press, Milton Keynes.

Fortune, J. and Peters, G. (1994). 'Systems analysis of failures as a quality management tool', *British Journal of Management*, **5**, 205–13.

Fortune, J., Peters, G. and Rawlinson-Winder, L. (1993). 'Science education in English and Welsh primary school: a systems study', *Journal of Curriculum Studies*, **25**, 359–69.

Glaser, B. G. and Strauss, A. L. (1968). *The Discovery of Grounded Theory: Strategies for Qualitative Research*, Weidenfeld & Nicolson, London.

Horlick-Jones, T., Fortune, J. and Peters G. (1993). 'Vulnerable systems, failure and disaster', in Stowell, F. A., West, D. and Howell, J. G. (Eds), *Systems Science: Addressing Global Issues*, Plenum Press, New York.

Jenkins, G. M. (1969). 'The systems approach', *Journal of Systems Engineering*, **1**, 3–49.

Juran, J. M. (1964). *Managerial Breakthrough*, McGraw-Hill, New York.

Mossiman, A. (1983). *A New Style of Cooking*, J. Sainsbury, London.

Perrow, C. (1984). *Normal Accidents*, Basic Books, New York.

Peters, G. and Turner, B. A. (1976). *Catastrophe and its Preconditions*, Open University Press, Milton Keynes.

Reason, J. T. (1990). *Human Error*, Cambridge University Press, Cambridge.

Smyth, D. S. and Checkland P. B. (1976). 'Using a systems approach: the structure of root definitions', *Journal of Applied Systems Analysis*, **5**, 75–83.

Solway, L. (1994). 'Urban developments and megacities: vulnerability to natural disaster', *Disaster Management*, **6**, 160–9.

Susman, P., O'Keefe, P. and Wisner, B. (1983). 'Global disaster a radical interpretation', in Hewitt, K. (Ed.) *Interpretation of Calamity*, Allen & Unwin, Winchester, Massachusetts.

Turner, B. (1979). *Man-made Disasters*, Taylor and Francis, London.

van Gigch, J. P. (1983). 'Towards descriptive and prescriptive theories of systems failures', Conference Proceedings, Society for General Systems Research, 325–9.

van Gigch, J. P. (1988). 'Diagnosis and metamodeling of systems failures', *Systems Practice*, **1**, 31–45.

Wahlström, B. (1992). 'Avoiding technological risks: the dilemma of complexity', *Technological Forecasting and Social Change*, **42**, 351–65.

Wilson, B. (1984). *Systems: Concepts, Methodologies and Applications*, Wiley, Chichester.

Young, O. R. (1964). *General Systems: Yearbook of the Society for General Systems Research*, **9**, 61.

Index